The Pacific Crest Trailside Reader

Oregon and Washington

THE PACIFIC CREST TRAILSIDE READER

ADVENTURE, HISTORY, AND LEGEND ON THE LONG-DISTANCE TRAIL

OREGON AND WASHINGTON

EDITED BY REES HUGHES AND COREY LEE LEWIS

ORIGINAL WOODCUT ILLUSTRATIONS BY AMY UYEKI

THE MOUNTAINEERS BOOKS

THE MOUNTAINEERS BOOKS
is the nonprofit publishing arm of The Mountaineers,
an organization founded in 1906 and dedicated to the exploration,
preservation, and enjoyment of outdoor and wilderness areas.

1001 SW Klickitat Way, Suite 201, Seattle, WA 98134

First edition: first printing 2011, second printing 2016

Distributed in the United Kingdom by Cordee, www.cordee.co.uk

Manufactured in the United States of America

Copy Editor: Julie Van Pelt
Cover, book design, layout, and map: John Barnett/4 Eyes Design
Illustrations © by Amy Uyeki

Library of Congress Cataloging-in-Publication Data
The Pacific Crest trailside reader , Oregon and Washington : adventure, history,
and legend on the long-distance trail / edited by Rees Hughes and Corey Lewis.
    p. cm.
  Includes index.
  ISBN 978-1-59485-509-2 (pbk.) — ISBN 978-1-59485-511-5 (ebook)
  1. Pacific Crest Trail. 2. Trails—Oregon. 3. Trails—Washington (State) 4. Trails
in literature. I. Hughes, Rees. II. Lewis, Corey Lee, 1972-.
  GV199.42.P3P35 2011
  917.9—dc23
                              2011022204

ISBN (paperback): 978-1-59485-509-2
ISBN (ebook): 978-1-59485-510-8

To my parents, Pete and Mary Hughes,
for instilling in me a passion for adventure and supporting my life's
journey with unconditional love.

—Rees Hughes

In loving memory of my brother, Bart "Black Bart" Lewis,
my most trusted guide and constant companion on all of life's most
rugged and beautiful trails.

—Corey Lee Lewis

CONTENTS

THE COLUMBIA AND VOLCANIC WASHINGTON: LAVA, MOSS, AND LICHENS

PREFACE

The Pacific Crest Trail has loomed large in both of our lives, ever since we first set foot on it. Like most PCT hikers and high-country travelers who went before us, we have found ourselves continually pulled back to the Pacific Crest, returning again and again, either through repeated trips or revisited stories. When unable to be on the trail, we find ourselves at home, scanning maps as we plan future trips, looking at pictures as we remember past journeys, and vicariously enjoying the memories and experiences of others. We have also found that we are not alone in this regard, that many other PCT hikers, like us, are called back irresistibly to that wild and rugged country snaking its way along the back of the American West.

As lovers of the trail, and of the stories surrounding it, we decided to compile a trailside reader that could stand as a testament to the PCT and those who have hiked it. Thus began a long and arduous literary journey, full of as many blisters and hardships as any PCT hike but also with just as many moments of inspiration, insight, and wonder. We sifted through countless historical accounts of exploration in the region, enjoyed reading the stories of contemporary PCT hikers, and collected some of the best work of our most well-known regional writers. We hope you will find this eclectic collection of stories to be as varied and enriching as your experiences on the PCT itself.

Perhaps, like many before, you will be inspired to write or tell your own story and will pass the PCT fever on to another lucky traveler. And if you are new to the trail, if *The Pacific Crest Trailside Reader* is your first exposure to the Pacific Crest, we hope that you too will be bitten by the bug and will find yourself compelled to explore the wilderness without as well as the wilderness within. For both of us, our first steps on the trail have come to stand out as significant moments in our lives, turning points and peak experiences, occasions for insight that have remained with us ever since. These first steps have led to countless others, both physical and intellectual journeys along the trail, to ultimately arrive as the book that you now hold in your hand. This volume is paired with its companion book, *The Pacific Crest Trailside Reader: California*, which contains stories from the southern half of the trail. Although each volume can be read alone, we see them, like the trail, as two parts of a whole that are meant to be read together.

REES'S STORY: THE BEGINNING OF A THIRTY-YEAR RELATIONSHIP

I have relived my first exposure to the Pacific Crest Trail countless times since 1981. The three of us, naïve young men, hoisted our packs and began the relentless 3000-foot climb to the rounded top of Big Huckleberry Mountain, just north of the Columbia River as the PCT enters Washington State. Upon reaching the grassy knoll near the summit, we each collapsed, dropping our too-heavy packs to the ground. I wrote in my journal, "The 50 pounds of food, clothes, and gear was devastating to my un-indoctrinated body." But around us was "a carpet of flowers and a panorama of the Gorge, mountains, and the awesome spire of Mount Hood." To this day I remember the overwhelming majesty of that view. However, we barely had the strength to eat and erect a tent. "All that beauty," I wrote, "could not mask the ache of my muscles. We pray for more good weather and quick relief for our beleaguered bodies."

A month later we reached Rainy Pass—leaner, wiser, and much more connected with the rhythm of the wilderness. We had crossed the deathly quiet blanket of ash blasted from Mount St. Helens the prior year that had smothered all life across a twenty-mile swath. We had camped in awestruck silence on a snowy flank of Mount Adams as we watched the setting sun illuminating distant Mount Rainier. We had supported each other across the precarious and icy Egg Butte ridgeline. We had endured days of soaking rain, snow, surging rivers, and lightning storms. We had watched the full moon rise over Waptus Lake. We had experienced the serenity of the mossy-backed Douglas fir forests in the valleys below Glacier Peak. We had witnessed the miracle of the dipper as its shadow danced along the water's surface. It is not hyperbole to say that we would never be the same. The Pacific Crest Trail was indelibly part of us.

On the final day of that trip I wrote that "the cleansing that I sought in the solace, the sweat, and the stimulation by nature has certainly occurred in the past four weeks. I feel renewed and aware, once again, of my purpose and vitality." I concluded,

Rushing stream; verdant forest glade,
Silent mountains, erupt with spectral colors,
The marmot whistle breaks the spell of the pilgrim.
Walking, walking, walking, walking, walking.
He has found his answer.

Since that first hike, Jim moved to Maine, Howard stayed in western Washington, and I relocated to California. But, as work and families have permitted, we have reunited to walk new sections of the PCT for a week or two at a time in the years since. Within a couple of days of our return to the trail, our bodies seem to rise to the demands we place upon them, we marvel at the view of Lake Tahoe or Mount Shasta, and we return to the familiar rhythm of the mountains. This bond begun nearly three decades ago has forever connected us with each other and the PCT.

COREY'S STORY: A SPIRITUAL QUEST

I first encountered the Pacific Crest Trail in the summer of 1998 shortly after having moved to the University of Nevada, Reno, to attend graduate school. Little did I know then that the next decade would find me taking countless expeditions along the PCT: backpacking alone or with my friends, day hiking with my young boys, and leading both trail-construction crews and classes of environmental studies students among its high peaks and ridgelines. Although an experienced backpacker and outdoorsman, I was new to the Sierras, having spent most of my mountaineering days in the Rockies of Wyoming and Colorado.

I entered the Desolation Wilderness, alone and expectant, hiking west from the Tahoe basin and then following the trail north toward Donner Pass. This area of the PCT is dominated by sparkling granite and clear water, blue sky and green pine. The first thing that struck me, as I hiked in silent awe, was the light. Great white shafts were everywhere: sparkling off quartz-studded granite, cascading through long feathery pine needles, reflecting off still mountain lakes, and raining down constantly from the cloudless western sky.

Lake Aloha held in its still reflection the perfect picture of the granite ridges of Mount Price and Pyramid Peak behind it. Without a schedule to keep or hiking partners to consider, I found myself drawn almost hypnotically to sit and watch the rippling mirror image for a long, meditative hour. In contrast to such stillness, Middle Velma Lake had me whooping and shouting as I jumped from lakeside cliffs into its icy waters.

As I headed north, through the Granite Chief Wilderness, and my gaze fell from the horizon line to the trail underneath my feet, I slowly became aware of the vast number and amazing variety of wildflowers bordering the trail. I marveled at the mountain sorrel and jewelflowers, along with the Lobb's buckwheat that clung so bravely to the tiniest cracks in cliffs and crevasses in rock. In the open pine forests, I sat down to study the saprophytic pinedrops and snow plants, while the moist meadows had me harvesting marsh marigold and Sierra onion. Everywhere I looked, the ground was studded with bright splashes of color, as if the artist had been tasked to use every hue on her palette.

Already, on that first trip, I was planning future hikes along the Pacific Crest Trail, camping trips with friends, field classes for students, and solo expeditions for spiritual solace. For weeks afterward, I walked long miles in my dreams, haunted by the desire to return and plagued by thoughts of starting preparations for a future thru hike.

After having walked more than sixty miles with a forty-pound pack on my back, and having weathered a brutally wild summer hail storm, I found myself walking and meditating on the conflict between freedom and security. At lunch breaks and campsites, after dropping my pack, I reveled in the freedom and weightlessness of packless hiking, bouldering, and rock climbing. But then, cold starry nights, and that long evening hailstorm that alternated between freezing rain and icy hailstones, filled me with gratitude for the forty pounds of tarp, sleeping bag, food, and gear that created my safe little port in the storm. As I headed off for the horizon of Donner Pass, I sang out loud to the world this hiking haiku that I wrote in my journal:

I am the ship
and all that I own
the anchor

YOUR STORIES

Our stories are not unique. They are, however, deeply personal stories. Stories, we suspect, that will strike familiar chords with those that emerge from your own journeys along the Pacific Crest Trail. These may come from a day hike in the Laguna Mountains, a week in the Pasayten, or a month in the Sierras. We all share the themes of discovery, insight, challenge, and success. We hope that the *Trailside Reader* will both complement your next hike and inspire you to share your stories with others.

—*Rees Hughes and Corey Lee Lewis*
Arcata, California

ACKNOWLEDGMENTS

When we embarked upon this project after a lunchtime walk into the Arcata Community Forest some years ago, neither of us had any idea of what we were really undertaking. It has been a wonderful partnership. Much like taking a long hike on the PCT with a good partner, we learned from each other, came to trust and appreciate each other, and above all emerged from the experience as friends.

No endeavor of this complexity is possible without the contributions and support of many. These books have become much better because of the suggestions, the feedback, the editing, the encouragement, and the patience of family, friends, colleagues, and the staff of The Mountaineers Books. We are eternally grateful for the many authors who submitted stories for inclusion in this anthology, including those we were unable to use. Great thanks go out to those hiker-authors included here, for their willingness to donate their stories in support of the PCT and for their patience and flexibility with us throughout the entire publication process. We would like to offer a special note of appreciation to Julie Van Pelt for her careful edits, and to the Department of English at Humboldt State University for its support of this project. Similarly, thanks go to the Association for the Study of Literature and Environment (ASLE) and the Pacific Crest Trail Association (PCTA) and all of their members, for their organizational support for this project in particular and for environmental writing and for the PCT in general.

Many have generously lent their talents and loving critique to individual stories, early drafts of sections, and to the publishing process itself: Rick and Susan Benoit, Bob Birkby, Barry Blake, Jan and Ingrid Brink, Joy Hardin, Michele McKeegan, Riley Quarles, Claire Reynolds, John Schafer, Kathy Statzer, Annie Stromquist, and Buzz and Judy Webb. And a special thanks to Cheryll Glotfelty for her professional advice on editing, anthologizing, and publishing. Your contributions have meant far more than you could ever realize.

REES'S ACKNOWLEDGMENTS

First and foremost, I would like to thank my wife, Amy Uyeki, who has patiently embraced this project as her own and has been willing to shoulder a backpack for nearly four decades to share the backcountry with me; my daughters, Chisa and Mei Lan, for understanding and supporting their crazy father; and the ever loving and nurturing Hughes and Uyeki clans.

I would also like to acknowledge my Pacific Crest Trail hiking partners from over the years, as well as the drivers and trail angels who have made it possible to be a section hiker. Howard "Rocky" Shapiro, Jim "Pierre" Peacock, and I grew up on the PCT. Over the past three decades of walking together, we have developed a passion for the trail and an unbreakable bond of friendship. In addition, I have had the good fortune to share trail time with my nephew, Taylor "Anti-Gravity" Smith, Steve "Crosscut" Benoit, Jim "The Epicurean" Elferdink, Gary "Nightcap" Fox, Steve Gustaveson, Chisa Hughes, Bruce and Nathan Johnston, Bob "Birdman" Lockett, Eli Robinson, Don Seifert, Kathy and Emily Shapiro, and my wife, Amy. I cherish each of these PCT experiences.

COREY'S ACKNOWLEDGMENTS

I offer a heartfelt thanks to my parents, Lon and Nancy Lewis, as well as to Grandad Lee and Grandma Dot Brunk, for instilling in me a love for the land and for backcountry adventure—thanks for all of those hiking, horsepacking, and backpacking trips that filled my childhood and adolescence with such amazing experiences. Thanks also to Bart Lewis and Tim Pyles for teaching me to love a good story and how to tell a good tale, as well as for their constant camping companionship and long, laughter-filled fireside conversations.

I would also like to thank Jerry Keir and everyone from the Great Basin Institute and the Nevada Conservation Corps for the opportunity to build hiking trails, lead university classes along the PCT, and gain valuable editorial experience and skill. Thank you, also, to Marge Sill, Roger Scholl, Sharon Netherton, and everyone else at Friends of Nevada Wilderness for mentoring me in wilderness advocacy and showing by your example how to live one's life on behalf of our wildlands. And a special thanks to Gary Snyder for connecting me to so many bioregional authors, to the bioregion itself, and to the mythopoetic power of literature. Your work has enriched both my life and our world.

INTRODUCTION

Outlined in *The Pacific Crest Trailside Reader: California*, the PCT's long and storied history bears repeating. Barney Mann's contribution to this second volume tells us that Catherine Montgomery is credited with first promoting the idea of a crestline trail along the length of the western United States back in 1926. By 1937, Fred Cleator, supervisor for Region 6 of the US Forest Service, had overseen the completion of the Cascade Crest Trail and the Oregon Skyline Trail, making it possible to walk from the Oregon-California border to Canada, through the Cascades. However, despite the early efforts of Clinton C. Clarke, known as the father of the PCT, and others, a high-elevation trail in California remained in limbo until the 1960s, when new resolve coalesced around the passage of the 1968 National Trail Act. The Pacific Crest Trail and the Appalachian Trail were the two original components of the National Scenic Trails System. But it was not until 1993 that the PCT was officially considered complete.

Today, the PCT spans the length of California, Oregon, and Washington, traveling 2650 miles from Mexico to Canada. It climbs nearly sixty major mountain passes and traverses seven national parks (including Crater Lake, Mount Rainier, and North Cascades National Parks), twenty-four national forests, and thirty-three designated wilderness areas. From the handful of hikers that conquered the length of the PCT in the early years, the number of long-distance hikers who tackle trail sections or its entirety has grown exponentially in recent times.

The Oregon and Washington PCT

The PCT climbs northeast out of the steamy heat of the Klamath River valley, slowly leaving the dense forests and coastal influences of the Klamath Knot. Following the Siskiyous along the southern Oregon border, the PCT hooks east to reconnect with the Cascades. This routing, initiated in the early 1970s, replaced the original PCT that relied extensively on road walking south of Sky Lakes and, at the state border, faced the arid topography north of Mount Shasta. Once the trail reaches Mount McLaughlin going north, it bisects Oregon and Washington, winding its way between magnificent volcanoes. As the trail passes one landmark, the next peak invariably comes to dominate the thru hiker's world. Mazama, Thielsen, Diamond Peak, the Three Sisters, Three Fingered Jack, Jefferson, and Hood—the peaks are like mileposts marking progress north. Each has its own personality, which is also changeable— at times a welcoming friend and at others a worthy adversary, depending on weather and trail conditions.

Between the peaks, the Oregon Cascades are blanketed in a verdant conifer forest that thrives in this temperate, moist environment. Varieties of fir, cedar, pine, spruce, and hemlock provide welcome habitat for abundant fauna, including the ubiquitous mosquito. The stories we have included in the first section of this volume capture Oregon's distinct community of inhabitants and canon of stories.

Once the PCT dips down into the Columbia Gorge and crosses the Bridge of the Gods, the second section of this volume begins. In 1984 the southern Washington PCT was realigned as it pulled itself out of the Gorge and began its way north. The trail climbs past the behemoths of Mounts Adams and Rainier, crossing the rugged Goat Rocks in between. As the trail approaches the timberland around Stampede Pass, the impact of logging along the trail corridor is pervasive, a subject treated extensively in the writings we have chosen about this section of the PCT.

North of Snoqualmie Pass, which begins the third and final section of this volume, the PCT enters the Alpine Lakes Wilderness. Serrated ridges, unforgiving terrain, late summers, and early winters replace the more benign character of the trail farther south. But nowhere are the phlox, lupine, tiger lilies, and fireweed more resplendent than in this often hostile climate. With tree line less than half the elevation of that in the Sierras, this is an inhospitable alpine landscape. Marmots, pikas, and black bears are the denizens of this world. The magic of an August day walking the exposed, high passes of the Pasayten, with flowering meadows dotted with the white sand traps of snow, is unparalleled, as is the challenge of pushing one's way forward, trail obscured and clothing saturated, in a driving rain or heavy snowfall. As Campo at the Mexican border marks both a beginning and an ending, so does Monument 78 at the Canadian border.

Collecting Stories

The process of collecting these stories has been its own journey. There have been many parallels with long-distance hiking—careful and thoughtful preparation, growth through the experience, countless serendipitous encounters and discoveries, and a continuing love affair with the trail. We have developed a few blisters along the way, but we both still have a sparkle in our eyes and a bounce in our step.

The search for stories connected us with a number of communities with strong affinity for the Pacific Crest Trail. First and foremost have been the PCT hikers, supporters, advocates, and trail angels. We spread our call for submissions through venues like the Pacific Crest Trail Association, the PCT Listserv, the Washington Trail Association, and more. We received contributions from members of OCTA (Oregon-California Trail Association) and others with a deep, abiding interest in the history of the region, particularly the important role of emigrant pioneers and mountain men in revealing the wonders and dangers of the high country. We reached out to US Forest Service staff and friends we had encountered on the trail. We requested and received contributions from members of ASLE (Association for the Study of Literature and Environment) and some of the seminal writers with strong connections to the trail. The warm embrace from these individuals has made these books possible and has resulted in the rich diversity of stories included here. In all cases, we did our utmost to preserve the texture and color of the individual authors, as a collection of this nature should.

We have been thrilled by the number of contributions from women but challenged, perhaps because of our own limitations, to ensure that the Native American voice has been represented. We have not been altogether pleased with our success in this regard. Certainly a fair critique regarding the contemporary PCT is that it is disproportionately, if not almost exclusively, used by white people. It is a resource that has failed to capture the interest of many people of color. As with the environmental movement in the United States, more must be done to extend the interest in and relevance of the PCT beyond the current narrow cultural range.

Stewardship and the PCT

From the beginning of this project, we recognized that it was a labor of love. We agreed that it felt most appropriate to return all of our profits from the sale of these books back to the support and protection of the Pacific Crest Trail. In almost all cases, contributors gave us permission to use their stories without charge or at greatly reduced rates (in the case of some of the previously published stories) because of their commitment to the PCT.

As a fragile 2650-mile ribbon, the PCT is constantly under assault somewhere along its length. Timber harvests, mining, grazing, off-road vehicles, wind farms, floods, fires, overuse, and development are but some of the threats to the trail. It takes many hands to maintain the Pacific Crest Trail as an extraordinary wilderness and walking experience.

While the stories we have collected recognize pioneering PCT advocates (see Barney Mann's story in this volume or Theodore Solomons's reflections in the California volume) and trail builders (see Robert Birkby's "Art of the Trail" in this volume), we have done little to acknowledge all of the roles necessary to ensure the health of the PCT. Countless volunteers and work crews clear the trail after each winter, donors provide the financial support to secure conservation easements, advocates work with local and national politicians or negotiate with the Tejon Ranch owners or ORV clubs, and others educate about appropriate use and appreciation of wilderness. While the importance of walking lightly on the land should not be trivialized, our commitment to the PCT does not and cannot end there. As Scott Russell Sanders observes in *Coming to Land in a Troubled World* (Trust for Public Land, 2003), "Every place needs people who will dig in, keep watch, explore the terrain, learn the animals and plants, and take responsibility. . . . No matter what the legal protections on paper, no land can be safe from harm without people committed to care for it, year after year, generation after generation."

In our relationship with the Pacific Crest Trail, it is not enough to walk the trail as a starry-eyed lover. We each have a responsibility, a duty to do what we can to preserve the PCT for those who will walk it in the years to come.

READING THIS BOOK

Each of us who has hiked along the PCT knows that our experiences mirror those of the thousands who have walked the trail before us. While the stories differ, the end result is the same. The trail is in our blood. Our feelings are not dissimilar to those who fell in love with the Cascades, the Sierras, the Siskiyous, and the San Gabriel Mountains long before there was a PCT.

We tread the same passes and cross the same rivers as the intrepid emigrants, mountain men, and native peoples of the West. The PCT winds its way through country that has inspired tall tales and has been inhabited by personalities larger than life. Its route includes sites of courage and cowardice, triumph and tragedy, and tales of the trail capture the unique mystique and power that the American wilderness has held throughout time.

In the *Trailside Reader* we have collected three types of stories. Half of the anthology is comprised of contemporary real trail tales contributed by PCT day, section, and thru hikers. Some of these stories capture the humor of the trail, such as Keith Liker's "Night Visitor at Maidu Lake" or Kim Todd's "Bear Bagging." Others provide a glimpse into the adventures of intrepid souls like sixteen-year-old Hawk Greenway or Marge "The Old Gal" Prothman. Still others recall grappling with the wild weather of the Cascades, as in Tom Griffin's "Editors on the Edge," which details the author's battles with torrential and dispiriting rains, or Cindy Ross's "Last Skies," which tells of oppressive snow and a winter eager to arrive. There are stories of encounters with animals. Stories of being lost and found. Stories of conquering fear. Stories of camaraderie and conflict.

In working with the authors of these real trail tales, we emphasized the importance of telling a story. We have worked hard to preserve the unique narrative voice of each hiker-writer. As a result, these stories tend to be easy to read, and they explore themes familiar to all of those who have experienced the trail.

We have complemented these tales with others that, because of their historical significance, enrich our understanding and appreciation of certain stretches of the PCT. Read "The Barlow Road Story" as you climb north around Mount Hood, sharing Joel Palmer's view down Zigzag Canyon. David Foscue provides added appreciation for what lies beneath Stevens Pass in "Triumph and Tragedy at Stevens Pass." Robert Cox profiles early Forest Service ranger Cyrus Bingham, who laid out long sections of the Oregon Skyline Trail and left a passel of arborglyphs that still hide among the forests of the central Oregon Cascades. These rich stories are reminders of the many layers of history that exist in the land now occupied by the PCT. They tend to draw extensively from journal excerpts, often reflect the vernacular of an earlier time, and can benefit from being read and reread slowly and thoroughly.

The final element in this anthology has been the selective inclusion of the writings of classic environmental authors, such as Barry Lopez's reflections on introducing wilderness to children and Ursula Le Guin's observations regarding the 1980 eruption of Mount St. Helens. We have included several pieces that touch on the aggressive timber-management practices that have altered the forest landscape in the Stampede Pass area—a short excerpt from George Perkins Marsh's prescient warning about the importance of the preservation of forests and a condensed version of Judge William Dwyer's 1991 ruling that led to the Northwest Forest Plan. Other well-known writers included here, such as William O. Douglas and David Wagoner, have helped define the way we think about the wilderness, walking, and the PCT itself. Unlike the real trail tales, with their strong narrative thread, these stories demand to be read differently. Savor them like the glorious color of an alpine sunset. Read them like a love letter. Underline passages. Write in the margins.

In their sum, these stories are a tribute to the Pacific Crest Trail. They capture a slice of the spirit and culture, the people and places, and the philosophy and history of this national treasure.

Although these stories are organized parallel to the geographical sections of the PCT so that you can read about a particular stretch of trail while you are hiking it, each story stands alone. You might also elect to pick and choose, moving across regions and types of stories. This, the second volume in the set, covers Oregon and Washington, concluding with the exhilaration of reaching Monument 78 after beginning months before at Campo and the Mexican border. Even though these volumes can be read individually, it has been our design and preference that they be read together.

THE OREGON CASCADES
FORESTS FOREVER

Covering Section A–Section G

Seiad Valley—Siskiyou Pass—Fish Lake—Crater Lake—Cascade Crest
Willamette Pass—McKenzie Pass—Barlow Pass—Columbia River

THE TRAIL NORTH

By Hawk Greenway

The year was 1976. The Vietnam War had been over for a year, Gerald Ford was president, the Apple Computer company had just been established, and a gallon of gas cost fifty-nine cents. At the ripe old age of sixteen, Hawk Greenway and his horse, Fatima, journeyed from Greenway's home in the California Coast Range to the Pacific Crest Trail, which they loosely followed north to Wenatchee, Washington, where Greenway's mother lived. As his father noted in the preface of the book that grew out of the trip, "Wonderfully, absurdly, anachronistically like someone out of another century, romantically, and most of all, with blind courage, this sixteen-year-old boy headed north on a heavily laden horse almost as old as he was."

Aside from the short excerpt that touches on Greenway's trip preparations, these selected entries from his journal profile an impressively mature and reflective young man. About two weeks into the journey, horse and rider crossed the Klamath, climbed into the Siskiyous, and entered Oregon, but not without some challenges. Anyone who has walked the long road along Grider Creek from the south has probably given serious consideration to fording the Klamath rather than making the long detour over the highway bridge. Greenway also makes this error, providing both himself and us—his readers—with one of his more memorable adventures.

Just as this volume of the Trailside Reader *begins at the Klamath River, so, really, do Greenway's PCT travels. For that reason, and the uniqueness of a sixteen-year-old on a solo journey as well as the importance of including an equestrian experience in the anthology, we selected this story to begin this volume.*

Source: Excerpted from *The Trail North*, by Hawk Greenway. Copyright © 1981 by Hawk Greenway. Reprinted by permission of Island Press.

I had thought about the trip so much for so long that the idea of it was completely familiar to me. I simply wanted to spend some time alone in the wilderness, traveling on horseback. I wanted an adventure, and I wanted to explore the Pacific Crest Trail. I had spent months going over topographical maps. [...] I had worked for 3 months as a dishwasher [...] to finance the trip. [...] [however] I had spent most of my dishwashing earnings to get outfitted, on things like a new fiberfill sleeping bag, new boots, and [...] saddle. I also had bought a lot of food. All I had left was $5, but I was so crazy to leave that I decided to believe that "it would work out" along the way if I needed something and couldn't work for it.

Monday, July 12

After 10 miles of [logging] roads, I got on a brand-new section of trail, down by the long Grider Creek. I met the man who was building this section, a good-humored guy, and stopped to talk with him and his crew.

Three miles more, the sun was sliding behind the ridges to the west, and I was facing the Klamath River. I could see town on the far side and what kind of looked like the forest service station. The river was about 150 yards across but looked shallow most of the way, with just a small channel of deeper water on the far side.

Fatima scrambled down the steep slope to the river bed, and we headed across. For the first hundred yards the river was only 6 inches or so deep. Then we got to the channel. It looked to be a couple of feet deep, but it was hard to tell because the water was dark brown and murky. A short way downstream the channel narrowed to rapids with waves a couple of feet high, churning and foaming. I looked down the river and watched the sun set above the water. We went upstream to avoid the rapids. Fatima stepped right into the current, and whoa! The water must've been 10 feet deep. Fatima was swimming immediately, striking out for the shore 50 yards away.

The current hadn't looked very strong from the bank, but it moved surprisingly fast. [...] We were closer than I would have liked to the rapids, and we were getting even closer fast. Fatima is a strong swimmer, even weighted down like she was. We reached the far shore about 10 yards above the rapids. Then I realized that the bank there was made up of huge, jagged blocks of old concrete that had been dumped into the river to slow down its sweep toward the town. Fatima was swimming strongly, so I turned her downstream toward the rapids. I didn't want her to break a leg on those rocks. I was looking for a spot to pull out before the rapids, and it looked like there was one right where the rapids started.

We weren't very far from the rapids when I realized that the spot I had picked wasn't going to do us much good because there was a huge eddy there. The eddy would swirl us every which way and make it very difficult to reach the bank. About 10 feet from the rapids, the edge of the eddy caught us and pushed Fatima right up against the rocks. Fatima then took over and decided not to get any closer to the rapids. She scrambled out onto the rocks; there she managed to get to dry land without breaking any bones.

We stood looking at the river for a bit. I don't know what thoughts went through Fatima's mind, but one of mine went back to what Bill, the trail guy, had said, "I send hikers across there all the time." I wondered what he had against hikers!

Tuesday, July 13

The trail is steep for the first few miles climbing out of the Klamath Valley, winding right over Three Devils Peaks, the lowest of which has an unmanned fire station on it. I stopped at the lookout to get one last view of the town of Seiad Valley 4000 feet below.

I turned and looked northward, the trail winding and curling away from me, going on for miles into southern Oregon. It looked like it had been a dry year there as well. I wondered about the high snowy peaks of the Cascade Mountains described by my father. Pretty soon I'd see for myself.

Soon we dropped down to Jackass Spring and some welcome water. There I found the biggest wild onions I've ever seen. I gathered enough for a huge meal of cream of onion soup. I like to save my "store-food" for as long as I can because I'm never sure how long my supplies will last.

We stopped for the night in the grassy meadows at Kangaroo Springs. Made camp right out in the middle of the meadow beside a big rock and unpacked everything.

Again the questions come into my mind. What am I doing here? What is this preoccupation with wilderness? How can I justify being out here? Is this all just a fantasy, some kid trying to be like an oldtime mountain man? I wonder at the insanity of it all. I so often criticize the management of this country, and yet this is the system that allows me to be here. I can imagine myself approaching the supervisor of a commune with a plan for a horseback ride for a whole summer. I can hear him laugh and say, "But what good would that be? How would the people benefit from your horse trip?" So all right, the people just might not benefit. Guess I have to work on myself before I can ever hope to benefit anyone else. Call it education, call it selfish, call it what you will, but don't stand in the way of someone who is trying.

So, I relax behind all this chatter in my head, stretch out on the meadow, listen to Fatima's new bell as she grazes nearby, and watch the stars coming into their glory before the last vestiges of the sun's warmth have left the air.

WEDNESDAY, JULY 14

I packed in the early light, making all the motions now so familiar. I fold the groundsheet and lay it on top of all the other gear, then sit on it while I dig into the saddlebags for my cup and spoon and a bit of granola. After eating I usually grab Fatima and start the daily ritual of horse care, brushing her down, cleaning her feet, painting them with a moisturizer, hoping to alleviate her problem of dry feet. I pack everything—hobbles, ropes, brush, and hoof glop—and start saddling her, which usually takes some time.

Half an hour later I was ready to go, leaving only a depression on the grass where I slept and cropped grass where Fatima ate. Good bye Kangaroo Springs, a fine meadow nestled amongst the red rocks.

A mile or so up the trail, I saw a sign: "Warning, Blasting in Progress." As I passed it, I wondered what I'd do if all of a sudden the mountain was blown out from under Fatima's feet. A voice yelled from the slope above me, "Fire in the hole!"

"Wait," I hollered back, and two guys stood up from behind a rock where they were crouched. They yelled that they were blasting a new trail and had put a charge about 50 feet above my head. They said I should go over to the road and I'd be safe. After about nine more shouts of "Fire in the hole," there was a huge pillar of smoke and dust above where the rock had been. Seconds later the sound reached us, and I had my hands full keeping Fatima still. More time went by, then there was a rain of rock chunks dropping into the brush all around us. A piece of rock about the size of a baseball landed in a small tree 20 yards from us, breaking off most of its limbs. The echo of the roar came bouncing back from all the way down the canyon. I was pretty impressed. I told the guys on the hill about the rocks raining down, and they said I should've been a bit further away.

I continued on, pausing occasionally when the boom from the blasting reached us, listening to the echo as long as I could hear it. [...]

The trail followed the ridge dividing the Applegate River drainage from the Klamath drainage. I watched Shasta all day. It slid from the east toward the south as I moved along the ridge. It seemed that if my arm were just a little bit longer, I could reach right out and touch that huge mountain.

The maps showed a meadow straddling the Oregon border, so I was really pushing to make it, hoping for good grazing. I did take time to stop in a small meadow along the way. I turned Fatima loose, tying the bridle onto the saddle horn, hoping she would get a good graze. I was almost asleep in the hot sun when out of the corner of my eye I saw her going down on her knees, in preparation for a good roll. I yelled at her and she stood up quick. I watched her more closely then, and sure enough she went behind a tree, and down she went, a good hearty roll in mind. I got there, yelling like crazy, just as she was about to go over onto the bulky saddle. She stood up, sort of sheepishly, and I tightened the cinch. We took off up the trail.

About 10 miles from the Oregon border I noticed a tall column of smoke rising from the vicinity of where I figured the trail had to go. The meadows where I wanted to camp were about half a mile west of the trail.

As I got nearer, I could see helicopters and small airplanes hovering overhead, but I couldn't tell what they were doing. I didn't want to get stuck on the southern side of a forest fire, so I figured I'd better get around to the north of it. The wind began to blow pretty steady from the west; the fire seemed to be just on the other side of the ridge from the trail. I kept Fatima moving along at a fast walk until we were just about due east of the fire. I watched for flames, envisioning the downward rush of the fire as it snowballed toward the road. All I could see was the outline of the sun just above the ridge, blood red because of the billowing smoke. I got the tired Fatima going at a trot and kept her at it until the forest opened out into a large grassy meadow on both sides of the road. I was pretty scared but hoped that Fatima could outrun a fire if she had to. Looking back at the western side of the ridge, I could see the flames as they crept up to the top. It was good to be beyond it. Whew, you're in Oregon, boy! Worrying about the fire, I had hardly cared about the border. Now I was too tired to think about it.

I reached a small spring just as the sun was setting and got the exhausted Fatima grazing in the gently sloping meadows. I took the saddle off her, and she finally had a good roll, squirming with pleasure, all four feet in the air.

From where I sit I have a full eastern view. I watch the last of the sun's rays leave Shasta, glowing red against the deep blue of the approaching night. Pilot Rock stands as a beacon, about a day away, lower than where I am.

I peer through the haze and smoke to the south, thinking of my old stomping grounds—from the Yolla Bollys' rough ridges to the peaks of the Trinity Alps to the Marble Mountains with their lakes and quiet trails. I look to the north, down into the valleys of southern Oregon—into new country, unexplored by anyone I've ever talked with. I look at the dry grasslands, spotted with scrub brush and oaks, and worry about the grazing ahead.

I build a fire to enjoy the evening by, sitting close to the tiny flame because the wind is chill. I stew up a meal of onions and grains, wishing for that imaginary rabbit to add a bit of strength. I watch the stars come out to start their swing to the west. And always the trucks crawl along the highway, their lights flashing out into the haze-filled valley as they make each turn.

So this is Oregon! I can't think of a place I'd rather be.

For those who want additional stories of horses and the PCT, read about the Mulfords. In 1959, Don and June Mulford defied prevailing wisdom and rode their horses the then 2400-mile length of the PCT, still an ambiguous jumble of trails, roads, and cross-country routes. After almost four months, they reached the Oregon Cascades, where Don commented in his journal, "You may think one would get tired of so much scenery, day after day, but June and I will never get tired of the outdoors, the scenery or the clean mountain air out here. We may get bone weary and tired, from pushing so hard to make a schedule, but not of the scenery, horseback riding or outdoor life." The Pacific Crest Trail Association sells a DVD about the couple's adventure, called Historic 1959 Trail Ride: Mexico to Canada, *and articles about the Mulfords appeared in both* The Oregonian *(September 25, 2009) and* The Communicator *(December 2009).*

LISTENING FOR COYOTE

By William L. Sullivan

William L. "Bill" Sullivan is the author of fourteen books and numerous articles about his home state of Oregon. He began hiking at the age of five and has been exploring new trails ever since. He and his wife, Janell Sorensen, spend summers in a log cabin they built by hand on a roadless stretch of a remote river in Oregon's Coast Range.

In 1985 Sullivan set out to investigate Oregon's wilderness on a 1361-mile solo backpacking trek from Cape Blanco, the state's westernmost shore, to Oregon's easternmost point in Hells Canyon. His journal of that two-month adventure was published as Listening for Coyote. *By the time he joined the Pacific Crest Trail in southern Oregon, Sullivan had already hiked 243 miles. He followed the PCT north to Mount Jefferson and then struck off across eastern Oregon, following the Ochoco and Blue Mountains to the Snake River.*

As he began that journey, Sullivan recounts his sense that it seemed "like someone else—someone very naïve—[who had drawn] the 1300-mile route in red ink across my maps. That red line blithely wander[ed] cross-country through canyons and mountains I [had] never seen." His father even insisted on buying a $100,000 life-insurance policy for Sullivan. At seventeen dollars a month, he said it was a deal he couldn't pass up.

In this selection from his journal, Sullivan has reached the Red Buttes Wilderness in southwest Oregon, where he joins the Pacific Crest Trail.

Source: Excerpted from *Listening for Coyote: A Walk Across Oregon's Wilderness*, by William L. Sullivan. Copyright © 1988. Reprinted by permission of Oregon State University Press.

AUGUST 29, 1985

9:10 AM, Cook and Green Pass. 64°F. Mileage so far today: 4.2. Total: 248.0. This morning I climb back onto the Pacific Crest Trail just as a young man is walking up. His ungainly backpack is topped by a rolled-up foam pad and an eagle feather. Pouches, wineskins, and bags are strapped around his shoulders and waist. His arms and legs are bronzed by the sun. His short beard is pale blond. He wears mirror-lensed sunglasses, a red bandanna sweatband, and a white-tailed Foreign Legion desert hat.

"Hello," I say.

"Hello." He gives the word a British accent. "Where are you headed?" I ask.

"Mexico to Canada. You?"

"The Pacific to Idaho."

For a moment we are silent, pondering the immensity of our crossed purposes. Then I suggest, "I'm going your way for a while, though. Perhaps we could hike the morning together?"

He grins, exposing a row of perfect white teeth. "Oh, say, I could use a bit of company."

We set off together, talking. Chris explains that he spent three years earning a degree in geography from the University of Manchester—a degree that failed to provide him with a profession, but succeeded in giving him an insatiable wanderlust.

"This PCT, you know, is the longest trail in the world." He talks over his shoulder as we hike along. "I daydreamed about it in school when I should have been studying. As soon as I graduated I worked at a campground in the Lake District, clerked in a grocery store, and washed dishes at night in a restaurant— three jobs at once, for a full year—to save enough for this trip."

"When did you start hiking?"

He sighs. "Too late. I didn't get to the Mexican border until mid-May. The chaps who plan to do the whole trail before winter started out in April. You've got to get through the southern California desert before the summer heat hits, you know, and then get to the North Cascades in Washington before the first snow."

"Doesn't anybody hike the trail from north to south?"

He shakes his head. "I've only met two. There's probably two hundred going my way, though."

"It must be frustrating, all going the same way, so you never meet the others."

"Not at all. We all know each other. We meet at campgrounds and outfitters. We leave notes in the trail registers, or pass word with slower hikers. A week ahead of me there's two girls packing their stuff on llamas. Two days behind me there's a lawyer who set aside his practice for five months to go hiking. One guy's already made it this year to Canada."

"How could you know that?"

"He wrote a postcard back to an outfitter near Shasta to let all the under-twenty-five-miles-a-day crowd know. Me, I don't think mileage is the main thing. I probably won't make it anyway, what with starting so late. It'll be October when I get to Washington."

I think of my own late start, and my scheduled October finish in Hells Canyon. It is troubling. I echo his words, hiding my concern. "No, mileage is not the main thing."

He waves his arm. "The main thing is all of this." Then he chuckles. "I guess it's not for everybody, though, is it? One of the two wrong-way PCTers I met was a girl who'd never been on a hike before. She'd just sold her business, bought a bunch of gear, and decided to do something wild and crazy. By the time I passed her she told me, 'You know, I don't care if I never see a tree again.'"

"Where do all the PCTers come from?" I ask.

He gives me the answer of a geography student. "About 50 percent seem to come from the eastern United States—Pennsylvania, Massachusetts, Maryland, that sort of thing. The next biggest group is Californians. Then come the New Zealanders and Australians, who, if you lump them together, probably outnumber us Britishers."

"Do you see a lot of local hikers?"

"Only on the John Muir Trail in the High Sierras. You meet armies of them there, and everywhere else, nobody. In geography we call areas like that 'honeypots.' All the bees buzz to a few choice spots. Maybe that's best. It leaves ninety-five percent of the trails to us."

We stop to rest at a pass, and trade hard candy—the essential mouth-moistener and calorie-booster of the long-range hiker. He chooses one of my butterscotch pieces. I inspect the strange Yorkshire candy he offers. It is vaguely pear-shaped, in a variety of mottled colors ranging from yellow to purple. It tastes a little to the left of watermelon, yet a little to the right of citrus. Strange, I think. This Yorkshire stuff, though good, resembles nothing I've ever seen. Perhaps it is the appropriate nonconformist fare for this nonconformist

Yorkshireman. His father, he says, works in a velvet factory. His brother works in a velvet factory.

But Chris? He's spending his last pound hiking the American wilderness.

"Is there," he muses, "any demand for high school geography teachers here? Social studies teachers?" I shake my head. "I'm afraid there are sixty applicants for every opening."

He sighs. "It's three hundred to one back home. Sometimes I think I should try to get a work permit so I could stay on here in America. And then sometimes I'm just not sure. Everything's so big and lovely. But maybe I'm just seeing the good part of it all."

And I think: Yes. He is.

MEASURING TIME ON THE
PACIFIC CREST TRAIL

By Mark Larabee

There are a number of reasons why few hikers begin their northbound walks on the Pacific Crest Trail in Seiad Valley. It is conveniently located, but the climb out of the Klamath River valley is severe, and summertime temperatures can be unforgiving. Nonetheless, this is exactly where Mark Larabee and Ian Malkasian began their 2005 quest to walk the length of the Oregon PCT. As they walked their first steps in Oregon several days later, Larabee remembers, "We passed a man who had parked on a nearby dirt road. I was amused—and a little annoyed—by the fact that the PCT's Oregon border was very close to the road. After all that heat, all those hours of climbing, why hadn't we started here? As we left the border behind, I wondered what other flaws were in our game plan."

It was close to 100 degrees Fahrenheit the day before we began our monthlong hike across Oregon on the PCT. We hadn't even started hiking and I was already wondering why I had wanted to do it. In camp that evening, pondering every lung-searing breath, I was cursing myself for even suggesting the idea. Sane people would have waited for the brain-bending heat to subside. Not us. We were on a mission and we were getting paid to hike.

In 2005, I was a reporter for the *Oregonian* newspaper and my hiking partner was Ian Malkasian, a former staff photographer and photo editor. We had spent four months researching the PCT's abundant wonders and immense challenges in preparation for a summer series. Our reporting had taken us to the heat of the California desert, the dense forests of Oregon, and the sweeping vistas of the North Cascades, and our hike across Oregon would help us put into context what we had learned. My words and Ian's pictures ran as a thirteen-part series in Portland's daily newspaper, and we maintained a daily blog. We filed as we hiked, using a satellite phone, a palm-sized computer, and a lightweight foldable keyboard that looked like a silver cigarette case. One couple said it reminded them of something from a James Bond movie. They gave me my trail name: 007.

Along the way we met trail angels, federal foresters, recreational hikers and equestrians, volunteer trail workers, and professional advocates, each in their own way giving back to this fragile ribbon that winds its way through the West, connecting mountain ranges and ecosystems. It was surprising to me—and remains powerful in my mind to this day—that because of the PCT, all these people had come to the same place, regardless of political ideology, religion, or any of the forces that seem to divide us these days. I'd always felt that the outdoors creates its own kind of magic, one that brings people together. After that summer, I had proof. Out on the trail, we find peace and understanding and we share a bond that is greater than all the others. But the PCT is more than a unifying force. One man I met told me that he thought the trail was a great equalizer. It's a subtle difference, one that I believe is spot on.

It was Friday, July 22, 2005, when Ian and I left Seiad Valley, California. As I look back half a decade, I can still feel those first heavy steps on the trail. We began where the Siskiyous rise high from the chasm carved into earth and stone by the unrelenting power of the Klamath River. I said goodbye to my girlfriend, Carol, who wisely gave up her plan to hike with us for part of the day in favor of an air-conditioned ride back to Portland. It had taken less than six hours to drive from home to the trailhead, where we pitched the first of many campsites. I remember taking in the Cascades, one by one, as we traveled south like lightning on Interstate 5, wondering what we might discover as we walked 488 miles back over thirty days. I will never look at that drive the same way again.

We started at 6:45 AM, when the river's cool air offered hope. It was 65 degrees. But the reprieve wouldn't last. By 10:30 AM, it was 80 and by noon it had reached 90. I dreamt of relief, blindly telling myself that the air would be cooler up high. But the hottest part of the day was still to come. The Klamath runs at 1600 feet above sea level through the Seiad Valley on its winding journey to the Pacific Ocean. We climbed to 5900 feet over the first seven miles, a brutal start, as the air continued to bake. We ended that first day fifteen miles into the backcountry at a crossroads called Cook and Green Pass, a windy saddle at 4770 feet. We were still more than a day's hike from Oregon, exhausted and a little demoralized. But once we settled down, ate a meal, and drank as much water as we could fit in, I had time to reflect.

I jotted notes in my journal about the beauty of the mountains in the Klamath National Forest. We had walked through proud ponderosa pines and towering oaks through the Devils Peaks. (There are three: Lower, Middle, and Upper.) At the top of Lower, we crossed a 1987 burn caused by lightning, where dead trees stood like skeletons, bleached silver in the sun. Mount Shasta and the Marble Mountains hung in the periphery most of the day as we traipsed through foothills covered in young huckleberry and wildflowers.

As I drifted off, filled with worry and wonder, doubt and exhilaration, I had only a vague idea about what the trail had to offer, and no clue about how deeply this journey would affect my life in the ensuing years, especially my sense of time.

We hiked another forty miles on that first weekend, reaching the Oregon border after a couple of hours of hiking that Sunday morning. The heat had dissipated and we were feeling good, pausing briefly to sign in at the state line register, snap photographs, and post a blog telling readers that we had walked "home." It actually felt like a homecoming of sorts, although we were still about 450 miles from the Bridge of the Gods and the Columbia River, with many challenges to come.

As we descended the Siskiyous toward Ashland, a blister formed on the bottom of my right foot the size of a cigar burn. When it burst, it was nearly impossible for me to walk. So, we paused for a couple of days at Hyatt Lake, east of town, while I let the sucker heal, or at least let the nerves die. I cut a hole in the lining of my boot to give the blister more room, and eventually limped north for several days, feeling every step. There was a lot of brooding at that lake, a beautiful spot I wanted to escape. I called home and spoke with friends and editors for support. Despite years of backpacking, I was not ready for the emotional challenges of a long-distance hike. But even during this struggle, I could feel myself changing, both mentally and physically.

I have hiked in many areas of the West and completed many sections of the PCT, going back to the 1980s, when I lived in San Diego, and after I moved to Oregon in the mid-1990s. Back in those days the trail was always part of what I did in the backcountry as my friends and I explored and climbed in the Santa Anas, San Bernardinos, San Gabriels, Sierras, and Cascades. But the trail never was the focus. I suspect it's that way for many people. They appreciate the trail's existence without understanding its significance, how it came to be or the backbreaking work it takes to keep it going. I learned about all this through my newspaper reporting, and I took great joy in the luck I had to be able to inform others.

If that wasn't enough to keep Ian and me hiking, the encouragement from our readers was more than adequate. We received hundreds and hundreds of email notes from people who wanted to offer their support, tell us about their own trail experiences, or ask specific questions about the places we had seen or the gear we carried. We tried to answer them all, even if it was just to say thanks.

Two of those notes stand out. One came from a group of young people who wanted to tell us about the hike they were going to do in the Three Sisters Wilderness. They were very excited about their outing, so much so that when we arrived the following Friday at McKenzie Pass near the town of Sisters, they were waiting at the trailhead. We talked awhile, took a group photo, and watched them walk south into the woods. Another reader wrote to us from the Veteran's Administration Hospital in Portland, where he was a patient. He told us how he and other patients had hung a map on the wall to plot our progress; how they wished they could be out there hiking with us. A nurse had brought them guidebooks so they could see pictures of the trail. How could we quit after that?

In reality, the thoughts of quitting, I later learned, are just part of the transformation process. Other hikers told us about how mind and body acclimate to the distances. We started out trying for twenty-plus-mile days, folly at best, especially with the heat. But by the second week of hiking, the blisters behind us, we were pounding out our first ten miles before noon. We were in a rhythm and looking forward.

We met dozens of people on the trail, many of whom knew we were coming. They saw Ian's oversized camera and would say, "You're the guys from the *Oregonian*." News along the trail travels through hikers like the Pony Express, passed up and down from one to another. This was a typical experience for us.

I could go on about the endless stream of incredible days: the hospitality of the summer rangers at Crater Lake National Park; the burgers and ice cream at Elk Lake Resort; sublime showers at Forest Service campgrounds; the choking smoke from a nearby forest fire; fly-fishing in the Sky Lakes Wilderness; or the pull of Mount Thielsen's summit, so close to the PCT that it's a shame to walk by. That's the hike in physical terms, easy to understand and to explain.

It's much tougher to explain the mental hike and what it does to you. I finished this long-distance journey a changed man. Walking hour upon hour, inside my head, day after day, I learned much about myself and was able to focus on what is important in life. I lived for a month with all I needed in a pack on my back, which made me appreciate the comforts of home as well as to look at them warily.

I also was able to shift my perception of the passage of time. Open spaces are our inheritance, a gift from those who made sure these places were protected. They are also a gift from time. In the present we measure time step by step; then it's gone, catalogued and vaporized. On the trail, time has its own quality, like musical notes played live. Yes, it goes by. But out there, time is a dance, a perfect tango of connected movements, precise and methodic. It moves slowly and offers clarity.

As minutes tick away to hours and days, landscapes pass slowly, at least slowly enough to ingest. An hour goes by and you're only a few miles down the trail, having enjoyed the scenery and pondered every detail of the latest life challenge. I asked Carol to marry me the day before we ended our hike. She met us at Government Camp and walked with us the last four days. At 7½-Mile Camp on Eagle Creek, I proposed as we sat on a rock, surrounded by clear, cool water. I spent many steps before that day pondering that decision.

It's difficult to hang on to this sense of time back home, in the "real" world. Like a freeway, it moves much faster here, with less purpose most days. But it comes back now and again like a familiar song, a feeling of focus and steady vision. It's a persistent reminder of what's possible and most meaningful in this life. This is why I've always hiked. I may not have understood it that clearly before I walked across Oregon. This insight is what the trail has given me.

After twenty-five years as a newspaper reporter and editor, I now work on the trail's behalf. All those steps I took before have led me here. The events of every second, minute, and day are forever linked in time's trail on the ribbon of life, however short.

THERE AND BACK AGAIN

By Chris Hall

In recent years, a growing segment of Pacific Crest Trail hikers' trail names have been connected to popular works of literature and film such as Star Wars *or J. R. R. Tolkien's* Lord of the Rings. *Comments such as "May the forest be with you," references to the Misty Mountains, and trail names like Strider, Bilbo, and Gandalf are commonplace among the younger generations of PCT hikers; and Tolkien's famous adage, "All that is gold does not glitter. Not all those who wander are lost," has become a veritable anthem. As Chris Hall observes in this essay, such a connection is perhaps fitting, since the wilderness journey experienced on a PCT hike and the mythic adventure captured in Tolkien's novels share many features in common. The most important of these similarities seems to be that both entertain and inspire us, and both enrich our lives by uplifting our spirits.*

As we leave the trailhead parking lot and cars behind, and wander off into the backcountry, there is often a distinct feeling of having entered another world, another time. And as the trail climbs up onto the high mountain crests and we find ourselves cloud walking, looking down on cloudbanks or even rain and lightning while the sun blazes above, we know that we have, indeed, been transported to another realm.

After a few steps on the trail we find ourselves transported to another world. Gone is the clamor and chaos of Interstate 5; instead we walk, immersed in the forest's silence, as though in a vast and tranquil sea. My wife, Rose, and I traveled from our northern California home to the Pacific Crest Trail near

Mount Ashland in Oregon to escape the din and drudgery of town living. Here we sought—and found—the ancient stillness that we knew would renew and refresh us like nothing else we have discovered upon this earth, the stillness of the wild. Perhaps many hikers turn their steps toward the PCT to enter this other world, and for this same twofold purpose: to find escape from the clamor of crowds and to seek the sort of renewal that one can only find in the earth's quiet and unpeopled places.

For many who make the time to hike through the earth's wilder regions, there is a desire to retreat from everyday life and reconnect with something older and grander than themselves. For Rose and me the toil of daily life often prevents us from making longer treks along the trail. Yet, for hikers such as myself, the experience may prove no less significant than the longer, more arduous journeys of the thru hiker. For the day hiker, the trailhead near Mount Ashland provides an ideal place to explore the trail's wonders. This section of the PCT is easily accessible by road, and views of the Siskiyou Mountains—gold by morning and purple by evening—abound within a few miles of the trailhead.

As we hike north to south (against the usual PCT grain) across the sun-rich southern slopes of Mount Ashland, I find myself thinking of an essay by J. R .R. Tolkien in which he explores the purpose of fantasy literature. Tolkien laments that fantasy may fade away, its importance forgotten, as the industrial world becomes ever more pervasive and dreams and myths become increasingly overwhelmed by the glitz and glamour of technology. But even as he warns us of the danger of losing fantasy and wilderness, he celebrates the value both have for us. Tolkien argues that fantasy and myth hold spiritual and psychological benefits, such as providing an escape from the stress of daily life and a means by which to renew ourselves in body, mind, and spirit. We might find these very same benefits from time spent wandering the wilds of our own modern Middle Earth.

Indeed, the very same things we seek in fantasy—escape and renewal—are basic human needs and are, in fact, the very same things we find in the wilderness. We escape into both fantasy and wilderness to experience renewal.

From miles spent on the trail and hours spent in the pages of fantasy books, I have come to believe that humans not only desire mythic and wilderness experiences, we require them. My experience tells me that the rejuvenating power of both wilderness and fantasy is necessary for physical and mental health. In spite of this vital need, today's industrial world, with its emphasis on efficiency and profit, often dismisses fantasy and outdoor exploration. It is a vicious cycle: the need for renewal is especially pronounced given the frenetic (and ultimately exhausting) pace of contemporary life; at the same time, renewal is increasingly hard to find. However, if we take the time to step onto the trail or into the realm of fantasy, we may yet discover places, both real and imagined, with the power to restore, renew, and rejuvenate us so that we may return to our daily lives with new energy.

For Rose and me, this form of spiritual renewal comes most noticeably in two separate and significant moments: during our first night and on our last morning on the trail. Although the whole trip rejuvenates us, these two moments in particular embody the restorative peace we have come here to find. Perhaps these moments stand out to us because they come at liminal times—the spaces between day and night—which traditional cultures and wisdom traditions the world over have long associated with visions, transcendental experiences, and the spirit world. Indeed, transformative moments of heightened or altered awareness often seem to come in these brief stretches between light and dark, between known and unknown, between fantasy and reality. During these in-between times, as day blurs to night and back again, crepuscular creatures crawl in the darkness, and spirits stalk the shadows of our minds.

Our first transformative moment comes at moonrise. As the sun sets, a last golden glimmer of daylight fading in the west, a silvery light rises in the east to replace it, the moon shining brighter than any I have ever seen. Our camp is tucked away, a few hundred feet to the northwest of the trail, but through the trees we can still make out the distant peaks of the Siskiyous to the southeast. We hear the chattering of small creatures from the branches of the subalpine forest surrounding our camp—squirrels or chipmunks no doubt. And yet the mind still plays tricks with the shadows, suggesting a host of other possibilities. In the distance we catch the subtle rustling of brush, and everything from bears and cougars to orcs and trolls stalk through our fearful minds. But no orc attacks; no bear lumbers toward our little camp in the forest.

And in the end this night holds no fear for us, only comfort and soothing serenity. Tonight is a night without darkness, a night where moon shadows seem almost to dance across the ground as a gentle breeze sets limbs of pine and cedar swaying. The distant rustling ceases and we are left in near silence and total tranquility. Before we know it we are immersed completely in the beauty of this winding mountain trail. Gone are the worries that came before this journey—the nagging concerns and stresses of the workplace evaporate in the high mountain air. We have found peace at last, and soon, though the moon still shines bright in the clear sky above, we have passed into a deep and tranquil sleep.

I have long been a seeker of other worlds. And as I discovered through exploring the PCT, the fantastic vistas of the mind and the real views of the wilderness—like the sight of the Siskiyous' craggy peaks towering high above groves of fir, pine, and cedar—share more in common than one might think. Here among high peaks and crests, I find myself walking almost level with the clouds, navigating a world as foreign to the lowlander as the sky to one who cannot fly.

As we climb ever higher along the gradual sloping trail that cuts across Mount Ashland's southern flank, we emerge from the wooded depths to stand upon a nameless ridge. We stop to savor a wide open view of verdant, marshy meadows below. Beyond, the great trunks of the Klamath National Forest shoot skyward, and far away, in the distance, Mount Shasta's snowy peak rises. Rose and I breathe the mountain air—crisp even in summer—and relish this moment of recovery and escape. It feels as though we've crossed another threshold, moved deeper into another realm, along this wildern track.

On such trails as these, some of us may find the same things we find in fantasy. Part of what draws many of us to both the trail and to works of fantasy literature may be the need to escape from the burden of our daily lives, to leave the ordinary world behind. We may discover here, in the wild places of the world (and in the wild places of our mind), retreat from the mundane workaday life, retreat that renews and rejuvenates us so that we can return to our lives refreshed.

Our final morning on the trail provides us with another moment of escape and renewal, a morning where the sap rises and my spirits soar as we pause to watch the sunrise limn the Siskiyous' peaks in pale gold. Here, even our simple morning tea, brewed in a crude pot and served unsweetened, seems a luxury. Together we sit and sip our morning brew, watch as it sends coils of steam circling skyward in the early morning chill. As I look ahead and above toward Mount Ashland's peak, wreathed in mist, I am transported to Tolkien's Misty Mountains. In this instant, this place, the very ground beneath my feet is no less wondrous to me than the farthest reaches of Tolkien's Middle Earth. I half expect to see a dragon circling in the distance, elves darting through the forest, or an earth-loving hermit ambling down the mountain trail, walking stick in hand. In this moment, I think only of the world around me; forgotten are the trivial details of daily life. I have escaped, for a time, the everyday, to bask in the ancient beauty and power of these gleaming and mythic morning mountains.

We have come out here to escape and to recover some sense of our connection to the more-than-human realm. But we have also come to remember this: without places such as these our dreams become but faded memories of what once was or what might have been. Without real places free from the sludge and smog of modern life, our fantasies lose some of their meaning, and without such meaning our lives are likewise diminished.

Places such as these are vitally needed too, in light of both our frantic pace of life and contemporary ecological upheaval. If our whole life becomes nothing more than a series of phone calls, emails, and committee meetings, we may lose sight of the things in life that matter most, the things that bring us happiness and restore us, mind, body, and spirit.

And, like a faerie story, our journey brings us a happy ending as we turn our steps toward home again. Coming out here helps us remember what it is, exactly, that we are holding on to, helps us remember that there are still real places in this world as wild and grand as any fantasy. Traveling to such places is one of the most valuable experiences a human being can have, and such travels help us to see the world anew. It is no mistake that fantasy stories are themselves, invariably, tales of journeys; indeed the most famous pattern of myth is itself that of a journey—the hero's journey. Like the hero of mythology, we return home from our wanderings along the Pacific Crest enriched, so that we might enrich our homes and our communities in turn. And like Tolkien's beloved hero, Bilbo Baggins, we are gladdened when we arrive home at last, a little weary, perhaps, but also a little wiser. For though the trail goes ever, ever on, in the end the path leads us home—to be complete a journey must take us full circle, must take us there and back again.

OF OUTLAWS AND TRAIN ROBBERIES

By Corey Lee Lewis

Under the shadow of Pilot Rock and just west of Interstate 5, the Pacific Crest Trail drops down from the slopes of Mount Ashland to Siskiyou Pass. The trail crosses above the 0.6-mile-long Tunnel No.13 of the old Southern Pacific Railroad (now owned by the Central Oregon and Pacific Railroad). On October 11, 1923, this was the site of the tragic and ill-fated D'Autremont train robbery.

Along the length of the PCT, there are periodic but generally brief encounters with railroads. These range from the busy tracks of Sullivans Curve at Cajon Pass to the Western Pacific's passage along the Feather River near Belden to the corridor on both sides of the Columbia River. Once a mainstay of American passenger and freight transportation, railroads have been in decline since the advent of the automobile; however, their tracks, both the old and unused and those still maintained and traveled today, often follow the same routes and use the same passes as many early pioneers who struggled to cross these rugged western mountains. Both this story and David Foscue's "Triumph and Tragedy at Stevens Pass" deal with railroads that the hiker crosses over, way over.

My brother's real name—not his trail name, but the one given to him at birth—was Bart. His trail name—or what some call a forest, spirit, wilderness, or street name—was Black Bart. And yes, he was a renegade, a wild one. Like a western outlaw, he too was bigger than life and couldn't be bound by rules.

Black Bart is a fitting hero and namesake for my brother (or for any boy growing up in the American West). The real Black Bart was an outlaw—a bandit robber—who held up stage coaches, and more importantly he did it with style. His real name was Charles Boles, and he became one of the most famous and notorious of western outlaws during the 1870s and 1880s. Black Bart primarily operated along the Siskiyou Trail in northern California and southern Oregon. He was known as the Gentleman Bandit because of his habit of leaving poems after his robberies and his polite manner of speech while committing the crimes. Some of his heists were dramatically popularized, and much fictionalized, in the widely read "dime novels" of the time where Black Bart grew to mythic proportions and national fame.

Perhaps one of the things that so enamors Americans with the West, and so endears us to wilderness, is that both mythically feel like the realm where anything is possible, where the rules don't apply, where one man can win with only his raw grit and determination. It is the land of the outlaw, the refuge of the revolutionary. As Edward Abbey once wrote, "Why this wilderness cult? . . . Because we like the taste of freedom; we like the smell of danger." A true western outlaw himself, Abbey also said we need wilderness if for no other reason than so that a lone, desperate outlaw has some place to run and hide from the long arm of the law.

It is no surprise, then, that when Black Bart and I were hiking we often found ourselves thinking and acting (*pretending*, if you must use the word) like we were outlaws on the run, renegade brothers fleeing from the law. We listened patiently across canyons for the sounds of human voices, intently scanned distant ridgelines for dots of color or human movement, and practiced leave-no-trace ethics when vacating a campsite, as if an entire posse, complete with bloodhounds, were on our trail. We were immersed in western history and tales of banditry, especially bank, stage coach, and train robberies. Of the three, there is no question that in the lore of the West the train robbery always rated as the most daring and intriguing for Black Bart and me.

One of my favorite sections of the Pacific Crest Trail, then, has less to do with scenic vistas or piled-high pancakes and more to do with its proximity to what easily rates in my book as one of the most interesting and infamous of western outlaw stories of all time: the failed "Gold Special" train robbery. In addition to the fact that it was the last attempted train holdup in Oregon, and was carried out by three brothers, it included dynamite, a high-elevation tunnel, a wilderness frontier, and an international manhunt. And of course, because the PCT passes directly through this area, and you can easily hike down to the veritable scene of the crime, the Gold Special story is a must-know for any PCT hiker crossing the Siskiyous in Oregon.

The setup for the heist was dramatic, with all the perfect ingredients of a great train robbery. First, it was to take place in a high mountain tunnel, identified only as Tunnel No. 13 of the Southern Pacific Railway. The brothers D'Autremont who planned and carried out the crime consisted of Ray and Roy, twenty-three-year-old twins, and Hugh, who was only nineteen at the time. It was 1923, and the brothers estimated the Gold Special to be carrying $40,000 in its fortified mail cars, which they planned to blow open with dynamite.

The brothers selected a perfect spot for the ambush and had each detail planned out carefully in advance. They would board the train after it stopped for its usual brake check and would use the cover of darkness provided by the tunnel to surprise the engineers. Then, they would blow the doors off the mail cars with dynamite, remove the cash, and disappear into the wilderness. They even presoaked their shoes in kerosene and had a pound of black pepper to throw the dogs off their scent. And deep in the Cascade wilderness, somewhere on the side of either Brushy or Bald Mountain, they had previously built a hideout; accounts differ as to the exact location of the hideout, but both Brushy and Bald Mountain stand together, not many trail miles to the east and north from the scene of the crime. There, on the side of one of these insignificant summits, the brothers dug out and built a hidden refuge to stay in until the inevitable manhunt cooled down.

But things didn't exactly go according to plan. It appears that the three brothers were much less like the Three Musketeers than the Three Stooges. First, they used several times more dynamite than was necessary to blow open the door of the mail car. In fact, they literally blew the fortified train car to pieces, tearing the mail clerk, who had locked himself inside the car, and everything in it to shreds. As the thunderous explosion echoed across the surrounding peaks, and smoke and burning debris filled the tunnel, the brothers accidentally shot and killed the train's brakeman, who came running toward the destroyed car. Then, either in cold blood, or by accident during an ensuing struggle (again, accounts vary), the brothers shot both the engineer and the fireman, bringing the death toll to four but still leaving them empty-handed. Without anything to show for their efforts, and with four murders on their hands, the brothers hastily fled the scene, disappearing into the wilderness and heading for their hideout. To make matters worse for themselves, however, they accidentally left easily readable signs that allowed law enforcement to identify them almost immediately. Roy dropped his Colt revolver on the railroad tracks as they ran away, which had a traceable serial number on it, and a piece of registered mail was forgotten in the pocket of an old pair of pitch-stained overalls the brothers left behind.

Further investigation revealed that this wasn't the brothers' first botched robbery attempt; they had previously failed at holding up both a candy store and a bank. In their first attempted robbery, they had been casing the candy store while hiding in a nearby ditch. Unfortunately, all three brothers fell asleep and missed their long-awaited chance to accost the elderly owner as he was locking up. Similarly, their second aborted attempt at grand theft saw them standing outside of a bank, armed and ready to enter, only to see a rival gang pull up, fully armed, and rob it right in front of them.

Despite being such bungling burglars, the D'Autremont brothers were actually quite good outlaws. They not only managed to escape what has been called "the most extensive manhunt in US history" but succeeded in remaining free for almost four years. Legend has it that Ray actually left the mountain hideout after only two weeks and made it to Medford, Oregon, where to his horror he saw the city was plastered with "WANTED" posters bearing pictures of the three brothers. The mountains, at this time, were crawling with National Guard troops, lawful posses and posses formed by railroad workers looking for revenge. Ray, in disguise, apparently joined one of these posses as he traveled back toward their hideout, only to silently slip away from the group when the time was right.

There were anywhere from two million to nine million wanted posters printed in a number of languages, including Spanish, German, Portuguese, and French. Despite the massive mobilization of manpower, the brothers managed to escape the lynch mobs and law dogs searching for them. Hugh eventually joined the army under the assumed name, James Price, and was even shipped out to the Philippines; even such a great distance, however, couldn't save him, as a fellow serviceman recognized him from a wanted poster and turned him in to the authorities. The twins, Ray and Roy, made it to Steubenville, Ohio, together, where they adopted the name Goodwin; both held jobs and Ray married and started a family. But the twins were recognized from a newspaper story about them and found themselves, like Hugh, on their way back to Oregon to face murder charges.

Although all three brothers initially claimed they were returning to clear their names, and Hugh initially filed a plea of not guilty, eventually they confessed to the crime and were given life sentences. Hugh was paroled in 1958 but died soon after from stomach cancer, while Roy was transferred to Oregon State Hospital in 1960 for schizophrenia and lived there for the rest of his life. Ray was paroled in 1961 and worked as a custodian at Oregon State University until retirement; he passed away in 1984.

So, although they weren't very successful thieves, Ray, Roy, and Hugh D'Autremont were tried and true outlaws, real renegades of the West. And although they didn't come away any richer from their daring heist, they did succeed in giving PCT hikers a very rich tale.

My brother would have liked this outlaw story and especially the fact that it was about renegade brothers in the wilderness. He would have really enjoyed hiking along the Pacific Crest, over Siskiyou Pass and down toward the East Fork of Cotton Creek and the infamous Tunnel No. 13. It's not a long scramble off the trail to the railroad tracks and the entrance to the tunnel, which one can still walk through and explore. Bart has been gone for two years now, off on his own solo hike, where no one can follow. But the next time I hike that high pass, I'm going to bring him along with me, and like a true outlaw I'm going to break my own leave-no-trace rules so I can scatter a few of his ashes. Then Black Bart and I will sit, high above the dark mouth of Tunnel No. 13, and laugh as we tell the story of the not-so-brilliant but definitely bold D'Autremont brothers, one of the most brazen and bungled of all Western outlaw stories, the failed Gold Special train robbery.

STOPPING, LOOKING, AND LISTENING

By Kaci Elder

Although most of the pieces in this anthology have come to us in prose form, we felt it was also important to collect some poetry about the Pacific Crest Trail and its environs. We have included the works of renowned poets like Gary Snyder, Jim Dodge, and David Wagoner in the Trailside Reader. *But we also felt that it was important to make room for new voices. Kaci Elder, like our other hiker-writers, brings a fresh, inspired perspective to the collection.*

While movement and making mileage is a ubiquitous topic of conversation among PCT hikers, we are reminded by Elder in this triptych of poems that stopping and taking time to soak it all in is just as important. Even the most ardent of thru hikers find themselves occasionally arrested by beauty, stopped by a sunset or held in place for a moment by the dance of a butterfly. In much the same way that poetry asks its readers to slow down, to pay closer attention to the rhythms and sounds of language, backcountry trails ask travelers to leave the freeway behind and to attune themselves to the slower rhythms of walking and resting. We enjoy the repetition of making and breaking camp, the punctuated pause of a lunch stop, and the exclamatory crossing of a high crest or raging river. This becomes our language of the trail, out of which we build our trail stories, songs, and poems, the hooks upon which memories are later hung. But if it is true that there is poetry in such movement, it is equally true that to truly appreciate it we must take the time to stop, to look, and to listen.

STOPPING

Lumbering north of the Siskiyou Pass I slowdown my self
To no movement, no progress,
No inch forward on the folded map—resisting momentum of muscle and
   mind—
and I Stop.

Green Springs Summit, it will wait. Yet—
What twitches?

It is my toes, pressing into shoe soles rhythmically
Lockstep with my heels, who lift themselves
Up and
        up and
                up again (like grasping toddlers).
My knees, they tighten release tighten into a
Corporal choir of impatience.

I want to move.

I pivot,
Face the path behind,
To those just-taken steps vivid in the ache of my thighs,
Remembered in the taut pull of calves pushing me forward, forward and
   toward.
I see the long stretch of trail I have just walked, yet

Was I there?

That last droopy fir on the south slope of Little Pilot Peak,
Did my eyes track the sinuous pattern of fire ants
Making warfare on a stout trunk,
Did I notice how many needles clasp in each cluster,
Where the bear tore bark, or where the cones
Hurled themselves toward the earth and now lay, spent, in slow decay?

Or was I elsewhere,
Walking through thoughts of next Christmas,
The friend who didn't call, the lists of all the things I need to do when I
Check this off that list.

I can't help myself.
Miles have turned the majestic into the mundane.
I have seen how many ant tracks, how many fir trees, perched eagles, and
  peaks,
How many sunrises, moonsets, creeks, outcrops, and
Starry starry nights   and I admit, at times, I observe
A new thought instead. I get lost in them.
Tomorrow there will be more.

I have a friend, eight years inside prison (for something he did, indeed, do
  and he is my next thought,
Waiting inside his dust-on-concrete cell, and I wonder
If he were here now, could he
Be Here Now?
Where his thoughts would be, and how swiftly he would stop them
To make room for this.

I feel the small rub of guilt weave into my chest, fined for complacence
  while walking
Amongst giants. I know the gods sleep here.
And so I have come to this stop, only to submit to the thought
That I am not able to stop,
Not ready to face the unease of my
Un-narrated self.

I am young, with many lifetimes to cycle and, at least, I know this.
Like a nudging mother, I gently watch myself move cautiously toward the
  stillness,
  and in so doing,
I am
Stopping.

LOOKING

She stepped off the trail.
It wasn't Mount Hood. Or Callahans Lodge. Or Crater Lake.
It was just here, in this regular place
Where she stopped, slid off shoulder straps and unlatched her hip belt,
Let her pack fall and felt the buoyancy of relief.

She bent low and lay down long on her belly in the unnamed grass
Which drew borders down the edges of the PCT,
Like a frame to the picture.

She
Closed
Her
Eyes.

She opened them.

She watched a fat black bug hug the top of a spear
Of grass,   and   like a grandfather clock
   the pendulum grass   ticktocked   tick   tock, tick   tock
Until the bug stretched one   long   leg
Onto the next spear, clasped it tenderly into grip and soon,
Legs two and three and four and five and six
Followed suit, the fat black bug having moved a slender strip of grass
   closer
To where he needed to go.

Now she rolled over onto her back,
Pointed her legs and arms straight up into the sky, squeezed her eyes
Shut, opened them again and thought,
I'm falling! I'm falling! Into the pale sky she pretended was the hole
She could fall up to, and, like a child
She almost believed.

LISTENING

There are rebels afield,

Moving soft rubble aside as they push up, up, up and

Forge cracks in the dirt with their tangled rhizomes,
   protruding petioles,
     leaves that'll sting ya until you learn
       just
         how
           to
             touch
               them.

These are the medicines we knew (before we knew too much).

In our tongue we name them

Yarrow. Nettle. Plantain. Cascara. Madrone. Oregon Grape. Chickweed.

They are the stoppers of leaking blood, the scrape healers, bowel movers,
  fever shakers,
       the magicians who coax out that damn splinter
          you've been limping with for days
      on the curvatures of this long, long trail.

When I chew the leaf of madrone, my molars grinding down astringent oils
  (Puckering tongue!)   and then slap on the spittled leaf poultice,
Easing the pulsing bite of the mosquito—

When I've taught you to see the budding needle tips of the Douglas fir
and the dandelion leaves and the tanoak acorns and miner's lettuce and
evergreen huckleberries, and to know them all as
Food—

When you've shown me that freshly picked yarrow leaves will stop the
bleeding, that cascara bark moves my digestion, and that the plantain
should be acknowledged on bended knees and a shout of "Hallelujah and
Blessed Be!"—

When we steep nettle tea overnight to bring inside its Vitamin B, and relax
into knowing that

All of this is medicine, and all of this is free, and it grows under feet and
   over heads—

Don't forget.

This is what they burned the witches for.
In the land my elders come from.
This is what they sent the children away for.
In the land you're passing through now.

For knowing this unregulated medicine chest,
For plying the wild anarchist's pharmacopeia,
For practicing the universe's healthcare
   The wild healers of the Western World
            were strapped to the burning stake,
   The wild healers of The People here
            were forced away to school
            for the re-education of a first nation.

And so,
When I walk this cresting Pacific trail—or heck, cut across the Fred Meyer
   parking lot—
I will notice my plant allies
   Gently and unrelentingly pushing themselves up through the
Dirt and soil and clay, or poking themselves through small fissures in
   sidewalks
      (If that's what it takes to get noticed these days), enduring denigration as
         our weeds
            to pull, and
            to poison.

They have been waiting for the
Remembering times, and now they are speaking
   Each time the thorn plucks pants,
      Each time the leaf brushes boots,
         Each trip over root—it is a small voice saying, Hey! We are still here.

Listen to them.
And listen when the oldest folks talk plants,
When the youngest folks talk plants, and if the
Original people of this place, where you are walking,
Ever take the risk to share their secrets that grow from soil and clay, oh my
  oh my oh my oh my
Just
Listen.

(And then tell the rest).

BE PREPARED

By George and Patricia Semb

Every Pacific Crest Trail hiker knows well the wisdom of the Boy Scout motto, "Be prepared." The wide variety of problems that may arise in the backcountry often require a number of different skills, plans, and equipment to solve. From getting lost or separated from our hiking partners, to medical emergencies, injuries, inclement weather, and failed equipment, the backcountry traveler must be prepared for it all. Even short hikes and day hikes on the PCT require us to be prepared with survival gear and emergency plans.

Even these briefer adventures can go awry, as George and Patricia Semb note in this piece. Authors of Day Hikes on the Pacific Crest Trail: California *and its companion volume for Oregon and Washington (both published by Wilderness Press in 2000), George and Patricia are experienced hikers and know the PCT well. In California, you can day hike more than 1491 miles of the PCT, or 86 percent of it; in Oregon and Washington, you can day hike 879 miles, or 87 percent. But don't let this accessibility to the high country fool you. As the Sembs' story demonstrates, even the most experienced hikers need backup plans, and for the unwary and unprepared the high country can be very dangerous indeed.*

Be prepared. That's the Boy Scouts' motto as well as a song made popular many years ago by Tom Lehrer, one verse of which reads:

SONG EXCERPT: "Be Prepared," by Tom Lehrer. Copyright © 1953 by Tom Lehrer. Reprinted by permission of the author.

Be prepared! That's the Boy Scouts' solemn creed,
Be prepared! And be clean in word and deed.
Don't solicit for your sister, that's not nice,
Unless you get a good percentage of her price.

Our first encounter with the Pacific Crest Trail, unfortunately, was during an "unprepared" moment at Saddle Junction near Idyllwild, California. It taught us the importance of being prepared—of always having a contingency plan, or two.

The night before, we had met our friends Mel and Carrie in Palm Springs for the weekend. Sunday morning, we decided to take the tram from the 115-degree desert floor—it was August—to the ridge high above. We would hike to Devils Saddle by one route and take another route back to the tram for the trip back down. In all, it would be a twelve-mile hike. Pat and I looked at it as a way to break in my brand-new, pink orienteering shoes—shoes so grotesque that Carrie would pretend not to be with us when we met other hikers on the trail.

As we approached Saddle Junction, the cumulus clouds that had been mounting all morning turned black, and as we stood under some trees they began to unload. Rain turned to hail, calm turned to wind, and the temperature fell as the storm unleashed its fury. We moved to the shelter of some nearby rocks but could not escape the hail, some two inches of it in less than ten minutes. It pounded our nylon jackets without mercy, leaving behind pockmarks on our arms and torso. Each of us was dressed only in shorts, T-shirt, and a thin nylon jacket. That was it. As the water and hailstones swirled beneath our feet, we began to shiver. We knew we were in serious trouble and that our only option was to start down the west side of the mountain to warmer air below and the town of Idyllwild. During that 2.5-mile trek to warmth, Pat and I also swore that we would never again go to the mountains without a day pack filled with emergency gear, a promise we have kept ever since.

It was not until several years later that we returned to the PCT, this time to hike the state of Oregon. We did several day hikes near Siskiyou Pass, Fish Lake, and in Crater Lake National Park. One of those hikes dealt us a healthy dose of reality. We started the day at the Sevenmile Marsh trailhead and hiked together six miles into Sky Lakes Wilderness. Pat turned around to go back to the car to drive to the Cold Springs trailhead. From there, she would hike in to meet me and we would hike out together. Pat's concern grew exponentially when she did not meet me on the trail. She walked back to the Cold Springs trailhead and waited until 5:30 PM, by which time I surely should have been there. The emergency plan we had made earlier in the day went into effect: Pat immediately drove back toward the Sevenmile Marsh trailhead, where we had begun the day's hike.

As much as we both love the outdoors, we also know there are risks in outings like these. A primary objective is to limit those risks. We cannot emphasize enough that you must know the limits of your endurance, both mental and physical, and that you must exercise caution, particularly when you are fatigued. On this particular day, I made some bad decisions as I approached the Devils Peak/Lee Peak Saddle (7320 feet). I was hiking from north to south, so I could see the wall of snow facing me as I started up toward the saddle. Many hikers coming from the south slide down these snowfields. However, this can be risky if you're not experienced in dealing with snowfields. You must pay attention to what you're sliding into. If you end up in rocks or encounter a tree on the way down, serious injury or even death may result. Needless to say, I did not have any experience with snowfields, nor did I have, or know how to use even if I did, an ice ax.

I had been climbing the snowfield for several hundred feet as I neared the saddle. I could see tracks in the snow in front of me, but I did not realize just how steep the ascent had become. I lost my footing and slid several hundred feet, hitting small trees, roots, and rocks along the way. Luckily, I only scraped my arms and elbows and bruised my ribs. Despite losing all but one water bottle, I was able to walk out. During that hike—7.5 miles to the Sevenmile Marsh trailhead, then 5.7 miles down the access road—I did not meet another soul. At about 6:30 PM Pat spotted me along the access road. She was relieved that my injuries were not too serious, and I was happy to put that day behind us.

That incident reinforced several important points. First, always establish an emergency contingency plan. In this case, we had agreed that if Pat had not seen me by 5:30 PM, she was to drive back to the original trailhead. If she did not find me there or along the way, she was to file a missing person report. Second, when an emergency arises, follow the plan. The reason you make a plan is to have a set of procedures to follow when, and if, an emergency occurs. In this case, the plan saved the day. We were prepared.

The other thing the incident did was to get us to rethink what kind of hikes we were going to do. We were using these day hikes to build up to longer backpacking expeditions along the trail. We also liked just doing day hikes. Much as we enjoyed backpacking, these day hikes were appealing and, what the heck, we had already day hiked from the California–Oregon border to the entrance to Crater Lake National Park. We wondered just how much of the Pacific Crest Trail we could day hike. At the same time, just for fun, we started to chronicle these day hikes. By the end of fall, we had day hiked every single mile of the 464.6 PCT miles in Oregon, from Wards Fork Gap just south of the Oregon border to the Bridge of the Gods at the Columbia River.

Next, we explored Washington and mapped out eighteen day hikes covering some 246.1 miles north to Snoqualmie Pass. The northern 261.1 PCT miles to Manning Park are more challenging for day hikers. However, we managed to map out thirteen day hikes that covered more than half of those miles.

Over the next two years, as we completed our day-hiking mission, there were a few minor incidents but none that ever led to major injury or distress. We had faithfully followed our motto, "Be prepared."

GREAT STRENGTH OF FEET

By Amanda Carter

*There are many things we take for granted in our daily lives that we gain
a new awareness of, and appreciation for, after having spent some time on
the trail. Whether it is our soft bed, warm and dry house, or the health
and functionality of our feet, the importance of these things is easy to overlook in our ordinary lives but often becomes painfully obvious once we are
on the trail. As Amanda Carter notes, taking care of one's feet is a critical priority for any hiker, one that is easy to miss until we are blistered,
bruised, and footsore. And, of course, the same holds true for our own
health; our physical ability and strength of spirit is often unappreciated
until it is tested, as are many of our closest relationships. In this story of
hiking the trail with her sister, Carter gains an appreciation for her sister's
courage and fortitude and reminds us to be careful that we don't take our
own blessings for granted.*

"When you're backpacking, the most important thing you need to worry
about is your feet." Until my sister said so, I hadn't really thought
of it that way before. I spent most of my preparation for this trip worrying
about food, firewood, extra blankets, and, if I'm perfectly honest, monsters and
zombies and serial killers stalking us through the backcountry of the Fremont-
Winema National Forest in Oregon.

I am what some would call a "car camper" and what others might call a
"wimpy camper." To me, roughing it means sleeping outside, cooking rudi-
mentary dinners, and then packing everything into the car every morning and
driving away. My sister, though, is a different story. Roughing it, to her, means

hiking strenuous distances and elevations carrying everything she needs on her own back, and even sleeping in snow. So when I told her I thought we should take a trip to hike the Pacific Crest Trail where it skirts Crater Lake in southern Oregon, we had very different attitudes toward the preparation. While I was busy concocting wildly paranoid scenarios involving the living dead, Cammy was worrying about her feet.

My sister is quite a bit more *rational* than I am. Or maybe rational isn't the right word; maybe *grounded* is the better choice. I'm a writer, a word person, always with my head in the proverbial clouds, always making decisions based on emotion and imagination. (Yes, I'll admit it: I slept with a hatchet next to me the entire trip . . . damned zombies.) Cammy, on the other hand, is a highly logical person. She's a scientist who makes a living by seeing exactly what's in front of her and whose judgments are rooted in common sense rather than fantastical impulse. That logical outlook is one of the many reasons I brought her with me: obviously, it makes her way better at this whole outdoors thing than I am, and it also makes her a damn fine geologist.

"Yeah you've always gotta take really good care of your feet—keep 'em dry, keep 'em protected—because they're the tools you use most of all on a backpack trip . . . even more than toilet paper." She chuckles. "You've gotta be extra careful in terrain like this too, because it's steep and unstable . . . crumbly, I mean." She's right. We've been hiking for only a couple hours and so far I've already slipped countless times, mostly regaining my balance but sitting down hard often enough I'm sure I'll have bruises tomorrow—what our mom always called a *tried and true blue moon.*

The trail we're on now is narrowing fast, the volcanic boulders encroaching on its space. In the distance, I can see pine and Douglas fir marching up the sides of high slopes and I wonder how anything can gain footing in this terrain. It's chunky and sharp and doesn't seem all that hospitable to vegetation. And yet I see wildflowers—columbine, aster, monkey flower—clinging to the sheer grades above me. I squint against the crisp glare of the July sun trying to get a better look, and suddenly I'm staring my waffle stompers in the face . . . I've gone down . . . again.

"I guess I'm falling for both of us! You've hardly slipped at all," I comment as I brush dust and cinders off my jeans.

"At least my ass has gotten big enough to protect my tailbone."

"Ha! You and me both!" I laugh.

"Maybe that should be in the PCT field guides," Cammy muses. "Those who wish to hike the Oregon section of the PCT can and should prepare by eating doughnuts and growing their butts to cushion their falls."

"Is it just my lack of experience or do you think lots of people spend this portion of the trail mostly on their backsides?" I wonder.

"I think they probably do. We're basically traversing a huge landslide," says Cammy the geologist, "or rather a series of them. The Cascadia Subduction Zone creates these stratovolcanoes—they're the high peaks you see on the topo map—that are made of mostly volcanic debris so they erode really easily. It's actually pretty exciting. Southern Oregon is one of the best places to see such young volcanics."

"Exciting, huh?"

"Oh yeah! Mount Mazama blew up only about seven thousand years ago, which is actually pretty recent." She glances at me sideways to see if I'm appropriately struck by what she's just said. I'm not.

"Okay, let me see if I can explain what's so cool about where we are. The Cascade Range is basically a long string of volcanoes that runs the length of the West Coast. About four or five million years ago, these big stratovolcanoes grew on top of an existing platform of rocks left over from melting oceanic crust. You've got Lassen Peak and Mount Shasta in California all the way up to Mount Mazama, Three Sisters, and Mount Hood in Oregon."

"So it's like a series of zits on a teenager's face: high peaks that erupt periodically."

"Really, Amanda, does everything have to be so disgusting with you?"

"Hey! I take great pride in my metaphors!"

"What's really interesting is that all those huge volcanoes are actually very young and vulnerable to erosion—that's why you keep falling. The rapid erosion of these steep peaks makes this part of the trail pretty slippery."

"*Vulnerable* is definitely not the first word you'd think of to describe deadly volcanoes."

"It's true and that's what I find so interesting! What's underneath the volcanoes is a much more extensive, much older platform of rocks with a completely different chemical composition that makes them much more stable; because that platform took longer to form, it's stronger and it's gonna last a whole lot longer than those fast-forming, explosive volcanoes." She pauses. "I dunno...I guess I think it's so cool because it's not what you'd expect. Your brain wants to tell you it's the high volcanoes that will last forever . . ." She trails off.

She doesn't continue right away. I look at her, about to ask a question and then stop. She looks like she's concentrating as she walks. Her body language hints at pain. I can't pinpoint what tells me that, but I learned to read that language well during her long months of physical therapy. I realize she's probably thinking about her feet, just like she has been the whole trip, just like she has been since her accident two years ago.

"You wanna take a break, Cam? I could use some water and rest. Falling down the whole damned Pacific Crest Trail is wearing me out."

"Yeah, I should probably take some ibuprofen anyway. We've got a ways to go and my foot's kinda starting to ache."

We find a fallen log that's not quite as rotten and bug infested as the rest, unshoulder our packs, and sit down. One of the things that characterizes this section of the trail, and Oregon in general for that matter, is all the deadfall. Having grown up in southern California, all the gray rotted logs scream *fire hazard*, but this climate is saturated with rain and snowfall for most of the year, so everything is still wet even in the height of summer. I can smell the layers of decaying leaves and wood—what I've always thought of as a *cellar smell*, organic and old. We chat pleasantly about our boyfriends, plans for grad school, and what's new with our family. Twenty minutes go by easily before we decide to get moving.

"Hey, do you know what time it is?" Cammy asks me as we start walking again.

"Yeah, it's about 1:30."

We look at each other. Our eye contact is enough to establish that we're both thinking the same thing. Good thing too, because neither of us wants to talk about it, especially not Cammy. But we both know . . . at this exact time on this exact day two years ago, Cammy, my little sister, lay on a desert highway, crushed and bleeding, waiting for the jaws of life to pry her from a crumpled vehicle, waiting to see if she'd survive or perish on Highway 1 in Baja.

When the van Cammy was driving rolled, it hit a tree and the steering column collapsed in on her, destroying her lower body—compound fractures in both femurs, tibia and fibula broken in one leg, one severed Achilles tendon, and of course the shattered left foot. She was in the hospital for a month afterward and off her feet for four months after that. She's endured countless reconstructive and plastic surgeries and had to completely relearn how to first stand and then walk. The process was slow and incredibly painful. Walking with her now, I wonder just how terrifying it must have been for Cammy to face all the things she'd have to give up—running, playing soccer, rock climbing—things she loved, things that defined her. And that is real fear, not zombie invasions or monsters in the closet, but loss of personal identity; how can I be me when I can no longer do the things that have made me who I am for as long as I can remember? My sister has faced that fear and given it the finger, and that is real bravery.

We've been walking in charged silence and I wonder what memories are creeping back to her. I'll probably never know because my sister is not like me: she doesn't talk everything into the ground and she doesn't complain when something hurts. Instead she lowers her head, sets her jaw, and pushes forward…always forward. She doesn't crumble like so many would—like I myself would—because Cammy's nothing if not solid.

And suddenly it dawns on me all at once why she's so taken with the geology of where we are. Doesn't the landscape of the Cascade Range mirror her own experience? Doesn't that long string of volcanoes resemble the long strings of scars where broken bones carved unruly holes in her legs? And aren't those scars fading just as those volcanoes are eroding? I look at my sister's legs—she's wearing shorts, yet one more sign of a kind of bravery I could never muster—and yes, those scars are fading fast. I never thought they would because they were so big and so severe.

But the lesson I've learned from my little sister on this trip is that, sometimes, the most extreme things are also the most ephemeral. What will be left when those high volcanic peaks have eroded to nubbins? What's left will be what was there all along: that solid platform that's so much older, so much bigger, and so much more permanent. Regardless of what drastic changes occur on the surface, that platform isn't going anywhere.

Cammy's the same person she always has been. No doubt things have changed on the surface: she's no longer the all-star fullback everyone's always known her to be, she'll probably carry ibuprofen everywhere for the rest of her life, and she'll always have to take extra special care of her feet. But where others would be justified in making excuses—"I can't hike the PCT, Amanda, it'll be too hard and hurt too much"—Cammy makes none. And how lucky am I to know someone who can triumph over so much pain and loss? Those shark-attack-looking scars are her personal volcanoes, but the sheer force of her will is her underlying platform…and that sucker is not going anywhere.

I stop and take a good look at my little sister; she's the most beautiful girl I've ever seen. I smile, reach out my arm and pinch her.

"Ow!" she giggles. "You're a bitch!"

"No, Cammy, you are. And I truly pity any zombie that ever gets in your way."

NIGHT VISITOR AT MAIDU LAKE: A TRUE PACIFIC CREST TRAIL STORY WITH VERY LITTLE EMBELLISHMENT

By Keith A. "St. Alfonzo" Liker

From ghoulies and ghosties
And long-leggedy beasties
And things that go bump in the night,
Good Lord, deliver us!

—Traditional prayer

Our imaginations thrive under the cover of darkness. Deep in the blackness of night tends to be when our worst fears prevail and paranoia overwhelms rationality. The unseen foe unleashes our inner child. And whether it is fear of the monster under our bed, or the one lurking in the parking garage or the dark alley, the feelings are the same. Nighttime on the Pacific Crest Trail is ripe for the adrenaline rush that accompanies an unexplained sound: that bump in the night. From the snap of twigs to the rustling of tent walls or the crackling of leaves, most PCT hikers have at least one story of dancing with their own fears in the dappled moonlight. While backpacking the PCT solo through southern Oregon, Keith Liker came face-to-face not only with his fears but with a formidable and unexpected nocturnal predator who proved to be his match. This is his story.

What the hell was that?

I am rising, slowly, from the subterranean unconsciousness of sleep, clawing my way toward the surface of the waking state, or at least I think I am. It had been a long day on the trail and I am exhausted. I can't quite place what I just heard, and, more importantly, what I just *felt*. Something is outside the tent and making contact with it, but I'm not certain if this is real or part of some anxiety-driven dream.

In my semiconscious state, I feel inside the tent, Braille-like, for my head-lamp. At that moment, I hear it again. Something is pushing and scratching on the tent trying to get *inside* the tent, and here's the part I don't like—*I'm* inside the tent. I am now fully awake, and I realize my mistake: before going to sleep, I had not hung my food. Instead, I "strategically" placed my food on the ground a few feet away from the tent where I could see it "just in case" the bear should pay a visit. Just my luck—my anxiety attracted the bear, and he is here!

As I shine the light outside the tent, I see that my food bag is apparently unmolested. I have a brief moment of relief, but immediately the thoughts come from all directions at once: Do I rush out and grab my food before the bear gets it? Do I shine the light and try to scare it away before it gets to my food? Or, do I just start peeing my pants now, knowing that the flimsy tent fabric is all that separates us? As I try to decide what to do next, I hear, and now *feel*, the scratching at the rear of the tent. I listen for the heavy snuffling of the bear, but it never comes. This bear is obviously operating in stealth mode. I feel it pushing against the tent, and now I see the tent move! The scratching sound continues, and I see the bottom of the tent *lift* just inches from my hip, as though a snout were under it.

At that moment, I find myself outside the tent in an instant of near panic. I don't even remember unzipping the door. I am armed with only my headlamp and a full bladder. My trekking pole, my only weapon, is nowhere to be found. I'm not thinking clearly. Where did I put it? Instinctively, I place myself between the bear and my food, but I have nothing with which to defend myself.

Shining the light, there is no bear to be seen. I am relieved to learn that it is not a bear. It is smaller and it's not afraid of me. It has gone under the tent and I can't see it. It *doesn't* want my food—it wants *me*.

It is quiet and still outside the tent. There is no wind, no visible moon, a few mosquitoes, and a circle of diffused light wherever I shine the headlamp. Surreal moments pass. I have no idea what to do next. Then I see the tent move again.

Whatever it is, it's *not* leaving on its own. Not knowing what to do next, I check my watch: 1:34 AM. "Come on, show yourself!" I shout aloud, and immediately realize how ridiculous that sounds. I try to laugh, but this is no laughing matter—there's a predator under my tent.

I remove a stake and lift the tent corner. There, on top of the ground cloth, underneath the tent, is the stuff of which nightmares are made: the biggest, fattest toad I've ever seen. Mystery solved. This should be easy.

The toad is perfectly camouflaged to match the forest floor: gray, brown, speckled, warty, and wrinkled. All I have to do is scare him to make him hop away. Nice Mr. Toad. It's time for you to move along, so I can go back to sleep and resume worrying about the bear.

Using the open palm of my hand, I gently push the toad from behind, hoping he will move away and start eating mosquitoes. As I push, I feel him tense up and resist my pushing. I push harder. The toad resists by using more force than before, and then I notice that he's not just resisting my efforts, but he's actually *pushing back*. The toad is using my own physical energy against me like an experienced martial arts master. Until this moment, I did not know that toads, or at least this one, could do this.

Changing tactics, I decide to shine my headlamp directly into his eyes on the brightest setting. As I do, the toad responds by flattening himself closer to the ground, and then he does something else I didn't know toads could do. He growls at me. The toad emits a low-pitched guttural sound from somewhere inside those tensed muscles covered with the lumpy, sometimes poisonous skin. Each time I shine the light into his eyes, he growls and flattens. This toad will not go easily.

Fortunately, I am confident that I am at least 1 percent smarter than the toad, or so I think. If he won't budge, then I simply need to exert more force and push from behind. I decide to use my trekking pole instead of my hands to avoid contact with his skin. I locate the pole in the light of the headlamp—it's the support holding up my tent. If I remove it, the tent will collapse. I conclude that it's not worth dismantling my tent, which probably saves my adversary from inadvertently becoming an amphibian kebab. But, I still have another card to play—compassion—something the toad doesn't know about but should appreciate.

I decide to use both hands to scoop him up and airlift him to safety. Gently, now. I feel the toad tense up and begin to push back as I slide my hands underneath him and then commence liftoff. The toad is as big as my cupped hands, and he's heavy too, weighing nearly two pounds. For a brief moment,

I'm worried about contact with his poisonous skin, but then, without warning, I suddenly have something ten times worse to deal with.

"What the hell?!" He just crapped on me! Forget the poisonous skin; this toad is a weapon of mass defecation.

I simply cannot describe what it looks and smells like. Let's just say that it's unlike any kind of animal poop that I've ever encountered before. It is a horrible liquid, sickly in color, and coming from a pure demon; it is shockingly cold and immediately drips between my fingers and onto my bare feet. This toad takes no prisoners, even if they are 1 percent smarter than he is. Thus, I find myself at almost 2:00 AM, in the dark, holding one large and very pissed-off toad that just unloaded on me.

Now it's personal. *Very* personal. I put him down roughly. He lands with a thud, and without hopping away as expected. My disgust at suddenly being turned into an amphibian porta-potty continues as I stumble to the lake to clean up. The water is warm in comparison to what's on my hands, and I know for certain that I will be filtering the lake water since I know what I just put into it. I walk back to the tent and Mr. Toad (who hasn't moved—what a surprise).

The toad has not budged from where I dropped him—he's not moving, but he's not growling, resisting, or deploying his doomsday doo-doo defense either. The toad simply is as he was intended to be, and I am relieved that he shows no visible signs of injury. With the excitement and most of the humiliation over (at least for me), I decide that the toad wins after delivering a knockout that I never saw coming. I resolve not to push, slide, nudge, lift, or otherwise make any sort of physical contact with this toad again. Forever.

My thoughts shift rapidly in an unanticipated direction toward outright astonishment at this amazing creature. I am moved at his resilience and resourcefulness, at his calm demeanor in the face of the overpowering threat that I must present to him. So amazed am I that I remember some ancient words of blessing upon encountering a unique creature such as Mr. Toad. It only seems fitting that I bless the toad in the dark, and I do. Really.

I find that I admire the toad and decide that the toad will be staying as long as he likes. I even feel guilty about dropping him.

I crawl back inside the tent and find it full of mosquitoes. In my hurry to flee, I didn't zip the netting shut. So much for being 1 percent smarter . . . . Through the tent's bug netting, I can see the backside of the toad guarding my food from the bear. If the bear should appear, I will deploy Mr. Toad and his arsenal.

As I begin to fall asleep, I hear the toad hop once, then twice. I am happy that he is unhurt. My watch now says 2:04 AM. In the past half hour, I have experienced an incredibly rich and complex, rapidly shifting series of thoughts and emotions, which resemble a high-speed thrill ride in their intensity. Something profound has just happened to me, but I won't fully understand it until I sit down and write this story months later.

In a very short span of time, I have just gone from intense fear to relief. From curiosity to frustration at a toad who would not move. From being way too pleased with myself to being outraged at the affront to my human dignity. From defeat to respect for this worthy adversary. From admiration, to affection, to blessing, and ultimately, to acceptance. This amazing process occurs entirely within me, yet meeting the toad is the catalyst. None of it would have occurred except for one bad-ass toad at Maidu Lake who became my teacher.

When it is light enough to see, several hours later, I pack up my gear and prepare to resume hiking toward Canada. As I fold the tent, I notice something I'd missed when I'd set it up the previous evening, and no, it isn't leftover merde du toad. The toad is nowhere to be seen, though I do look briefly for him. Instead, I find a hole in the ground located directly underneath the tent. Apparently, I had set up my tent directly *over* Mr. Toad's doorway. The only plausible way out for him was to try and go through the floor of my tent.

Now I understand. The toad had two additional emotions for me to experience that he saved for daylight: I now feel unbelievably stupid and humble at the same time.

As I hike out of camp in the predawn light, I wish the toad well . . . and better bowel control.

LOST HORSES AND MULES ON THE PCT AND OTHER FOREST SERVICE STORIES

By David Kolb and Rees Hughes

Many of the trails, cabins, and lookouts that populate our rugged back-country in the West have been historically, and still are today, built and maintained by an equally rugged sort of character. From seasoned back-country rangers and old-timers running pack mules and still doing double-diamond hitches, to the dirty trail-crew workers and sooty smoke jumpers, this diverse Forest Service family are the unsung heroes of the Pacific Crest Trail. The vast majority of the PCT's 2650-mile-long route, of course, runs through public land managed by the Forest Service. So, as PCT hikers, we owe as much to the unnamed generations of devoted Forest Service employees as we do to advocates John Muir and Theodore Roosevelt, who were key to the creation of our national forests. Here, David Kolb, a veteran of the Forest Service, shares a few stories from his many years working in the high country.

By the time I had the opportunity to talk with William David Kolb, it had been years since he had been in the backcountry. He has a cochlear implant and his hearing has deteriorated to the extent that he does not answer the phone anymore. His scope of life is much more modest these days. But it becomes immediately apparent that, while Dave's body may be failing him, his mind is sharp and his memory vivid. Dave represents an era of foresters whose contributions have done much to shape the way contemporary hikers experience the backcountry.

Dave grew up a city boy in the suburbs of Baltimore. Like many of his generation, Dave had no choice but to grow up quickly because of the realities of World War II. Immediately after graduating from high school, Dave went directly into the army as a "voluntary draftee," and he served through the end of the conflict. Although Dave entered the forestry program at the University of West Virginia after the war, his dreams were of the West and the opportunity to work and live in the wilderness of the Oregon Cascades. By the fall of 1951, Dave had become a full-time employee of the Umpqua National Forest. It was a land of rugged peaks like Mount Thielsen and Diamond Peak, pristine lakes like Diamond, Odell, and Summit, and endless miles of magnificent forests.

In the early 1950s the centerpiece of the nascent high-country trail network in this area was the Oregon Skyline Trail (OST), the precursor to the PCT. Introduced in 1920 by the Forest Service, the route initially stitched together old wagon and logging roads, and Indian paths, and involved very little building of new trail. Over the years, the Forest Service consistently improved the trail infrastructure—routing, trail quality, signage, shelters—and served as stewards of these backcountry byways.

Among Dave's responsibilities during his years with the Umpqua National Forest was oversight of trail maintenance for the Skyline Trail. Crews of seasonal workers spent the relatively short window between melting snow in the summer and inclement weather in the early fall brushing, repairing, and improving the OST and the web of trails that form the circulation system of the Oregon backcountry.

Much of Dave's supervision occurred on foot or from the saddle of his white Arabian named Bird. Whether he was checking in with fire lookouts, visiting trail crews, or monitoring fire-suppression efforts, horseback was the most practical mode of covering substantial ground in limited time. Learning to be a skilled equestrian did not prove to be too difficult.

However, as a city boy, Dave found that he had a lot to learn about mules, the mainstay of backcountry pack teams. Words like *temperamental, stubborn, bullheaded,* and *unyielding* never seemed adequate to capture the personality of these animals. There was Tuck who, when being loaded into the stock truck, would refuse to stand sideways to make room for the other pack animals. Who would take a ten-foot detour to avoid a gum wrapper that had been dropped on the trail. Who would just stop on the trail and wait until Dave noticed that his train had diminished by one and returned to coax him along.

Not to be outsmarted by a jugheaded mule, Dave once tied Tuck's lead rope to Minnie's pack saddle. Minnie was a good pack animal and had been much more reliable than ole Tuck. It wasn't long before Tuck reared back dragging Minnie's pack saddle off her back and took off down the trail, breaking Minnie's saddle in the process. By the time Dave began the return trip, he had concluded that it made more sense to put the broken saddle on Tuck and the good saddle on Minnie and load her for the return trip. Of course, the trip home was uneventful. As they made their return to the ranger station, it became clear to Dave just how clever Tuck had been. As Dave observed, "I had a long frustrating day, Minnie did all the pack work, and Tuck had a nice stroll through the woods!"

The packers, who ferried food, equipment, and other supplies in support of projects throughout the backcountry, using teams of pack animals, tended to be an interesting breed in their own right. Well before thru hikers popularized trail names and eccentricity along the PCT, packers seemed to be a profession dominated by nicknames and characters. They had monikers like Blackfoot Smith, Broken Hand, Big Boy, and Grizzly. Dave remembers the diminutive Shorty who stood in stark contrast to his wife, the substantial Babe. After his own experiences with mules, Dave considered it a testimony to Babe's skill with animals that she would saddle and ride one of the mules without a whit of protest from the mule. There was the old misogynist packer who summarized his world view by noting, "There are mean horses and mean cattle, but ain't nothin' meaner than a mean woman." Dave was always suspicious that the isolated nature of the packer's work was one of the principle benefits of the job for that fellow.

Then, there was the veterinary student from Davis. That packer preferred not to use hobbles—only to have his stock frequently slip back to the barn at the ranger station, leaving him afoot in the high country. There was one time when this packer had delivered supplies to a crew working on the PCT in the extreme northeastern area of the Diamond Lake District. The stock, not so familiar with this region, disappeared as usual. However, this time they failed to show up at the barn or any other manned station in the district.

The packer, frustrated because his charges had gotten away from him, solicited Dave's assistance to find and return them to the ranger station. Together in the stock truck they drove to Windigo Road. It was agreed that Dave would walk up the Maidu Lake Trail to the PCT farther south and the packer would return to the site where the work crew was encamped at Windigo Pass. The terrain was heavily forested, which limited Dave's ability to scan for the way-ward animals; regardless, there was no evidence that they had ventured down toward Maidu Lake. He reached the intersection with the PCT and followed it north. After a couple of miles he noticed a stretch of disturbed underbrush and, after a little more investigation, it became clear that this was where the stock had left the trail. Who's to know what exactly motivated them to take this detour, as their cross-country adventure took them steeply down the mountainside into a dense, swampy stand of lodgepole pine. It seemed clear that they began to wonder the same thing—evidence suggested that they had milled around this area for some time. But where had they vanished to now? As Dave pondered, he became aware of the protests of a distant truck engine working hard as it slowly pulled along a rough track toward an intersection with Windigo Road.

It quickly became clear that the packer had reached the errant stock first, herded them to the truck, and was now heavily loaded and creeping home. Unless Dave was able to make his presence known or, impossibly, beat the truck to the road, he was destined to spend a long, cold night in the backcountry. Given the competing engine noise there was no way the packer was going to hear shouts or shots as Dave made his way through the thick growth of young lodgepole. Dave had almost resigned himself to his fate when the truck stopped as it reached Windigo Road. Perhaps, after the rough passage along the track, the packer thought it best to check his stock in the back. Whatever the reason, it gave Dave a brief window of opportunity. He pulled out the pistol he carried and fired three desperate shots, with penetrating sound. Dave made it home that night.

The northbound Pacific Crest Trail in the Umpqua National Forest snakes beneath Mount Thielsen, crossing Tipsoo Peak (the highest point along the Oregon PCT) and veering northwest across Windigo Pass, climbing past Cow-horn Mountain and over the eastern flank of Diamond Peak. For Dave, there is no more special view than the panorama from Cowhorn Mountain overlooking the Timpanagas Basin, which is sprinkled with lakes like Indigo and Opal, and even Amos and Andy (which according to Dave were named for the two mules used to stock those two lakes with fish).

In the early years of Dave's work in the Umpqua National Forest, the PCT was lightly used by hikers, horse packers, and the occasional hunter. At times it provided access to firefighters. However, as the public profile of the PCT grew, backpackers were attracted to this wild alpine country from across the United States and increasingly from across the world. It is not quite the secret it once was. But for most, the exposure to this country is limited to a weekend or the few days required to transit the sixty miles of PCT in the Umpqua National Forest. Most miss the many moods of the Oregon Cascades. It is not just the euphoria of summer but the muted colors of autumn, the periodic sparkle of winter contrasting with the endless days of gray, and the chatter of a verdant spring that complete the picture.

For Dave Kolb it has been more than six decades since his first visit to this Oregon high country and several since his last. Yet, he still knows all the nuances, the subtleties, the charming quirks in the personality of his old friend in a way that those of us who just pass through will never understand. It is deep love, not just the infatuation most of us experience. And, as with Forest Service personnel along the length of the trail, Dave represents the contribution and commitment that most of us are oblivious to as we climb past Cowhorn Mountain or sit on the shore of Summit Lake.

Thank you, Dave.

INTERLUDE: A BUG'S LIFE VII

By Hermann Gucinski

Anyone hiking the Pacific Crest Trail through the Cascades soon recognizes that these lush, green mountains, so commonly bedecked in cascading rain, are aptly named. The English "cascade" comes most directly from the Italian cascata, *or waterfall, and indeed, this is a land of falling waters. Of course, as the wary PCT hiker also knows, where rain falls and water pools, mosquitoes fly. In this humorous tale Hermann Gucinski describes his own run-in with, and subsequent retreat from, a hoard of the bloodthirsty little devils. Anyone who encounters such a pack of ravenous, winged wolves is bound to wonder if perhaps the most dangerous predators in the wilderness are actually the smallest. Forget the cougar and the bear, or the blizzard and the blister, the greatest challenge and fiercest enemy a PCT thru hiker might face on his or her 2650-mile journey is a group of little, buzzing girls.*

I don't know how many *A Bug's Life* stories, movies or otherwise, have been released, but "A Bug's Life VII" is our very own. This story explains how we Americans got to be here, in Oregon, and the important role a bug played in that history, as farfetched as that may seem. The bug in question is *Anopheles*, the lowly mosquito, whose Latin name means "worthless." Our story also involves *Aedes*, meaning "repugnant," a cousin to *Anopheles*—the repugnant part will become clear momentarily.

This story goes back to the early 1800s, when Napoleon was foiled from expanding his empire to the Americas by these buzzing beasts—the tiny *Anopheles* spread disease among his armies and decimated them. And so when

Thomas Jefferson made the overture to acquire French lands in the Louisiana Purchase, Napoleon, having incurred heavy losses in the Caribbean, agreed. Vast tracts of land west of the Mississippi became US territory, to be explored by Lewis and Clark and later extended to the West Coast—and so we probably would not be living in Oregon today were it not for the so-called worthless *Anopheles*.

Although the mosquito *Anopheles* may have made it possible for us to get here, the mosquito *Aedes* makes it almost impossible to stay here. We discovered this unfortunate fact after dropping down into the Diamond Peak Wilderness, which is transected by the Pacific Crest Trail. From Cowhorn Mountain, a few steps off the trail, you can see Mount Yoran, and we hoped to find peace and solitude in its shadow. Our aim was to lose ourselves to the simple pleasures of a walk in the woods, to forget the challenges of yesterday, and to start afresh tomorrow. We know that a walk, especially an overnight hike, focuses our thoughts on the surrounding environment, on the will needed to climb a steep section and the need to look for adequate shelter, to find water, to cook a meal, to listen to the night noise, and to keep to the trail when it becomes indistinct. This trip served to focus our minds with astounding single-mindedness.

It focused our minds on *Aedes*.

Although *Aedes* means repugnant, this is too narrow a description. So far our PCT hiking had been in weather and at elevations that brought freezing cycles during the night, which keeps *Aedes* and a lot of other critters in a stupor and away from us. We knew this was changing; as the sun reached the Equator, the days grew longer, and the forest started to come alive with creatures big and small. In anticipation, we were carrying our eighteen-ounce bug tent, weight that we'd been happy to leave behind before. A few repugnant beasts had circled us sluggishly as we alit from the car and laced our walking shoes—a hint of things to come.

We thought we could rely on our good karma to keep them uninterested, and for a while that seemed to be working. As we climbed, we enjoyed the transition from second-growth Pacific silver fir to mountain hemlock, with trunks and boles growing, adding interest and diversity. Our first attempt to rest showed our problem to be more serious, and we opted for a nearby lakeshore, where the breeze might blow our "signature" of heat and carbon dioxide away, before those repugnant creatures could home in on us. But between gusts, they found us, and I put on my light nylon wind pants, which I wanted to test for impermeability to the *Aedes* proboscis.

Do you know just how complicated the apparatus of the mosquito's proboscis is? The little sucker (pun intended) has an end, the labium, designed to fasten on to your skin and allow the sucking of blood. In addition there is a four part "nose" that has needlelike penetrating power as well as a sawing tool (the stylets), which, once their work is done, allow two ducts to be inserted into the nearest capillary of your skin's blood supply. The damn things actually bend and go into the capillary a ways, much like a nurse inserting a syringe into your vein in order to draw—a.k.a. suck—blood. Here's the itchy part—only one duct "draws," the other injects the *Aedes* saliva, which is supposed to prevent premature coagulation and stimulate blood flow. If you're allergic, and most of us are, that's when the itch let's you know you've been had.

So here we were, at Lake Yoran's shore, on a snow-free south-facing slope, the white face of Diamond Peak dominating the view to the southwest, its snowfield invitingly pure and presumably *Aedes* free. Not so at our place—we found ourselves surrounded. The *Aedes* military strategy was clearly dictated by generals that like to sacrifice many, many troops as they overwhelm by sheer numbers. We settled on a camp spot, we made all possible haste to set up our little bug tent and rushed inside. I got stung simply while trying to leave our shoes outside the tent. My lips were already swelling from bites, and the concept of taking head nets on a hike matured at this point. All ideas of a cooked supper went by the board as the repugnant bastards swarmed en masse around every part of our bug tent. They even appeared to be using the tarp above it as shelter!

My hiking partner and I shared a slice of bread with jam and one apple and found it surprisingly satisfying—perhaps because neither of us wanted to crawl outside to the food bags. The night was peaceful because we did not have to get up to go to the bathroom or to crawl outside at all. The nearby hoot of an owl, probably a great horned one or the rare great gray owl, awoke us, and we listened, awed. Much, much later the clatter of our hiking sticks—cheap mop handles that make superb trekking poles—signaled that critters were about. Daybreak was near and we'd better get up.

But we lay still for a while, listening for the telltale buzz of *Aedes* and mulling over our options. Yes, they were here, hovering outside the bug tent in big numbers, clouds in fact, waiting for us to make the first move. Breakfast? Out of the question. Brushing our teeth? No way. Wait for the breeze to blow them off course? What breeze? If it weren't for the repugnant buzz, the forest would lie in perfect stillness. The only strategy we could think of was not "being here" but being "outta here," and we've never left a campsite so fast and so clean. No water, no coffee, no oatmeal, just stuffing things into our packs and trotting away. We even delayed the needed pee break until we'd shaken off a few of the *Aedes*. Needless to say, we were back at the trailhead in record time, with breakfast taken at a nearby lodge, where only the early guests were drifting into the dining area.

Were we angry, sore, disappointed, intimidated, ready to switch to other pursuits? No way! After all, we had never once used repellent. Instead, we discussed tactics for next time—buying head nets and sewing nylon shell mittens in addition to the nylon pants and shirt that even the *Aedes* find impenetrable. In fact, these lightweight hiking trials convinced us that we could hike the entire PCT, not just the Oregon section we had laboriously conquered over many weekends and the yearly vacation trip. We've now finished section hiking the entire PCT, but that particular hike remains fixed in our minds—never again did we encounter *Aedes* in such numbers, so ravenous, and with such dogged persistence. *Repugnant* barely begins to describe them.

BLAZES ON THE SKYLINE

By Robert H. Cox

The year was 1968. Robert Cox had stopped to fish Upper Island Lake on what was to become the beginning of a thirty-year quest. Noticing a faint trail heading off into the forest, Cox stashed his gear and followed it. After a mile the trail began to drop off sharply, so he stopped and prepared to retrace his steps—then he noticed a large mountain hemlock with the outer bark chopped away. Four names and the date, "Aug. 10. 1905," had been hewn into the tree. For ten years that discovery lay dormant until, at last, Cox found his way back to that tree. He prepared a rubbing of the carving. He shared it with a Forest Service ranger, who, after some scrutiny, concluded, "I have no idea whose names those are." Cox received the same response at the Forest Service headquarters in Eugene.

With his curiosity sufficiently piqued, Cox persisted with his search. Aided by resources at the University of Oregon, he began to unfold the forgotten tale of Cyrus Bingham—miner, cowboy, ranger, and sheriff. After tromping countless hours through the Oregon high country, Cox documented some thirty of Bingham's arborglyphs, many of them along the route of the Oregon Skyline Trail and the contemporary PCT between Cowhorn Mountain south of Diamond Peak and McKenzie Pass. Here, Cox tells Bingham's story, tracing his arborglyphs and love for the land along the PCT's Oregon skyline.

Who marked these trees so long ago,
With axe to show the way?
It stirs the mind to see them now,

Old remnants of yesterday.
Indians left no marks like these.
Their tracks were soft and frail.
White men feared they might get lost,
And marked their every trail.

The tradition of arborglyphs, also known as dendroglyphs or tree writing, is one that has spanned many cultures, times, and locations. Trees have been used to express love, as message boards and boundary marks, as locational maps, and as an artist's palette. Cherokee Indians tagged beech trees along portions of the Trail of Tears in the 1830s; Civil War soldiers would carve names and dates in trees as they passed; pioneers left their mark as they migrated west; and Basque sheepherders etched images on the high-country aspen of Nevada, Oregon, and California beginning in the late nineteenth century.

However, this historical record is, at best, transitory. Trees grow, trees change, trees die; arborglyphs are botanical relics with a limited life span. As a result, it is increasingly rare to find an arborglyph outside of old-growth forests. Such is the case with the disappearing wooded legacy of Cyrus J. Bingham.

In March 1903, Cy Bingham was commissioned to serve as a US Forest Ranger, with orders to enter the high country as soon as practicable. Initially he was the entire personnel of a vast territory that extended from McKenzie Pass to the California border and lapped over both sides of the Cascade Range. He was lookout, ranger, fireman, peacemaker, and, as necessary, forest supervisor. For half a decade he lived in the mountains with his wife, never saw a boss, and would only emerge to resupply very periodically. For his first several years he found himself right in the middle of the Oregon Cattle and Sheep War, a tussle to see which species would be allowed to destroy the sensitive mountain meadows. And, perhaps most significantly, he laid out the Skyline Trail along the backbone of the central Oregon Cascades. "That was the best five years of my life," Bingham told the *Blue Mountain Eagle* newspaper in 1928. "I laid up more real money. I received $75 a month. There was all the deer I wanted, fish everywhere, game in plenty, and one season Mrs. Bingham canned 150 jars of wild blackberries. We traveled the mountains making trails and would go all summer and never meet but a few people." Bingham loved this Oregon backcountry.

Trails he would often mark with simple blazes on trees. But, periodically, using a timber scribe he would carve the date in trees along with his name and those of any companions to leave an enduring record of his camps as he crisscrossed his territory. This record almost allows for the reconstruction of Ranger Bingham's high-country travels. For example, set in the saddle of Cowhorn Mountain and along the route of the PCT, one of Bingham's early arborglyphs documents his presence on August 8, 1904. From this location one can imagine him scanning the region for miles. Then on horseback Bingham slowly moved north and two days later settled into camp on the edge of Summit Lake, where he again left his mark. The fish of Summit Lake would have been a wonderful source of food. Three days later, he reached Waldo Lake and again etched his name, the date, and elevation in a tree adjacent to his camp facing the now rerouted trail. He spent extended time using this location as a base of operations until relocating to Bobby Lake, just east of the PCT. Joined by a private timber cruiser by the name of Nathaniel Martin, they left their names on a tree near a protected bay where the horses could feed on grass. Bingham and Martin finished the season on Odell Lake, where they left their fifth arborglyph.

Over the years, enough other trees have been found to follow Bingham's peregrinations. In early August 1907, Ranger Bingham made the long climb up Foley Ridge toward the Three Sisters, stopping initially in Separation Meadow, along the route of the Oregon Skyline Trail, before moving south to Mesa Creek, through the Wickiup Plain to Houserock Meadow, and on to the Mink Lake basin. He left his mark four times en route. By the time of his retirement, this early-day Kilroy had carved his name on so many trees that it is alleged that the Forest Service jokingly presented him with a bill for all the timber he had "cut."

It is difficult to know just how many of Cy Bingham's carvings remain undiscovered or have fallen to the forest floor, covered by the detritus of many seasons. Even he once said, "I expect that I have scribed my name in a good many places" that will never be seen. The dendroglyphs that have been catalogued offer a glimpse of a time long past in these wildlands.

Bingham was a daunting figure. Reputed to weigh 275 pounds with a fifty-inch chest, he could take a hundred-pound sack of flour in his teeth and toss it over his head. He was born in Michigan in 1870, came west, and worked as a miner and cowboy before becoming a ranger and, lastly, the sheriff of John Day. His reputation was such that it was said that,

When a pine needle falls, the eagle sees it,
The deer hears it,
The bear smells it,
And, Ranger Bingham ponders it.

And, as sheriff, it was alleged that the intimidating Cy Bingham never had to pull a gun on anyone.

Bingham returned to Lake Odell for a visit in 1924 and penned a requiem for his beloved high country, alarmed by the changes he saw. Here we see some of his colloquialisms, including "meatbird," which refers to the gray jay, and "dollies," which refers to Dolly Varden trout. His words are a fitting plea for the careful stewardship of our precious wilderness:

Not long ago, I drifted back to an old familiar spot called Lake Odell, that
    nature built on the Cascade Mountain top.
I met Bill Brock, an old timer pal, who shook me by
the
hand
and said, "Old man, where have you been since we once roamed this
    land?"
And when I asked, "[What] does this mean so many camps I see and autos
    parked where once we tied our horses to the trees?"
Then we sat down where we used to sit, then Bill told me all
"The Natron Cutoff's being built—from Oakridge to Klamath Falls."

"They have ruined all," said Bill to me, "The deers about all gone;
The 'dollies' they must seek a stream in other lands to spawn.
The pine squirrel he must move away and hunt another home.
The chipmunk and the meatbird leave the land they long have roamed;
The big lake trout will disappear, the hills will all turn brown.
The creeks will all be waterless when the timber's all cut down;
The forest will all soon fade away, George Kelly's mill is here,
to trim the hills, that George has watched for many a long, long year."

And as we looked across the lake, those horrid sights I've seen
I saw the spot I often camped beneath the evergreen.
It sent a chill, my eyes did fill, for those camps once dear to me,

were all torn up with the railroad grade, long drills, and T.N.T.
At Beaver Marsh, they have graded high and dug up most of the grass,
cut a grade around the south lake side; drilled a hole clean through
  the pass.
They widened out the old pack trail over which the autos spin
that I once built from the Sisters, south clear to the crater rim.

Those days are gone forever when a ranger's life I led,
and camped beneath those hemlocks; used fir boughs for my bed.
When I used to spear the dollies; shoot the blacktails from the licks,
and keep tab on the horses bell from the glades along the creeks.
How I used to ride that summit—look for fires east and west;
then night would overtake me, I would camp, cook, eat and rest.
Those were the days when work was a pleasure, in the land I knew so well.
And I often think of the days I spent on the inlet of Lake Odell.

Cyrus J. Bingham died in 1937.

CHILDREN IN THE WOODS

By Barry Lopez

Whether one hikes the Pacific Crest Trail with children or without, we all find ourselves rekindling that childlike sense of wonder, that young and vibrant thirst for adventure and exploration, when we are on the trail. Whether it means taking the time to sit and enjoy a long, slow sunrise with a steaming cup of tea in hand, or becoming mesmerized by the bumbling dance of bees around brightly colored phlox in the meadows along the trail, we often discover that these moments are more meaningful than the miles we cover each day. In "Children in the Woods," Oregon nature writer Barry Lopez discusses our childhood sense of wonder and how we can help to foster it within children rather than drive it out of them. When hiking the PCT, with or without children, we would do well to heed some of Lopez's advice. As we trudge along with our field guides and guidebooks in hand, calling out the litany of names of flowers, feathers, peaks, and passes, we may find our hearts jump and our sense of wonder begins to soar if we worry less about naming and more about knowing, if we focus less on information and more on sensation.

Whedn I was a child growing up in the San Fernando Valley in California, a trip into Los Angeles was special. The sensation of movement from a rural area into an urban one was sharp. On one of these charged occasions, walking down a sidewalk with my mother, I stopped suddenly, caught by a pattern of sunlight trapped in a spiraling imperfection in a windowpane. A stranger, an elderly woman in a cloth coat and a dark hat,

SOURCE: "Children in the Woods" excerpted from *Crossing Open Ground*. Copyright © 1988 by Barry Holstun Lopez. Used with the author's permission.

spoke out spontaneously, saying how remarkable it is that children notice these things.

I have never forgotten the texture of this incident. Whenever I recall it I am moved not so much by any sense of my young self but by a sense of responsibility toward children, knowing how acutely I was affected in that moment by that woman's words. The effect, for all I know, has lasted a lifetime.

Now, years later, I live in a rain forest in western Oregon, on the banks of a mountain river in relatively undisturbed country, surrounded by 150-foot-tall Douglas firs, delicate deer-head orchids, and clearings where wild berries grow. White-footed mice and mule deer, mink and coyote move through here. My wife and I do not have children, but children we know, or children whose parents we are close to, are often here. They always want to go into the woods. And I wonder what to tell them.

In the beginning, years ago, I think I said too much. I spoke with an encyclopedic knowledge of the names of plants or the names of birds passing through in season. Gradually I came to say less. After a while the only words I spoke, beyond answering a question or calling attention quickly to the slight difference between a sprig of red cedar and a sprig of incense cedar, were to elucidate single objects.

I remember once finding a fragment of a raccoon's jaw in an alder thicket. I sat down alongside the two children with me and encouraged them to find out who this was—with only the three teeth still intact in a piece of the animal's maxilla to guide them. The teeth told by their shape and placement what this animal ate. By a kind of visual extrapolation its size became clear. There were other clues, immediately present, which told, with what I could add of climate and terrain, how this animal lived, how its broken jaw came to be lying here. Raccoon, they surmised. And tiny tooth marks along the bone's broken edge told of a mouse's hunger for calcium.

We set the jaw back and went on.

If I had known more about raccoons, finer points of osteology, we might have guessed more: say, whether it was male or female. But what we deduced was all we needed. Hours later, the maxilla, lost behind us in the detritus of the forest floor, continued to effervesce. It was tied faintly to all else we spoke of that afternoon.

In speaking with children who might one day take a permanent interest in natural history—as writers, as scientists, as filmmakers, as anthropologists—I have sensed that an extrapolation from a single fragment of the whole is the most invigorating experience I can share with them. I think children know that nearly anyone can learn the names of things; the impression made on them at this level is fleeting. What takes a lifetime to learn, they comprehend, is the existence and substance of myriad relationships: it is these relationships, not the things themselves, that ultimately hold the human imagination.

The brightest children, it has often struck me, are fascinated by metaphor— with what is shown in the set of relationships bearing on the raccoon, for example, to lie quite beyond the raccoon. In the end, you are trying to make clear to them that everything found at the edge of one's senses—the high note of the winter wren, the thick perfume of propolis that drifts downwind from spring willows, the brightness of wood chips scattered by beaver—that all this fits together. The indestructibility of these associations conveys a sense of permanence that nurtures the heart, that cripples one of the most insidious of human anxieties, the one that says, you do not belong here, you are unnecessary.

Whenever I walk with a child, I think how much I have seen disappear in my own life. What will there be for this person when he is my age? If he senses something ineffable in the landscape, will I know enough to encourage it?—to somehow show him that, yes, when people talk about violent death, spiritual exhilaration, compassion, futility, final causes, they are drawing on forty thousand years of human meditation on *this*—as we embrace Douglas firs, or stand by a river across whose undulating back we skip stones, or dig out a camus bulb, biting down into a taste so much wilder than last night's potatoes.

The most moving look I ever saw from a child in the woods was on a mud bar by the footprints of a heron. We were on our knees, making handprints beside the footprints. You could feel the creek vibrating in the silt and sand. The sun beat down heavily on our hair. Our shoes were soaking wet. The look said: I did not know until now that I needed someone much older to confirm this, this feeling I have of life here. I can now grow older, knowing it need never be lost.

The quickest door to open in the woods for a child is the one that leads to the smallest room, by knowing the name each thing is called. The door that leads to the cathedral is marked by a hesitancy to speak at all, rather to encourage by example a sharpness of the senses. If one speaks it should be only to say, as well as one can, how wonderfully all this fits together, to indicate what a long, fierce peace can derive from this knowledge.

SILENCE IN THE SISTERS

By Anicca Cox

The Three Sisters Wilderness and surrounding areas are a favorite for many Pacific Crest Trail day and section hikers as well as for those long-miled thru hikers. And given the area's name, it is no surprise that upon entering the Sisters region we might find ourselves, like Anicca Cox, reflecting on the role women have played in the environmental movement, wilderness preservation, and trail designation. Although historically wilderness has been identified as a male-dominated space, many illustrious women pioneers have shown us that women belong in the wilderness as much as men. From Rachel Carson's environmental advocacy to Catherine Montgomery's initial idea for the PCT and Teddi Boston's first female thru hike, there are many sisters who stand tall in the West's environmental history. And, both anecdotal and survey evidence suggest that the growth of female participation in outdoor activities actually outpaces that of men. For further perspectives on gender and the wilderness, we encourage you to read "The Ghost of Muir Pass" and "A Rite of Masculinity" in the California volume of the Pacific Crest Reader. *In this piece, Cox reflects on the significance of sisterhood and the importance of companionship on the trail, while reminding us to enjoy the silence of the wilderness.*

On this summer's PCT hike, I expect to find many things: abundant wildlife, a bustling trail, and the lively sounds of wilderness. Instead, I discover stillness and wild things that are quiet. I enjoy the felicity in hiking with another woman amid the solitude of empty wilderness. The absence of human presence, as always, is marked by items left behind: a disembodied foil balloon in blue and white, a coconut shell bracelet languishing in the dust of a cross-roads in the trail, a few footprints. I imagine some distant birthday party or a wrist donning the emblem of a carved elephant and wonder if these things are missed as I scoop them up and pack them out. But mostly what I notice is the pervading silence, what quiet does to my thoughts, to our conversations on the trail, to the way I view myself, listening to the creak of my shoes and pack and my breath as it changes with incline and decline.

❧❧

In early August, just after the first acorn squash and eggplants begin to peek out of my garden, I leave the warm, dry air of New Mexico, my dog, and ripening plants and head west to the PCT. An old college girlfriend of mine, now living in Eugene, and I aim to hike a forty-mile section of the trail through the Three Sisters Wilderness. Stef and I meet in Bend, she coming from the west, I from the east. Borrowing an old van from an acquaintance, we finish the numerous last-minute preparations that it takes to hike in the woods. These include visits to two ranger stations to get the right map, to REI, and to Safeway for a several days' supply of DEET. We put our feet to trail at Devils Lake, kicking our shoes through dusty and well-traveled paths along the Wikiup Plains to where the trail converges with the PCT.

The convergence is meadowlike before heading up and across a ridgeline and back down onto a trail with dense and fallen trees. The PCT is open and dry, providing views of ridgelines and winding through parts of the Sisters that have been touched by fire. In fact, as we get on the trail there is a fire to the north and east of us, but its plumes of smoke are intercepted by the South Sister. On the trail, we see two or three other hikers as we climb, and then we see no one else for the next three days.

We quickly settle into movement with each other, meandering in silence. And, while we have goals on the trail, we have no agenda. Women hikers, I find, are better with this sort of uncertainty. We enjoy the freedom to change directions, plans, routes, at any time if it suits us, and neither of us feels the disappointment of not covering enough mileage or not reaching the highest summit. We both recall, with mild grimaces and a little humor, being pushed to the point of injury or threat to our lives with boyfriends who needed to accomplish something on the trail. As for our own plans, originally we thought we'd summit the South Sister; but when we found out there was ice above 6500 feet and, being unequipped with axes, we decided on another loop instead, easily revising our plans in favor of wandering and pleasure. So we pass just south of the Sister, wave to her glacial rise above tree line, and bow to the beauty of her crown covered in ice.

As we amble up the trail we decide to traverse the South Sister and explore the mountain lakes we see marked on our map. We head down the other side of the ridge into the thick trees toward Nash Lake to spend the night. This side of the ridge is nearly silent. Aside from legions of mosquitoes, barely deterred by our armor of toxic chemicals, we see only a lone predator bird in the late afternoon. Circling above the lake disinterestedly looking for food, the winged watcher finds only our quiet conversation as we prepare tea and dinner. Stef and I enjoy the last of the sunlight and quickly take asylum from the bugs in our tent.

There are no winds in the trees; the magnificent ponderosas stand still and watchful. There are no animals rustling or birds ushering in the change of light. A drift of usnea moss as it dislodges itself from the branch of a tree falls across the trail and we sleep silently, not stirring until the early light, when we quickly gather our things and keep moving along the trail. I begin to notice the soreness of my shoulders, quietly adjusting my pack without a word, and later I see Stef do the same. As the miles increase, we begin a relationship with our aching bodies—soberly carrying the weight of our things.

As we round a bend in late morning, the forest changes again. Instead of the density of an unmaintained trail—thick fir and ponderosa surrounded with other low-lying branches—the trees on the southeastern side grow taller and distant from each other. This part of the forest feels older, more comforting and open. There is light on the forest floor here. We head back up a rise in elevation toward Horse Lake on our return to the PCT and follow it north again.

Suddenly I hear a sound and see a creature scurrying up a thin tree. My excitement quickly turns to apprehension as I realize what it is: a baby feline. Stef will later humorously refer to it as "a cute little kitten." The next week I will look it up and conclude that it was either bobcat or lynx, both known to roam that area. It has dark gray and black markings, no tail, and tapered ears. It stares right into my eyes. I am stunned by its grace for a moment before I grab the back of Stef's pack and hold her in place as I whisper, "Cat, it's a cat!" She verbalizes my own thoughts, as she calmly whispers back, "It's a baby." She doesn't state what that implies, but I know. She tells me to keep moving, quickly, and if we encounter the mother to get really big and scream as loud as possible. She tells me to not be afraid; exuding fear pheromones isn't a good thing. This is difficult to do, as I irrationally imagine the worst.

Despite the fact that adult bobcat or lynx are unlikely to ever attack a human, it is difficult to shake the apprehension caused by disturbing their young. They say you never hear a wild cat before you see one, and it is humbling that we humans, for all our prowess in the world, are no match for their stealth. A few yards down the trail, another baby drops out of a tree to our left and scurries up a rise above us. We walk in tandem, trying to make loud conversation and moving as quickly as we know how to.

For the first time on our hike, our own discussion isn't subdued by the silence of the woods themselves; fueled by exhilaration and fear, we discuss safety. It is not only the desolate landscape we are traversing, with wild animals and emptiness, but the landscapes of our lives and, most specifically, the issue of protection that we consider. Like many women I have spoken with, we mostly learned how to be in the woods from the men who know. I spent my first camping trips with my step-father and, later, with boyfriends. Stef has had the same experience, recalling stories of her first love, Garrett, taking her camping in the snow, exploring the limits of temperature and teenage lovemaking. As unfounded as it is, I have often felt most able to suppress my fear of bears when in the company of a man.

I confess to her that until a few days ago I never even owned my own first-aid kit. I only recently learned to decipher a topo, though I have nodded my approval to the reading of them several times with male companions. I have limited know-how with wilderness first aid. I left those skills up to the men in my life who loved the outdoors, who explored it avidly and, later, shared it with me. The very concept of wilderness is also, often, of a male space. From Muir to Abbey, and beginning with Thoreau, Wordsworth, and others, our American consciousness about wilderness has often (not always) been narrated by men— men whose focus is on the glory of leaving society to strike out alone in nature. As I learn to embrace my own unmediated experiences in the natural world, and form a set of skills that I can rely on, I find a wellspring of empowerment that I never suspected I would possess. From this newfound strength, I learn to value my time spent outdoors as a gift that I can share with my women friends, male companions, and larger community.

So, while I have spent time alone in the backcountry much to my benefit, it is not the only way I like to be in the wilderness. I don't ascribe greater spiritual value to time spent alone than I do to time shared on the trail. More and more,

I work to be independent and autonomous in my wilderness endeavors *while* in cooperation with others—be that a friend or a lover.

As the adrenaline subsides, and after climbing a thousand feet in elevation, we reach the next lake. We strip off our clothes, lay down our packs, and dive into the cold water of the mountains. Gliding, weightless, our sore muscles and feet are forgotten. We swim out across the lake to the rocks on the other side, our long hair swirling in the clear green water. We stretch in the warm afternoon sun, momentarily free of the mosquitoes.

The human instinct for protection and escape seems much less urgent, while the magic of seeing wild animals in their natural environment begins to grow. We can finally laugh at our fears and marvel at the good fortune of seeing wild cats, something that has never happened to either of us on a hike—a rarity, as we know these animals are seldom caught unaware.

We lounge in the sun and survey the map again before leaving, making sure we are where we think we are on the trail, planning the miles we want to hike for the rest of the day. We read elevations, look for features and water crossings together. Learning to be independent as women on the trail feels good, liberating, but the cats remind us that, whether we know it or not, we are never alone in the woods. The trees watch us, and wild things abound underfoot, out of sight or otherwise. They are quiet and share their silence with us, a silence not empty or solitary but one filled with the comfort of being a part of the big, wild world.

THE RELUCTANT GUIDEBOOK WRITER

By Jeffrey P. Schaffer

For a good three decades, the Wilderness Press Pacific Crest Trail guidebooks served as the essential resource for section and thru hikers. They were virtually as indispensable as food and water and, in many ways, made the trail far more accessible to potential users. The heft of these books resulted in the creation of much lighter guides that emphasized the barest of PCT essentials; and, as Jeff Schaffer notes here, GPS technology and applications may soon render paper guides obsolete.

In 2008, these PCT guidebooks received a National Outdoor Book Award as the "best of the best," and, as of 2011, have sold well over 100,000 copies. Schaffer, as a coauthor of these two PCT guides, will forever occupy an important place in trail history. Here, he tells the story of his serendipitous entry into the PCT guidebook project, including a more detailed recounting of one particular field reconnaissance, back in 1973, from the Three Sisters to Irish Lake in central Oregon.

Life is what happens to you while you are out making other plans. I never planned to be a guidebook writer. I could ace exams at Cal Berkeley but struggled with term papers. If I were going to hell, Satan would have given me an eternity of term-paper assignments. Furthermore, I never was a gung-ho hiker. Walking is something I did out of necessity, sort of like swimming, which beat drowning. From the age of six, if not younger, I was a tree hugger, but not in the enviro sense. Rather, if I saw a tree, I tried to shimmy up it. With age, I became an increasingly better climber, and not just of trees. Our house and garage were fair game, as was anything vertical. Eventually, in high school, I discovered rocks. So it was not surprising that while at Cal Berkeley I became a Yosemite Valley climber in 1963, at age twenty. Although I almost died on my first climb, I (foolishly?) kept coming back and cheating death. By 1972, I had lost virtually all of my climbing partners, not to death but because all had graduated from Cal Berkeley.

One person I lost, because he had major injuries and so gave up technical climbing, was Ron Felzer. It turned out that Ron had written two High Sierra hiking guides for Wilderness Press (about Devils Postpile and Mineral King), and, being competitive, I decided that if he could write books so could I. So in the spring of 1972, I dropped by the publisher's office, not to write a PCT guidebook (I was antiguidebook and mostly still am today due to their overall poor quality), but rather to write a geology/geomorphology do-it-yourself field textbook to the Owens Valley/eastern Sierra Nevada. (By 1969 I had completed eight years of general science plus naturalist studies in zoology, botany, geography, and geology.) Not knowing anything about the company or outdoor publications, I found out from publisher/editor/writer/backpacker Tom Winnett that someone had essentially already done *my* book: *Deepest Valley* (1969), by Genny Schumacher. But Tom, seeing samples of my writing and my maps, proposed that I join his PCT project. Tom already had the PCT guidebook project in mind and by this time he had lined up all authors but me, an unknown.

While many stretches of the PCT already existed, such as the John Muir Trail, others were along old trails or on roads. Tom had received an advance copy of the federal government's *Pacific Crest National Scenic Trail Route Selection* in April, and so in the summer of 1972 we five authors of the California guidebook (myself, Winnett, John Robinson, Andrew Husari, and Jim Jenkins) hiked or drove the government's route (a lot of driving occurred in the mostly trail-less southern California section). At this time, I had a full-time job at Cal Berkeley and would drive to a trailhead Friday night, put in a long day of hiking on Saturday and most of Sunday, and would return to Berkeley late at night, only to repeat this cycle the following week. Thank goodness I had a shuttle driver, Ken Ng (brother of one of my former climbing partners), who would drop me at one trailhead and then use the appropriate Forest Service map(s) to drive to a spot where another road crossed the trail, about twenty miles farther along. Amazingly, he never got lost and my lemon of a VW never broke down. At Tom's suggestion, I used a tape recorder besides making sparse notes in a small notebook and on the topo maps. The tape recorder was a mistake, because being a trained naturalist I mentioned virtually everything I saw, and then was damned to listen to hours of my panting self. So I learned to write abbreviated notes, such as "MA" for moderate ascent, "RF" for red fir.

In the fall, I spent most of my free time (I was single with no time for dating) writing up the prose (first longhand, then manually typed) and calculating my mapped trail mileages. At the end of 1972, it became apparent to me that guidebook writing required full-time effort. So in January 1973, I quit my job, took a serious pay cut, and began working full-time for Wilderness Press, drafting all the 127 maps for *the* (not *The*, which came later) *Pacific Crest Trail, Volume 1: California* (PCT 1). With nearly illegible maps, the book was a near disaster, but that's another story.

Well, the book size was determined so that *Pacific Crest Trail, Volume 2: Oregon and Washington* (PCT 2) conformed with PCT 1 to create a matched set. But while PCT 1 covered 1646 miles in 276 pages, PCT 2 covered only 972 miles in 342 pages. The reason for fewer miles per page was, first, that I standardized the scale of the maps, making them much more legible. But (surprise, surprise!) PCT 2 is still much larger than it should be. PCT 1 description covers 1646 miles in 102 pages, or 16.24 miles per page, while PCT 2 covers 972 miles in 162 pages, or 6 miles per page. You can probably figure out why: I was the principal author, doing all of Oregon and about 60 percent of Washington, and I write more—more trail description and more natural history (mostly geology). Tom had (probably rightly so) a problem with this. I think he removed excess natural history from every book I wrote, especially around Lassen and Crater Lake (the latter description was reduced by 45 percent).

No sooner was PCT 1 out, than Ken and I rose early on May 30, 1973, drove north up Interstate 5, and recorded road mileages west to Seiad Valley to then do the PCT stretch north and east to I-5. On May 31, I hiked north to Cook and Green Pass and on to Copper Mountain, beyond which the PCT was snowbound. The research for PCT 2 was underway.

Most of our work was done as day hikes, but Section K, from Stevens Pass to Rainy Pass, was a six-day backpack, with a few other shorter backpacks in other sections. To illustrate how we approached the task, let me briefly describe our fieldwork from McKenzie Pass south to Irish Lake that produced eighty-eight pages of notes (plus annotations on the maps). On July 1, Ken and I drove a lot of roads to the south and east of Three Sisters Wilderness, taking mileages at all critical points, and then from Highway 242 we began hiking south at 2:43 PM (yes, my field notes were that detailed). I mapped about six miles that afternoon, stopping near Minnie Scott Spring after having taken the photo at

4:10 PM that appears on the "12 Trail Chapters" page. We got up at 5:45 AM on July 2 and headed south, Ken leaving me in the afternoon to return to the VW and drive to Irish Lake.

The USFS 1973 Three Sisters Wilderness topo map showed the PCT route going from Camelot Lake south past Red Hill to near Horse Lake along the old Oregon Skyline Trail (OST), while the official route in the *Pacific Crest National Scenic Trail Route Selection* put it correctly south over Koosah Mountain. However, this route was not obvious, and I hiked about a mile on the OST before deciding to backtrack and look for it. Then I continued south on the OST again, camping near Red Hill. On July 3, at 5:15 AM, I proceeded southwest to Horse Lake and some 2.25 miles past it, where I discovered the signed PCT, heading east on Trail 3517. So, the official route did exist. Rats! More hiking to do, and I had not counted on it. (For all hikes I would give Ken my ETA at the appointed pickup spot.) I dropped my pack and day hiked this stretch north, then reversed it, reaching my backpack 7 hours later. At 13.5 hours, this was one of my longer days. The next day, July 4, was a walk in the park, and after 37 hours of total hiking I reached Irish Lake around noon, and we drove back to Berkeley. In the first edition of PCT 2, I showed both routes but then I dropped the OST, since the PCT came within a mile of Elk Lake and its lodge, should one need help or R & R.

As new segments of the PCT were built, I'd go and map them. Sometimes I felt that certain stretches of the old OST, which tended to go from lake to lake rather than adhere to the crest (as the PCT bill mandated), were better than their replacements. One example is Section D's OST from Windigo Pass north to Odell Lake, which has both more lakes and more access. However, perhaps the best alternate route was Section G's descent to the Columbia River Gorge. Does anyone take the official route, when the descent along the Eagle Creek Trail passes a spectacular series of waterfalls?

I've called my story "The Reluctant Guidebook Writer," but my experiences on the PCT—other than blisters, mosquitoes, and bad weather (on one revision trip it rained 21 of 25 days)—were rewarding. My satisfaction with my PCT assignment grew as I got increasingly better at mapping, at interpreting geology, and at identifying plants; plus there was the benefit of seeing new scenery.

As I write in 2010, seven years have elapsed since any new edition, and none are in sight. With each year there will be more people on the trail properly cursing me for not making corrections or updates. The reason they have not come out, and may never come out (no revisions by me, at age sixty-seven, with multiple climbing injuries and more expected each year), is that these days the Wilderness Press guidebooks are 100 percent digital—that means text, photos, *and* maps. With about 1500 map overlays to scan for all the editions, the cost is prohibitive, and so the guidebooks need to die. They served their purpose. But these days, what with cell phones with GPS capability, I expect that sometime soon there will be a PCT application on a GPS unit that will tell you exactly where you are on the trail as well as what lies ahead (campsites, water, stores, weather, snow conditions) and how far. This is the future as we start the new millennium. Guidebooks, and not just the PCT guides, are history. So in later years, tell your grandchildren about your epic adventures of yore, when humans went into the mountains without any electronic gadgets whatsoever, using only guidebooks. If they ask you what a book is, dig out your battered PCT guides.

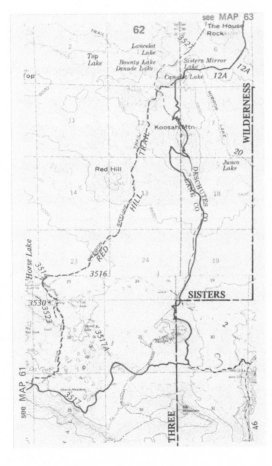

Schaffer's original map 62 from *The Pacific Crest Trail Volume 2* (Wilderness Press, 1974)

THE RESCUE OF OVER THE HILL JIM

By Jim Rea

How fitting that this story follows Jeff Schaffer's "The Reluctant Guide-book Writer." While most Pacific Crest Trail hikers continue to use some manner of hard-copy guidebook in the planning and execution of trips, many of us take for granted what real life savers these guides are. Not only do they keep us from getting lost, but, as Over the Hill Jim notes here, they also can be indispensable when calling for help. Other than getting lost, perhaps getting sick or injured on the trail ranks as the wilderness hiker's greatest fear and worst nightmare. This story of illness and rescue takes place at the foot of Mount Jefferson, the second-highest peak in Oregon. As in many other rugged wilderness areas, hundreds of hikers each year owe their lives and safe return to the heroic efforts of search and rescue teams, law enforcement personnel, and medical professionals. In Oregon alone, search and rescue operations were mounted for 138 hikers in 2008 (hikers consistently represent the highest category of SAR subjects). Nobody earns greater gratitude in the heart of the PCT hiker than these "trail angels" who have helped to bring us home safely and heal us, so that we can once again return to our beloved trail.

The day began uneventfully. I awakened in my tent at 6:00 AM, dressed, and went out. I was camped in the woods along the PCT in northern Oregon, near an unnamed pond at the base of Mount Jefferson. The scene was peaceful and lovely. It was Tuesday, September 9, 2008, and the day's hike would be easy. I had hiked 365 miles over the past several weeks, and the end of this year's trek was within reach. Breitenbush Lake, a popular fishing spot, was only eleven miles ahead, and I was supposed to meet my wife and daughters there the next morning. Zhita, my wife, was staying with a friend in Springfield while I was hiking. Darbi was arriving from New Mexico and Kirsten from California that day, to go with Zhita to Salem for the night. On Wednesday morning, Zhita would deliver our daughters to Breitenbush Lake to hike with me the final three days of this year's PCT trek. I had hiked 300 to 400 miles on the trail each year since 2004, and we had long looked forward to hiking together somewhere along the way. It would be wonderful.

The tranquility did not last. By 7:00 AM I was experiencing a searing pain in my belly like nothing I had ever known. It might have been appendicitis, I suppose, but I could only imagine that I must have food poisoning from the dehydrated seafood I had eaten the evening before. There was no way I could get relief from the pain. By 8:15 I gave up. I could not continue hiking. I knew this problem must be serious. I had adopted the trail name Over the Hill Jim, and now I wondered how apt that name might prove to be. I pulled out the satellite phone and called my wife.

Zhita had persuaded me several years before to rent a satellite phone for each year's hike. I usually hike alone, and she slept better knowing I could call for help. I used my prepaid bundle of minutes to call her briefly each morning so she could hear my voice and I could tell her where I was, on schedule or ahead or behind. In recent years I had been using a few of those minutes to play correspondence chess with a friend, leaving messages for a move each day. I had enjoyed all that, but now I suddenly recognized that carrying the extra pound of a phone all those miles was really worth it. I asked Zhita to call search and rescue, and we agreed that 911 would work as a start. I explained where I was, referring to the pages of the trail data book and the PCT guidebook in my pocket. I wasn't sure if I was at the foot of Mount Jefferson, but I knew I had just passed the Woodpecker Trail junction on Woodpecker Ridge, and I knew I was eleven trail miles south of Forest Road 42 and Breitenbush Lake.

Zhita's call to the 911 office was just the start of her telephone circus. She was directed to call the Lane County Sheriff's Office, but they realized that I was not in Lane County. Her stress mounted as the hours passed while she was referred to a series of sheriff's offices and other resources, people trying to be helpful but not having the answers. Finally, Neil Mackey at the Deschutes County Sheriff's Office determined that I was near the Marion County–Linn County border, and he contacted those offices for her. He then called the head of SAR (search and rescue) for the Marion County Sheriff's Office, who initiated the SAR operation, figuring out where I might be on the PCT and how best to gain access. He called me on my satellite phone to check on my condition and assure me help was on the way. He asked if anyone was with me. I told him that hikers had passed occasionally and offered help but I saw no reason for them to stay. SAR disagreed. They like to have someone stay with the person being rescued, so I agreed to stop the next hiker. Shortly after that I heard someone coming along the trail, and a young man called out, "Are you okay?" It was my friend Lakota John!

I had met John Freeman the previous week, when my brother, also named John, was hiking with me. John had invited us to share his idyllic campsite that night. John Freeman's grandmother is Lakota Indian, so I referred to them as Lakota John and Brother John while we were together. Lakota John had an older brother who had died in an accident and he enjoyed hearing my brother and me talking in a manner that reminded him of times with his own brother. We all enjoyed being together that evening and the next morning, but I did not guess we would meet again. Now Lakota John told me he had met some hikers on the trail a few miles back who said they passed a guy with a white beard who wasn't well. They confirmed that the guy wore a hat with a shiny top. Expecting that it was me, Lakota John had hurried ahead to see if he could help.

SAR sent out two volunteer rescue teams, a Marion County team starting from the north and a Linn County team from the south. Then they called the National Guard. The first to arrive on the scene was the Guard in a Blackhawk helicopter. Lakota John stayed with me as the helicopter roared in at about 2:00 PM, at long last. The crew spotted the pond at the base of the mountain, a landmark I described to SAR by phone, and then they saw us. Lakota John waved my hat with the Mylar top. They seemed to search for a place to land, and then they hovered above the treetops and lowered a medic on a cable to the ground. I was very glad to see him, but he could not be sure what my problem was. He could not give me anything for the pain before the cause was determined. I gritted my teeth. After some difficulty with the hoist (while I wasn't on it, thankfully), the cable was lowered once again. The medic had me sit on two of the three flat prongs of the anchorlike device at the end of the cable, and then he looped a safety strap around me and attached it to the anchor. He fastened my backpack, my trekking poles, and even my hat to the anchor (the prop wash would be terrific), and he stood on the remaining flat prong. Then, he asked if I was afraid of heights. Mercifully I am not. With a signal to the hovering crew, we were hoisted above the treetops to the side of the helicopter and its open door. As we neared the door, I let go with one hand and waved goodbye to my friend Lakota John.

Being hoisted above the trees, swinging into the helicopter, and then flying over the forest and the mountains to the Salem airport was spectacular. It was over the top for an E Ticket ride (Disneyland's top-priced rides in the early days), but it wasn't worth my price of admission. My anxiety subsided now that I was being rescued, but the pain did not.

At the airport a waiting ambulance took me from the helicopter to the hospital. With my first CT scan a doctor determined that the cause of the pain was intestinal blockage, a kink in the small intestine stopping the digestive process. It was just a coincidence that it happened on the trail; it could have happened anywhere. With that knowledge, they could give me blessed pain relief. At last! It had been a long day, nearly ten hours since the pain began.

More tests and signs of infection led to a surgeon finally peeking inside my belly with a laparoscope. He immediately proceeded to open me up and removed thirty inches of intestine, black with gangrene and grossly perforated. Several doctors confirmed what he later told us: that few people reach such an extreme condition and fewer survive. I'm a lucky guy.

Several days passed while I recuperated in my hospital bed. Staples adorned the long incision on my belly. As I progressed to eating solid food once more, the sweet young nurses began to ask me hopefully if I was passing gas. I would not be released from the hospital without that sign that my digestive system was functioning. I slowly recovered, digestive system and all.

We were glad we didn't know how near death I was until the danger had passed. I learned that the "72 Year-Old Hiker Rescued" news item was on local TV and in several Oregon newspapers. (My fifteen minutes of fame, something I would rather not have achieved.) Zhita's cousin heard about the rescue on NPR in Portland, and she called Zhita to ask if that hiker was really me. Susan, a nurse I had met on the trail the day before the rescue, remembered I was from Los Angeles, got my home phone number from the white pages, and called to leave a message asking if the news report was about me and if I was alright. Gary, whom I had met several days before the rescue, managed to call me in the hospital to wish me well.

I convalesced in Springfield until the staples could be removed from my incision. Zhita drove us home carefully, stopping every hour to give me a break. Driving only four hours each day, we took five days to get home. The incisions, internal and external, healed in six weeks, and then I cautiously resumed exercising. Six months passed before I could do sit-ups. There was one brief recurrence of intestinal blockage due to adhesion of scar tissue, but that passed without any surgery. Every day for months I exclaimed, "I'm alive!"

I'm happy to report that I have fully recovered. In August 2009, Zhita and I returned to Jackrabbit Ridge and I continued my PCT adventure, hiking another three hundred miles well into Washington. I hiked a little more slowly that year, but I wrote that off to being older. Susan hiked with me for two of the four weeks, and my wife and daughters were very pleased to know I was hiking with a nurse. Susan pointed out that her specialty is obstetrics, which I wasn't likely to need. Still, her general knowledge and experience was reassuring. And there was no problem with my belly!

In 2010, I'll finish the last four hundred miles of the trail, hiking into Canada to complete the grand adventure. Thanks to the great skills and diligence of my rescue team and my medical repair team and to the loving support of my family and friends, my wife most of all, I'm alive and well and I'll hike again. I proved to be Over the Hill only in the better sense and ready for the next one. Bring it on.

Jim finished the final four hundred miles of the PCT, reaching the Canadian border on September 7, 2010. He reported that he had no medical challenges, "not even a cold."

WASCO LEGENDS OF EARTH AND SKY

By Barry Lopez and Ella E. Clark

Historically, the Wasco people were fishermen along the Columbia River, known for building elaborate scaffolding over waterfalls from which they would use long-handled dip nets to capture salmon. As settlers arrived from the east in the mid-1800s, a series of treaties were negotiated with the Wascoes and the Warm Springs bands to cede some ten million acres and in return to establish the Warm Springs Reservation. The Pacific Crest Trail passes through the Warm Springs Reservation, spending more than forty miles inside or near the heavily forested western boundary of the reservation north of Mount Jefferson.

Through the telling of tales, tribes kept their beliefs and ways alive. Stories such as the two that follow are part of the rich oral tradition of the Wasco. Typical of many Native American stories, animals play a central role in both tales and, in the case of "The Elk Spirit of Lost Lake," speak to and strive to help humans. Lost Lake lies just below the PCT in between Mount Hood and the Columbia River.

Coyote Places the Stars, by Barry Lopez

One time there were five wolves, all brothers, who traveled together. Whatever meat they got when they were hunting they would share with Coyote. One evening Coyote saw the wolves looking up at the sky.

"What are you looking at up there, my brothers?" asked Coyote.

"Oh, nothing," said the oldest wolf.

Source: "Coyote Places the Stars," reprinted from *Giving Birth to Thunder, Sleeping with His Daughter,* copyright © 1978 by Barry Holstun Lopez, used with the author's permission; "The Elk Spirit of Lost Lake," reprinted from *Indian Legends of the Pacific Northwest,* by Ella E. Clark, copyright © 1953 by the Regents of the University of California, © renewed 1981 by Ella E. Clark, published by the University of California Press and used with their permission.

Next evening Coyote saw they were all looking up in the sky at something. He asked the next oldest wolf what they were looking at, but he wouldn't say. It went on like this for three or four nights. No one wanted to tell Coyote what they were looking at because they thought he would want to interfere. One night Coyote asked the youngest wolf brother to tell him, and the youngest wolf said to the other wolves, "Let's tell Coyote what we see up there. He won't do anything."

So they told him. "We see two animals up there. Way up there, where we cannot get to them."

"Let's go up and see them," asked Coyote.

"Well, how can we do that?"

"Oh, I can do that easy," said Coyote. "I can show you how to get up there without any trouble at all."

Coyote gathered a great number of arrows and then began shooting them into the sky. The first arrow stuck in the sky and the second arrow stuck in the first. Each arrow stuck in the end of the one before it like that until there was a ladder reaching down to the earth.

"We can climb up now," said Coyote. The oldest wolf took his dog with him, and then the other four wolf brothers came, and then Coyote. They climbed all day and into the night. All the next day they climbed. For many days and nights they climbed, until finally they reached the sky. They stood in the sky and looked over at the two animals the wolves had seen from down below. They were two grizzly bears.

"Don't go near them," said Coyote. "They will tear you apart." But the two youngest wolves were already headed over. And the next two youngest wolves followed them. Only the oldest wolf held back. When the wolves got near the grizzlies, nothing happened. The wolves sat down and looked at the bears, and the bears sat there looking at the wolves. The oldest wolf, when he saw it was safe, came over with his dog and sat down with them.

Coyote wouldn't come over. He didn't trust the bears. "That makes a nice picture, though," thought Coyote. "They all look pretty good sitting there like that. I think I'll leave it that way for everyone to see. Then when people look at them in the sky they will say, 'There's a story about that picture,' and they will tell a story about me."

So Coyote left it that way. He took out the arrows as he descended so there was no way for anyone to get back. From down on the earth Coyote admired the arrangement he had left up there. Today they still look the same. They call those stars Big Dipper now. If you look up there you'll see that three wolves make up the handle, and the two grizzlies make up the other side, the one that points toward the North Star.

When Coyote saw how they looked, he wanted to put up a lot of stars. He arranged stars all over the sky in pictures and then made the Big Road across the sky with the stars he had left over.

When Coyote was finished he called Meadowlark over. "My brother," he said, "When I am gone, tell everyone that when they look up into the sky and see the stars arranged this way, I was the one who did that. That is my work."

Now Meadowlark tells that story about Coyote.

THE ELK SPIRIT OF LOST LAKE, BY ELLA E. CLARK

In the days of our grandfathers, a young warrior named Plain Feather lived near Mt. Hood. His guardian spirit was a great elk. The great elk taught Plain Feather so well that he knew the best places to look for every kind of game and became the most skillful hunter in his tribe.

Again and again his guardian spirit said to him, "Never kill more than you can use. Kill only for your present need. Then there will be enough for all."

Plain Feather obeyed him. He killed only for food, only what he needed. Other hunters in his tribe teased him for not shooting for fun, for not using all his arrows when he was out on a hunt. But Plain Feather obeyed the great elk.

Smart Crow, one of the old men of the tribe, planned in his bad heart to make the young hunter disobey his guardian spirit. Smart Crow pretended that he was one of the wise men and that he had had a vision. In the vision, he said, the Great Spirit had told him that the coming winter would be long and cold. There would be much snow.

"Kill as many animals as you can," said Smart Crow to the hunters of the tribe. "We must store meat for the winter."

The hunters, believing him, went to the forest and meadows and killed all the animals they could. Each man tried to be the best hunter in the tribe. At first Plain Feather would not go with them, but Smart Crow kept saying, "The Great Spirit told me that we will have a hard winter. The Great Spirit told me that we must get our meat now."

Plain Feather thought that Smart Crow was telling the truth. So at last he gave in and went hunting along the stream now called Hood River. First he killed deer and bears. Soon he came upon five bands of elk and killed all but one, which he wounded.

Plain Feather did not know that this was his guardian elk, and when the wounded animal hurried away into the forest, Plain Feather followed. Deeper and deeper into the forest and into the mountains he followed the elk tracks. At last he came to a beautiful little lake. There, lying in the water not far from the shore, was the wounded elk. Plain Feather walked into the lake to pull the animal to the shore, but when he touched it, both hunter and elk sank.

The warrior seemed to fall into a deep sleep, and when he awoke, he was on the bottom of the lake. All around him were the spirits of many elk, deer, and bears. All were in the shape of human beings, and all were moaning. He heard a voice say clearly, "Draw him in." And something drew Plain Feather closer to the wounded elk.

"Draw him in," the voice said again. And again Plain Feather was drawn closer to the great elk. At last he lay beside it.

"Why did you disobey me?" asked the elk. "All around you are the spirits of the animals you have killed. I will no longer be your guardian. You have disobeyed me and slain my friends."

Then the voice which had said, "Draw him in," said, "Cast him out." And the spirits cast the hunter out of the water, onto the shore of the lake.

Weary in body and sick at heart, Plain Feather dragged himself to the village where his tribe lived. Slowly he entered his tepee and sank upon the ground.

"I am sick," he said. "I have been in the dwelling place of the lost spirits. And I have lost my guardian spirit, the great elk. He is in the lake of the lost spirits."

Then he lay back and died. Ever after, the Indians called that lake the Lake of the Lost Spirits. Beneath its calm blue waters are the spirits of thousands of the dead. On its clear surface is the face of Mount Hood, which stands as a monument to the lost spirits.

THE BARLOW ROAD STORY

By Walter Bailey and Joel Palmer

When driving paved and graded roads to well-marked trailheads, and hiking a carefully laid out, constructed, and maintained trail, PCT hikers can easily forget how arduous it was for early pioneers to move through such rugged country—especially when we consider that these early travelers were carrying and ferrying everything from horses, mules, and wagons to supplies, furniture, and mail. One of the most important of these early routes, which crosses the PCT, was known as the Barlow Road.

The old Barlow Road wound its way up the White River drainage to Barlow Pass, where it intersects with the current PCT, not quite ten miles from Timberline Lodge. The road continued west through Summit Meadows and down the infamous Laurel Hill Chute west of Government Camp. Here grades reached 60 percent and necessitated the use of ropes winched around trees and sheer strength to lower wagons down near-vertical slopes. Nonetheless, Judge Matthew P. Deady, a noted Oregon jurist, is reported to have said of this road, "The construction of the Barlow road contributed more towards the prosperity of the Willamette Valley and the future State of Oregon than any other achievement prior to the building of the railways in 1870." It was estimated that nearly three-quarters of the early immigrants to Oregon used the Barlow Road.

When Samuel Barlow established his route as a toll road in the late 1840s, wagons were charged five dollars (about a week's wages) and each head of stock was assessed ten cents. In its first season of operation, Barlow recorded the passage of 152 wagons, 1300 sheep, and 1559 mules, horses,

SOURCE: Excerpted from "The Barlow Road," by Walter Bailey, *The Oregon Historical Quarterly* 13 (March–December 1912): 287–96; excerpted from *Journal of Travels Over the Rocky Mountains*, by Joel Palmer (J. A. James, 1847).

and cattle. Nonetheless, the road was always a financial struggle, and despite ongoing maintenance the general condition of the road was considered to vary from "rough to barely passable."

Our understanding of this early exploration of the route benefits from the first-hand accounts of Joel Palmer and William Rector. (Rector, along with Barlow, led that first group of pioneers in 1845 over what became the Barlow Road.) Palmer, Barlow, and Porter Loch followed a route similar to that of the PCT as it climbs from Barlow Pass and traverses the southwestern flanks of Mount Hood, and they scouted from vantage points near the glacier that now bears Palmer's name (located due north of the current site of Timberline Lodge). We have incorporated a slice from Palmer's journal into this excerpt of Walter Bailey's summary of the history of the Barlow Road.

Among the numerous obstacles overcome by the American frontiersmen in the monumental task of building a wagon road across the continent, the last, and one of the greatest, was the Cascade Mountains. Unlike the Appalachian and Rocky Mountain ranges, the Cascades presented, to the eager eyes of the road hunter, no natural pass. To those who would cross with wagons, two alternatives were presented; first, the narrow gorge through which the swift turbulent Columbia sweeps and second, the range of steep rocky mountain tops which join the white hooded peaks of the Cascades.

The stalwart pioneers who led the first wagon train of American homemakers, from the valley of the Mississippi to the falls of the Willamette did not dare, because the season was late and their stock fagged, to try the mountain heights. With rafts and the few available boats, they descended the troubled stream, suffering severely en route from rapids and storms.

During the latter days of September, 1845, the third great company of Western immigrants arrived at The Dalles, then the terminus of the wagon road. The old mission station became a great frontier camp. Hundreds of prairie wagons, large droves of stock and crowds of way-worn people lined the Columbia. Only two boats were running down to the Cascade rapids and transportation prices were high.

Among the last to arrive that year was the company commanded by Samuel K. Barlow. Captain Barlow did not like the situation at The Dalles [nor] the prospect of exhausting his provisions by a long delay and his money for a dangerous passage down the river. Barlow began looking for a new route into the Willamette valley. Two trails, he was told, had been opened across the mountains by stock drovers and horsemen. One way was to swim the stock across the Columbia, skirt the mountains along the north bank and ferry back at Fort Vancouver. A second route was the old Indian trail south of Mount Hood, a path said to be steep and difficult.

Captain Barlow determined to attempt the southern route with wagons. If there was already a trail it would probably be possible, he reasoned, to widen it into a wagon track. Says his son, William Barlow: "After resting a few days and recruiting his followers [...] notice was given that the company's captain, S. K. Barlow, was going to cross the Cascade mountains. [...] An invitation was extended to any and all who felt disposed to join his expedition; but he wished none to follow him who had ever learned the adaptability of the word 'can't." When the start was made in late September the party consisted of seven wagons and about nineteen persons.

For forty miles the way led over rolling mountain land. At the end of this distance a halt was called for rest and repairs. From the Blue Mountains a small gap had been observed south of Mt. Hood. Through this opening the leader hoped to build the future roadway.

Having reached The Dalles after Barlow's departure, Joel Palmer followed Barlow and induced about twenty-three wagons and nearly as many families to accompany him. [Ultimately] it was mutually agreed to join forces and push on with the road building. On October 11th, it was determined that Barlow, Palmer, and Porter Loch would see if they could find a passage over the main dividing ridge. With some food, an axe, and one rifle they made their way some twenty miles to the Indian trail that followed a wide, stony plain of several miles in width, extending up to Mount Hood, about seven or eight miles distant, and in plain view.

Here we take up Palmer's account from his journal:
I had never before looked upon a sight so nobly grand. We had previously seen only the top of it, but now we had a view of the whole mountain. No pen can give an adequate description of this scene. [...] A perfect mass of rock and gravel had been washed down from the mountain. In one part of the bottom was standing a grove of dead trees, the top of which could be seen; from appearance, the surface had been filled up seventy-five or eighty feet about them. [...]

We followed this trail for five or six miles, [...] to where it connected with the main ridge; this we followed up for a mile, when the grass disappeared, and we came to a ridge entirely destitute of vegetation. [...]

We then went around the mountain for about two miles, crossing several strips of snow, until we came to a deep kanyon [sic] or gulf, cut out by the wash from the mountain above us. A precipitate cliff of rocks, at the head, prevented a passage around it. The hills were of the same material as that we had been traveling over, and were very steep.

I judged the ravine to be three thousand feet deep. The manner of descending is to turn directly to the right, go zigzag for about one hundred yards, then turn short round, and go zigzag until you come under the place where you started from; then to the right, and so on, until you reach the base. *[From this description by Palmer evolved the name of Zigzag Canyon.]* In the bottom is a rapid stream, filled with sand. After crossing, we ascended in the same manner, went round the point of a ridge, where we struck another ravine; the sides of this were covered with grass and whortleberry bushes. [...]

October 12. After taking some refreshment, we ascended the mountain, intending to head the deep ravine, in order to ascertain whether there was any gap in the mountain south of us, which would admit of a pass. From this peak, we overlooked the whole of the mountains. We followed up the grassy ridge. [...] My two friends began to lag behind, and show signs of fatigue; they finally stopped, and contended that we could not get round the head of the ravine, and that it was useless to attempt an ascent. But I was of a different opinion, and wished to go on. They consented [...] requested me to go up to the ledge, and, if we could effect a passage up and get round it, to give them a signal. I did so, and found that by climbing up a cliff of snow and ice, for about forty feet, but not so steep that by [...] cutting holes to stand in and hold on by, it could be ascended. I gave the signal, and they came up. In the mean time, I had cut and carved my way up the cliff, and when up to the top was forced to admit that it was something of an undertaking; but as I had arrived safely at the top of the cliff, I doubted not but they could accomplish the same task. [...] After proceeding about one mile upon the snow, continually winding up. I began to despair of seeing my companions. I came to where a few detached pieces of rock had fallen from the ledge above and rolled down upon the ice and snow, (for the whole mass is more like ice than snow); I clambered upon one of these, and waited. [...] I could see nothing of my two friends, I began to suspect that they had gone back, and crossed in the trail. I then went round to the south-east side, continually ascending, and taking an observation of the country south, and was fully of the opinion that we could find a passage through.

The waters of this deep ravine, and of numerous ravines to the north-west, as well as the south-west, form the heads of Big Sandy and Quicksand Rivers. [...] I could see down this stream some twelve or fifteen miles, where the view was obstructed by a high range coming round from the north-west side. [...] All these streams were running through such deep chasms, that it was impossible to pass them with teams. To the south, were two ranges of mountains, connecting by a low gap with this peak, and winding round until they terminated near Big Sandy. I observed that a stream, heading near the base of this peak and running south-east for several miles, there appeared to turn to the west. This I judged to be the head waters of Clackamis [sic], [...] I was of the opinion that a pass might be found between this peak and the first range of mountains, by digging down some of the gravel hills [...] I could also see a low gap in the direction from where we [had come] up the creek on the 11th, towards several small prairies south of us. It appeared, that if we could get a road opened to that place, our cattle could range about these prairies until we could find a passage for the remainder of the way.

The day was getting far advanced, and we had no provisions, save each of us a small biscuit; and knowing that we had at least twenty-five miles to travel, before reaching those working on the road, I hastened down the mountain. I had no difficulty in finding a passage down; but I saw some deep ravines and crevices in the ice which alarmed me, as I was compelled to travel over them. The snow and ice had melted underneath, and in many places had left but a thin shell upon the surface; some of them had fallen in and presented hideous looking caverns. I was soon out of danger, and upon the east side of the deep ravine I saw my two friends slowly winding their way up the mountain. They had gone to the foot of the ledge, and as they wore boots, and were much fatigued, they abandoned the trip, and returned down the mountain to the trail, where I joined them. We there rested awhile, and struck our course for one of the prairies which we had seen from the mountain. On our way we came to a beautiful spring of water, surrounded with fine timber; the ground was covered with whortle berry bushes, and many of them hanging full of fruit, we halted, ate our biscuit, gathered berries, and then proceeded down the mountain.

After traveling about ten miles, we reached the prairie. It was covered with grass, and was very wet. [...] We [...] arrived in camp about eleven o'clock at night; and although not often tired, I was willing to acknowledge that I was near being so. I certainly was hungry, but my condition was so much better than that of my two friends, that I could not murmur.

Here we return to Walter Bailey's history:
The main party had begun the arduous task of cutting a road through the timber. The eastern side of the Cascades was not heavily timbered, however, and progress was rapid, though there is recorded some complaint about the incompatibility of big trees, rusty tools and tender muscles. It being the dry season, fire was used effectively in clearing the mountain sides.

When they came face to face with the steep mountain sides several families gave up the enterprise and returned to The Dalles. Palmer and Barlow were still determined to push on. They set out again to find a way over the main dividing ridge. After several days travel Barlow and Palmer found a passable route for wagons to the western descent. But their own journey was fraught with so much hardship and suffering on account of the snow that they were forced to conclude that the season was too late and the journey too long to risk being snowed in among the mountains. It had previously been determined that, should the passage prove impossible, the wagons and impedimenta should be cached and the company should proceed with the stock over the mountains. Therefore, on the return of the leaders a rude house was constructed about five miles east of the summit. Packing a few necessary articles upon the horses and oxen, only the weakest having saddle horses, the remainder of the company pushed on toward the scattered Oregon settlements.

Even greater hardships were experienced on the western slope of the Cascades. On the very summit they encountered treacherous swamps; there was no grass for the stock and they broused [sic] the poison laurel bushes; provisions gave out entirely and the woods became so dense and the canyons so deep and precipitous that some despaired of ever reaching civilization. William Barlow relates how his sister, Mrs. Gaines tried to cheer her disheartened companions, saying, "Why we are in the midst of plenty; plenty of snow, plenty of wood to melt it, plenty of horse meat, plenty of dog meat if the worst comes." Ultimately, a pack-train with flour and other provisions from Oregon City came to their relief and all passed safely through to the Willamette.

Captain Barlow, early in December, applied to the territorial legislature for a charter to open a road across the Cascade mountains. As soon as the snow left the mountains in the spring, Barlow engaged a force of about forty men and opened the road to the camp where the wagons were left.

The Barlow road was extensively used by immigrants until the building of the railroad along the Columbia [in 1870]. The diaries and letters written by the travelers express a strange mixture of happiness and sorrow, contentment and dejection, hope and despair, ecstasy and misery. Says one, "Some men's hearts died within them and some of our women sat down by the roadside and cried, saying they had abandoned all hope of ever reaching the promised land. I saw women with babies but a week old, toiling up the mountains in the burning sun, on foot, because our jaded teams were not able to haul them. We went down mountains so steep that we had to let our wagons down with ropes. My wife and I carried our children up muddy mountains in the Cascades, half a mile high and then carried the loading of our wagons up on our backs by piecemeal, as our cattle were so reduced that they were hardly able to haul up our empty wagon.'

Of Laurel Hill an emigrant of 1853 complains: "The road on this hill is something terrible. It is worn down into the soil from five to seven feet, leaving steep banks on both sides, and so narrow that it is almost impossible to walk alongside of the cattle for any distance without leaning against the oxen. The emigrants cut down a small tree about ten inches in diameter and about forty feet long, and the more limbs it has on it the better. This tree they fasten to the rear axle with chains or ropes, top end foremost, making an excellent brake."

On the other hand many make no mention of hardship but are enraptured and captivated by the charming blushes of the snowy peaks, "by the spectacle of Mount Hood's snowy pyramid standing out, clearly defined against the pale grey of dawn; not white as at noonday, but pink, as the heart of a Sharon rose, from base to summit. A little later it has faded, and by the most lovely transitions of color and light, now looks golden, now pearly, and finally glistens whitely in the full glare of the risen sun."

WALKING IN 5-7-5

By Rees Hughes

It may have been Gary Snyder who introduced "haiku hiking" to the backcountry of the United States. In Dharma Bums, *Jack Kerouac and a fictionalized Snyder, Japhy Ryder, create poems in the 5-7-5 format as they hike toward Matterhorn Peak. (This story is included in the California volume.) It is a practice that continues to be reported periodically in hiking blogs and forums and that many Pacific Crest Trail hikers enjoy improvising such poems while on the trail.*

In this case, two families unite to introduce their twenty-year-old daughters to backpacking on a short trip north on the PCT from Timberline Lodge, on the slopes of Mount Hood. In lieu of paternal interrogations at the end of each day, it was agreed that all would write at least one haiku daily, to be shared as the sun set.

A new reverence
For every footstep—now
That I've made my own.
—Chisa

I am a walking zealot. A pilgrim born a millennium too late. I am at peace when following a high-country trail that offers a banquet of wildflowers or a feast of panoramas. Truthfully, conditions can be pretty miserable and I will still be content.

Not surprisingly, I have this strong conviction that we true believers of my generation must pass along the spirit of the trail and appreciation for the land to

Credit for this story also belongs to Amy Uyeki, Chisa Hughes, and Howard, Kathy, and Emily Shapiro. Without their poetry and companionship this account would not have been possible.

the next generation. As Chief Sealth said, "Teach your children...that the earth is our mother. Whatever befalls the earth befalls the sons of the earth." We have a moral duty to teach such important values in our own homes.

This, of course, was my fervent belief before I had children of my own. When I became a parent some two decades ago, I quickly came to understand that when we are successful at raising independent thinkers they generally select a path different from the one so ardently imagined by their parents.

Even so, perhaps the only one who was surprised that neither of my daughters had evidenced any enthusiasm for backpacking in general—and for the Pacific Crest Trail specifically—was me. For my younger daughter, *hike* and *walk* and *camp* had become the cruelest of four-letter words. So when my older daughter, Chisa, casually mentioned an interest in trying a backpacking trip somewhere on the PCT, I had to suppress my desire to return a few hours later with a two-week itinerary mapped out.

But her innocent suggestion did take hold. It was proposed that we undertake this inaugural hike with my longtime hiking partner, Howard Shapiro, his wife, Kathy, and their daughter, Emily (who happens to be a close friend of Chisa's). Kathy and my wife, Amy, would serve as the unofficial vice presidents in charge of moderation, an assignment they took very seriously. When I selected the perfect route, they cut it in half. My usual Spartan kickoff? No way. We'd be at Timberline Lodge. Ground coffee and gourmet chocolate were in, cold breakfasts were out. When you are trying to plant the seeds of trail passion, I guess these steps are necessary to properly prepare the soil.

For me, shared reflection has always been an important component of PCT hiking; it certainly was part of what I hoped to model on this trip. However, it has been alleged that my parental debriefings tended to resemble interrogations. As my intent to share our thoughts and feelings at the end of each day became clear to Amy, warning bells must have been clanging loudly. "Let's do trail haiku," she preemptively suggested. Amy and her mother had recently published a book of her grandmother's poetry written in traditional Japanese 5-7-5. Those simple poems had come alive in our household and creating them could easily be applied to trail life. "We'll have each of us share at least one haiku every day," Amy continued. It was a stroke of genius.

The Shapiros made the long drive from Washington and my family from northern California for our mid-August rendezvous. Timberline Lodge was the perfect starting point. You cannot help but feel a sense of awe both from the setting and the lodge itself; like Crater Lake Lodge and Drakesbad farther south, they are among the few such venerable oases located right on the PCT.

> Timberline welcomes,
> Friends meet and embrace each other,
> Trail calls family.
> —Howard

> Lingering glances
> At the mountain before us,
> Heavenly backdrop.
> —Amy

Our first day dawned crisp and clear at nearly 6000 feet. Morning light illuminated distant Mount Jefferson and radiated from Mount Hood, looming above. Somehow the one component of the trip that we were unable to control could not have been more cooperative. The late afternoon thunderstorms of the prior day were mercifully replaced by ideal conditions. The seeds of trail passion do best when left unwatered.

> The Pacific Crest
> Taken in skips, leaps, and bounds,
> First day confidence.
> —Chisa

We left the comforts of Timberline Lodge and joined the crowds of day hikers traversing the mountain's southwestern arm to Paradise Park, where the meadows were carpeted with shaggy western pasqueflower, lupine, and iridescent Indian paintbrush, accented by spears of bear grass. The views were unrestricted. We lingered on this broad terrace soaking in the warmth, the freshness, and the scale of this alpine world. Once we left Paradise Park, we made the steep forested descent paralleling Rushing Water Creek to its confluence with the Sandy River.

Chisa and Emily set the pace. I lagged behind them content to be absorbed in my own thoughts. When had I learned my own love and appreciation for nature? When had I been transformed from periodic worshiper to pilgrim? I could not help but remember my first experience toiling along the Frisco railroad tracks under the hot Kansas sun. Our destination was a stretch of pasture no more than three miles from home where we were content to sleep laid out like strips of bacon on a tarp. But I will always remember the glorious heavens on that moonless night far from the ambient light of civilization. Constellations came to life. It was like a universe laid bare. That brief outing, lugging old canvas backpacks with wooden frames, helped me know forever that there were rich rewards to be reaped for a little hard work.

> Late spring fashion show,
> Floral display surprises
> This August hiker.
> —Amy

> Day comes to an end,
> Tents set and packs emptied where
> Bouncing waters live.
> —Rees

There was a sense of joy and genuine pleasure as we broke camp on the second day. A thru hiker joined us to replenish his water supply and dawdled to field questions from Emily and Chisa. Hot water for coffee. A few extra moments to absorb the laughter of the creek. The wisdom of Kathy and Amy in making this experience about the process and not the goal was continuing to pay off. Being under no pressure to "make miles," meant more flexibility in our schedule and routine.

> New trail traditions
> Meld with long established ones
> We sleep until eight.
> —Rees

> Isn't it nice to
> Be without the Internet
> And without a mirror?
> —Amy

Sore calves, butt and hips,
Learning some humility,
Thanks vitamin "I."*
    —Chisa (*vitamin I is ibuprofen)

We carefully crossed the turbid Sandy River, stopping shortly after to soak up the magic of Ramona Falls. The treacherous footing and precipitous washouts along the valley wall and the subsequent crossing of the Muddy Fork of the Sandy River provided just the right amount of adrenalin rush. I watched in amazement as Emily bounded as sure-footed as a mountain goat from rock to rock. We took a long and leisurely lunch after the final crossing, enjoying the warmth, the dramatic landscape above us, and wriggling our toes in the frigid pools.

Cascading thunder,
Rock hopping our fears abound,
We conquer Hydra.
    —Howard

We then made the long contour up the valley wall toward Bald Mountain. Near our campsite was a magnificent view up the valley to the glaciated northwest face of Mount Hood and west toward the setting sun and east to the rising full moon. We spent the final hour of the day watching the unfolding drama as day turned to night. There is a powerful feeling that comes from being even a small player on such an immense stage. It was dark when Emily and Chisa returned to camp, some time after the rest of us. I was thrilled by their efforts to squeeze every last drop from this experience.

As I licked mustard
from crackers and fingertips,
night licks day above.
    —Emily

Cascading river
competes for my senses with
The evening sunset.
    —Amy

What more could you ask
Than to perch on a hillside
Soaking in the view?
   —Amy

The moon rising high
Above the flanks of Mt. Hood
Kissing sun goodbye.
   —Kathy

Our route on the third day began to take us away from Mount Hood along a ridge, offering distant views north to Mount St. Helens, Mount Adams, and even a glimpse of Rainier. The rhododendron forest dominated this day's walk as we dropped to Lolo Pass before climbing up to the restricted watershed above Bull Run Lake. Lunch became complicated when Howard thought he had left a small bag containing his essentials at the previous night's camp. Shortly after he began running back to find it, the missing bag was located under the log where it had fallen when pulling out lunch makings. Quick action by Emily and Chisa minimized the consequences, as they raced to catch him a mile back down the trail. It all seemed to contribute to an increasing sense of belonging they were feeling in the backcountry; now they had their own stories to tell.

If we had decades
for a hike, talk, and laughter,
time would pass as quick.
   —Emily

Almost thirty years earlier I had walked this stretch of trail, but in very different circumstances. Then the forest was at the wet, dripping end of the alpine winter with snow just recently gone. Yet there were compensations: the landscape was lavishly festooned with the pink and red blossoms of *Rhododendron macrophyllum* and the mosquitoes had yet to hatch. That was not the case this year. The final miles included an introduction to Oregon's legendary mosquitoes, but by then there was a large reservoir of good spirits.

A feast was announced,
Winged guests flew from far and wide,
We're on the menu.
—Rees

There was an audible sound of regret as we reached the spur trail to Lost Lake. "This has come too soon." "Can't we exit from Indian Springs?" We each felt an eagerness to walk farther—that familiar pull that every PCT hiker knows when the trail has established a foothold in one's soul. With a certain reluctance to do anything that suggested our hike was near the end, we made our camp just south of Lost Lake.

Quick miles, slow walking,
Friends move conversations,
Lost Lake draws us close.
—Howard

As we spent the final night of our short trip around the fire, discussion turned to future PCT trips. No one questioned her or his ability to walk with a load, or to overcome challenges, or the ratio of effort to return. The meadows of Paradise Park, the gaping maw of Zigzag Canyon, the distant views across layers and layers of mountains, the mellifluous bubble of Rushing Water Creek, the laughs and quality of our time together, and the looming presence of Hood will be shared in our collective memory.

The final walk took us around the eastern shore of Lost Lake and into the weekend crowds and our rendezvous with our shuttle back to Timberline. Although we all emerged with a sense of achievement, Emily and Chisa, Kathy too, were particularly pleased. Our accomplishment had come with little of the envisioned pain and suffering.

Our footsteps take us
Out of the serenity
Where our minds remain.
—Amy

Waters gently sipped
From a bottomless river,
First tastes of the trail.
　—Rees

This was a good trip. But, I would be presumptuous to think that our short adventure was sufficient to create passionate backpackers and custodians of the backcountry out of Emily and Chisa. This modest walk can be how it begins. Wilderness is to be lived, breathed, walked, and, then, ultimately loved.

I have been scouring the maps for our next PCT trip together. I have them spread out on our dining room table, pen in hand. I feel a rush of adrenaline as I think about the High Sierra. Perhaps the stark, sparse beauty of the San Jacintos. August in the Pasayten can be unparalleled. I can sense Amy and Kathy peering over my shoulder, and I voluntarily shorten the line I am drawing.

What a difference
Mattress, outlet, toilet, lights,
I'd trade for the trail.
　—Emily

THE OLD GAL AND
SWEET GOAT MAMA HIKE THE PCT

By Carolyn "Sweet Goat Mama" Eddy

For many years, horses, donkeys, and mules have been the beasts of burden of the backcountry. However, increasing in popularity is the "packgoat," that sure-footed ungulate more known for chèvre and chin whiskers. Advocates, such as Carolyn "Sweet Goat Mama" Eddy, contend that goats have a number of advantages over their more traditional rivals. Goats are browsers, content to eat brush and weeds, and when they are managed well they take a nibble here and there, leaving little sign that they ever passed by. They are sure-footed in rough terrain, can go without water for extended periods, and form close bonds with humans. Some contend that they even make great heaters on cold nights. Castrated male goats, or wethers, like Festus in this story, are most commonly used for packing. They can easily weigh two hundred pounds and are able to carry up to fifty pounds.

Carolyn paints a delightful profile of Marge "The Old Gal" Prothman, whose mantra is "Life begins at sixty." Painter, traveler, writer, weight lifter, mother, grandmother, backpacker, para-skier, and part-time goat wrangler, Marge is a testimony to the richness of living life fully and a reminder that most of our limitations are self-generated. Pacific Crest Trail hikers of any age who have suffered an injury on the trail will connect with this inspiring story of overcoming the odds and embracing our challenges with enthusiasm.

I think that one of the highlights of hiking the PCT has been meeting the other people who hike it too. There is often an immediate connection, especially when you have shared a section and can compare notes. And when you've hiked it together with one of these fellow travelers, you often have a lifetime connection.

One of the more eventful hikes I have done on the PCT in Oregon is the section from Lolo Pass to Cascade Locks. Not that this is a particularly difficult section, but it seemed that the week that Marge and I hiked it there were plenty of funny and dangerous occurrences.

Some people from the Backpacking Light e-group put this hike together, to show some east coasters the beauty of the PCT and to support Marge in finishing the northern segment of Oregon on her section hike. For those of you who don't know Marge, she can best be described as a force of nature—unstoppable, even when the fates have thrown their best at her. That year, 2000, she had fallen on the trail in California in April, cracking her ankle, but had decided she had healed enough to get back on the trail. Her children, even though used to their mom's adventurous lifestyle, insisted that she have some companions along, just in case.

Since developing arthritis in my thirties I could no longer carry a backpack, or even a fanny pack, so I'm dependent on packgoats to carry anything I need. A goat can easily carry around thirty pounds, so I can have everything with me that I need and have a luxurious camp by thru-hiker standards. Of course, I'm limited to around fifteen miles a day, but this was fine for Marge and me. The guys, who wanted to cover more ground, took off from Timberline, with plans to meet us at Wahtum Lake in two days. Marge and I took off from Lolo Pass with the goats. After a night together at Wahtum Lake, the group would pick up Marge and they would go out the Eagle Creek Trail and I would take the stock out the Herman Creek stock route.

Immediately, one of my goats decided to give Marge her first lesson in goat psychology and trail etiquette. In goat herds, one goat is called the social director, and his job is to make sure that the herd stays together and no one is lagging behind or getting too far ahead. This goat in my herd is named Festus. He takes himself very seriously and prides himself on a job well done. Marge also got a lesson in goat physiology, which was that they randomly drop "goat berries" every few minutes, indiscriminately. The berries are small and dry really fast, but if you are hiking with goats, the berries just don't have time to dry up before you encounter them.

Goats do best when there is a human in the front of the line and one in the back. I put Marge in the back, since the goats have a tendency to push you for the first few miles and I thought she would be more comfortable back there. And Festus's training program immediately went into effect. Marge tried to lag back to keep from stepping in the goat by-products. This act of apparent individuality didn't fit with Festus's worldview at all. The farther back she got, the more frantic he got, and he kept stopping the whole line till she caught up, and she would stop till he moved on, and pretty soon no progress was being made. After I switched places with Marge, the line once again started making progress. And since I'm used to hiking with goat berries underfoot, Festus once again became happy with our progress.

Our first day required that we hike through the Bull Run watershed. This nine miles of trail is closed to camping because it contains the water supply for the city of Portland. Once we covered this stretch we continued on to Indian Springs, where there was a good water source. The wind was howling and there was dust everywhere but the view was fabulous.

We ate dinner while the goats browsed on the trees and shrubs and then we made our beds. I had lost my tent earlier (it fell off the goatpack but was returned by one of our party when he caught up to us). Marge put up her tarp, crawled inside, and promptly had the whole thing blow down on top of her. We both slept under the stars that night.

I got up early the next morning and turned the goats loose to eat. Marge was still sleeping until Festus, who was in a forgiving mood after the misunderstanding the day before, decided to come over and bestow a big sloppy goat kiss right across her face. She came up spitting and spluttering, while I stood there laughing and apologizing for my goats' bad manners.

We packed up, hiked the last four miles to the lake, and spent the day exploring and waiting for our other hiking companions to catch up to us. The next morning Marge headed out with them to the Eagle Creek Trail, one of the most scenic areas on the PCT and well worth the diversion from the "official" PCT. There are no less than seven world-class waterfalls that are only accessible from this stretch of trail. Also, it's much less steep than the official PCT or the Herman Creek stock trail, which both have a "let's get it over with" approach to elevation.

I took the goats and headed out the PCT toward Benson Plateau. This is a wild, fairly remote section; although it's close to Portland, its 4000-foot altitude gain from the Columbia River side makes it less accessible than the Eagle

Creek Trail, which has a much gentler elevation gain. It is a "ghost forest" and in the right weather can be pretty creepy. There have been Bigfoot sightings since the area has been settled, and once a cougar followed me when I was hiking without the goats or my dog.

But today was gorgeous and warm and sunny, and there were no boogey men in the woods. I was making great time and decided to go down to the Herman Creek Bridge and camp just past it. But the fates, at that point, decided to intervene. I was about one hundred feet above the bridge, where it's graveled and steep, when I turned to call my dog, who was attempting to cut down to the creek. I had a hiking stick, but as I turned, my foot slid and both feet went out from under me and I landed on my face. Imagine my surprise when I turned over, sat up, and watched my foot rotate 90 degrees sideways. Both bones were broken completely through.

I managed to get my bandana wrapped around my hiking boot to splint the ankle, used my stick to get back up, and hopped on the treacherous footing down to the bridge, using the bridge railing to work my way across. I unloaded the goats as they came by and dropped everything right where I was. I knew that fishermen came up here a lot, but it was 5:00 PM already so figured I would be camping on the bridge for the night. I took some pain meds and sat down. About that time fate came back over to my side and a guy who I had met in this area before came by on his evening run. He returned to the trailhead and called 911. Within about an hour and a half, the search and rescue team was there with an ATV Stokes (a stretcher with a huge tractor wheel in the middle), ready to rescue me. And I was ready to be rescued.

They put my gear back on the goats, put me on the Stokes, and we headed out—whereupon Festus, the social director, swung back into service. The rescuers stayed together to suit him, but in order to make sure they weren't going to run off with me or drop me over the side of the trail he pushed himself in between the two handlers at the back of the Stokes and kept his head on my shoulder all the way out. A friend came and got the goats and me and took me to Hood River Hospital, and after pins and rehab the ankle was as good as new. I spent a couple of days in the hospital recovering from the surgery.

Marge finished Oregon and went on to complete many more parts of the trail. We keep in touch and she has had subsequent travels, some involving broken bones, but all grand adventures. She is a hero to her friends and, as one of the few women in their seventies to have walked long stretches of the PCT, remains a part of PCT history. When her last adventure landed her in a wheelchair, she completed a long and intensive rehab, and then at eighty-one she began learning to para-ski. I submit that her motto should be, "If you're going to sit around on your butt, there better be a ski under it."

SOUL, SWEAT, AND SURVIVAL ON
THE PACIFIC CREST TRAIL

By Bob Holtel

*This day in 1986 of Bob Holtel's quest to run the length of the PCT is told
from the perspective of his running companion, Court Mumford. Holtel
began the run the summer before and finished August 22, 1987. Here,
Court joins Bob for the two days they had allocated to run the Timberline
Lodge–Cascade Locks section of the trail. Janis, Court's wife, planned to
meet them at Cascade Locks. Court begins his account noting that "Bob
paraphrased [ultramarathoner] Jay Birmingham's motivational words,
'dream, plan, endure, achieve' as a guiding mantra for his undertaking.*

*Back on the trail again in 2010, Holtel attempted a repeat of this feat,
planning to end at Campo on his eightieth birthday in 2011. Holtel, who
has covered 195,000 running miles and completed 154 marathons in his
lifetime, will be the oldest to run the PCT should his plans succeed. As he
says, "It is better to wear out than to rust out. . . . Some day I am going to
be ninety and I won't be able to do this. That's why I want to do it now,
while I still can enjoy this majestic and dangerous trail." It does seem safe
to assume that he will not forget the ambiguities of the Ruckle Creek Junction this time around.*

I awoke in the night to the howl of the wind. The temperature had dropped
appreciably and I heard thunder in the distance. Weather changes quickly in
the mountains. At dawn my fears were realized. There was cold rain and the

SOURCE: Excerpted from *Soul, Sweat, and Survival on the Pacific Crest Trail*, by Bob Holtel (Bittersweet Press, 1994). Reprinted by permission of the author.

wind was blowing hard. Hot coffee and some fantastic mountain mush, along with plenty of layers of clothing, took the chill off.

After this breakfast feast we were ready to set out. Bob started with long pants, but I figured I'd be okay in shorts once we got moving. I also had on four layers of cotton, including a hooded sweatshirt, and a nylon windshell. Not ideal, but I suspected adequate. The first couple of miles back up to the Pacific Crest Trail were just that—up. How better to get the body fuel and heater working. I knew that going up also meant going into the moist clouds.

The rush of the wind became louder as we climbed from the lake valley. No matter, the trail was wooded, hence protected. If we kept running, the cold would not be a problem. Wet shoes gave way to soaked feet. We traversed several ridges, never leaving the elevation of the clouds. It wasn't getting any warmer or drier.

Occasionally the ridge would become exposed to the south, the direction of the weather. That made it very cold. Some of the trail was across lava flows. That made it very slow. Some of the trail was both. I kept hoping to descend or at least have back our lovely soft trail. Instead it was this loose lava trail and blasting, bitter-cold wind and rain. Uck! As the degree of difficulty peaked, the trail became so exposed to the howling weather and the footing so rocky that it seemed it couldn't have worsened.

The next bit of track, very lush, beautiful, and protected, was pure ecstasy. It took us to the Eagle Creek Trail, and after four-plus hours on the ridge it was wonderful to go down, out of the clouds.

Eagle Creek empties into the Columbia near Cascade Locks. After some 20 miles of wet and cold running, to come upon this sight completely erased any fragments of negative thinking from the earlier experience. No matter that it was raining, we were in a very special place. Our pace slowed, indeed often stopped, to enjoy this treasure of magnificent waterfalls, clear and deep pools, fern-covered cliffs, spectacular gorges, tranquil ponds, and beautiful woods. It was all here, bombarding every sense of the imagination. The trail was once again soft and welcoming.

It was late in the afternoon when we could first see the mighty Columbia River. The rain became torrential. If we were to take the direct route, the Old Columbia Gorge Highway, we were fairly close to our destination. On the trail, the purest route, it would be just over twice as far and infinitely more scenic. We were anxious to get back into the woods anyway. So obviously it was press on.

We felt we had 4.5 miles on Ruckle Creek Trail to the Bridge of the Gods, our terminus and the conclusion of Bob's 66th day this summer.

The trail went directly up. And up and Up and UP. As the rain abated we stopped once for me to let my heart sink back into my chest, to eat what was left of the energy bars, drink some water, and enjoy the vista from high above the river. Then it was back to steeper uphill running than I've ever experienced, but we knew we had just a few miles to go.

Finally we reached a plateau where we were sure the trail would then cut back north. But trails do what they do, and we kept going east and up. How can this be, we wondered? Surely we've gone four or five miles. I hated to mention it to Bob, but we had perhaps just one more hour of daylight. Though it had already been a long day, our pace quickened. It was hardly raining now but we were still soaked. Wouldn't this trail please turn north?

A rule of trail running, indeed of survival, is never leave the trail. As dusk settled in, it was becoming increasingly difficult just to see it. Right after dark, we finally came to a junction with the sign: Pacific Crest Trail to Cascade Locks: 9 miles! Our worst fears were realized. We had doubled back on Ruckle Creek Trail. So there we were, at dark, with nine miles still to run.

Poor Janis, I thought, she'll be worried sick.

Although we had expected to be finished long before dark, Bob, being ever prepared, produced the smallest of flashlights. As long as we kept moving we could stay warm. As long as the critical beam kept working, we could make our way.

At first it seemed awkward, as it was pitch black in the forest on this overcast night. It took some experimenting to determine the best way to shine the light for both of us to see. What seemed to work best was for me to run in the front, carry the light, and shine it down at my feet. Bob, one step behind, could then see his footing. Of course, our progress was dependent on the flashlight working.

We were doing just fine. The trail was leading us on a most circuitous route in and out of the deep forest, but we knew we were on the right path, headed north and west. And Bob would say, "Just keep moving, endure, be patient, and pray for the flashlight."

At once it happened, the unthinkable. The son-of-a-gun blinked. What was that? Bob reported that he had just replaced the batteries and bulb, but again it blinked. Then it was black. Everywhere. Pitch black.

Threatening it with expletives didn't help, nor did banging it on the palm of my hand. Bob was verbally angered at all mechanical and electrical things in the world—"they always let you down." Old engineer Court was taking the damn thing apart by Braille, rearranging the batteries, wiggling the spring, anything. All the while we were trying to press on.

For some unexplained reason the light did come back on briefly, at which time we tripled our pace. Not a major feat, considering how slow we were moving. But then it would go out again, so it became place-and-test-each-step-one-foot-at-a-time. This was going to be a very, very long night. Poor Janis.

Once removed from the setting, it could have appeared comical. Our most efficient method was for Bob to literally hang onto my butt pack while I groped for the trail. The groping was at a snail's pace and somewhat dangerous, but we found it possible to keep moving. For one thing, the trail had a distinguishable pitch. Also, wearing shorts, it was immediately obvious when we got off the trail and into the bushes or rock. To my surprise the trail appeared as the darkest part of the all-black surroundings, unless that blackest part just happened to be a tree. In that case, we would walk directly into the tree.

I discovered that by unscrewing the flashlight, when I'd screw it together again, we got a couple of seconds of light. It was definitely worth the effort. So this is the way we traveled over the next few miles. We'd step and test to see if it felt like the trail. Twist for a glimmer of light and watch out for roots, rocks, and bushes. "You okay?" "Okay!"

Bob lamented somewhere along the way that in his experience on the Pacific Crest Trail he'd learned how appropriate was the "Crest" part of its name, which it continuously stays on. Below we could see the lights of Cascade Locks, but we weren't going down. It was frustrating, but we were inching along slowly. Movement was important as the night was still wet and cold. We were making progress, but it was quite late. Poor Janis.

Occasionally our spirits would wane, like the time we thought we'd traveled a spur to a dead-end overlook. Thank Bob for feeling out the trail which had taken an uncharacteristic switchback.

Finally starting down, the trail went into the deepest of black forest. After a couple of flirtations with the ledge, one direct hit by a tree, and my head-first fall over some rocks, we came upon a footbridge. Our sense antenna fully extended, we stopped to discuss this apparition in the darkened wilderness. What was it, we pondered, though not for very long. Very cautiously we chanced this bridge and to our amazement a road lay just across. A one-lane dirt road to us resembled a major freeway. But here it was and going in the right direction.

It wasn't long, maybe two miles down this wonderful road, when we emerged on a back street in sleepy Cascade Locks. It was something like 1:30 AM and not a creature was stirring, save two, and no telling what we looked like. We walked toward the center of town until the sole moving vehicle came into sight. Running and waving to intercept it we realized it was the local police who had spotted us. On approaching, the policeman rolled down his window, smiled, and said: "I was wondering if we were going to find you two tonight. I'll call Janis!"

I turned to Bob, smiling, "Tell me again what comes after endure?"

Courtland "Court" Mumford was killed in a small-plane crash in 2007. During his summer 2010 PCT run, Bob carried a special medal that Court had received for finishing twenty Catalina marathons. Bob continues his quest in honor of his good friend Court.

THE COLUMBIA AND VOLCANIC WASHINGTON
LAVA, MOSS, AND LICHENS

COVERING SECTION H–SECTION I

Columbia River—Bridge of the Gods—White Pass
Mount Rainier—Snoqualmie Pass

GIFT FROM THE TRAIL

By Lynn Wunische

Companion animals of virtually every ilk have traveled the trail, including dogs, llama, donkeys, mules, and Carolyn Eddy's goats. We even heard a wonderful story of a father and daughter whose beasts of choice were two camels. Apparently camels are surprisingly skittish, even though they are the biggest creatures along the trail. The twosome hiked and rode south one summer day, past the Three Sisters and along the Wickiup Plain, where they loosely tied the camels to available vegetation as they left the trail to use the bathroom. Along came a group of hikers, apparently spooking the dromedaries, who panicked, pulled loose, and scattered. The daughter, who was telling the story, will always remember the looks she encountered as she raced along the trail frantically asking each backpacker, "Have you seen my camel?" Not a question you expect along the Pacific Crest Trail.

This sweet story exemplifies the serendipitous events that make life, and trail life, so unexpected and so addictive. You just never know what awaits you, over the coming rise or around the next bend. In this case it was a feline furball named PCT.

As any hiker of the Pacific Crest Trail knows, the PCT gives in many ways. But this was the most unexpected gift that came literally from the trail.

Scotty, our tired, old Lhasa apso, was a dog with nine lives, and in the summer of 2007 he was living on borrowed time. He had logged many trail miles with us, but now it was hard for him to limp to the mailbox with me. As we had done for previous long hikes, I hired Carol, our house sitter/critter sitter/trail supplier, to stay at our house so we could do a three-week trek from White

Pass south to the Columbia River. (Yes, I'm an old, slow hiker myself, with arthritic feet, but I'm not ready to give up yet.) We had nearly lost my little Scotty so many times before that I was emotionally prepared to lose him soon, but I hoped he could last long enough for us to finish this hike. Mostly, I didn't want him to die on Carol's watch, as I knew she'd feel terrible. I know she loved him as much as we did.

Unlike the previous year's section hike, where things went like clockwork, this hike had some unwelcome surprises in store for us, including a moment of sheer terror as I slid down a 45-degree glacier in the Goat Rocks and crashed on the rocks below. That wasn't the terrifying part. The terrifying part was the knowledge that, had I been a few steps farther on the trail, I wouldn't have crashed on the rocks; instead, I would have shot out into midair for a 2000-foot drop. I later discovered that I hadn't attached my crampons correctly. My heart still races if I allow myself to think about it.

A week later, as we were completing the placid Indian Heaven section, I saw Carol and another friend, Karen, hiking up the trail toward us. Teary-eyed, Carol explained that I needed to go home and take care of my dog. He had had a stroke and could no longer walk or eat, but the vet would not put him down without the actual owner's permission. Carol was willing to take me home and then bring me back to join my husband, Dave, farther along the trail the next day. So I left Dave with another hiking partner, Asa, and went home while they completed the stretch from Road 60 to Panther Creek Campground over the next two days.

Carol had left little Scotty at my mom's to be cared for. Sure enough, he was nearly comatose, so I did what I knew I had to; I gathered him up and we drove to a clinic in Portland to say our last goodbyes. I stroked him and told him I loved him and then asked the clinic workers not to put him down till I was gone.

Funny how habits die hard. After that long drive home, I couldn't help but look for Scotty to greet me on the porch as always—but just for a second. Then it sunk in that he would never greet me again. That night, the house was colder, darker, and emptier than I had ever remembered it, with Scotty gone and my husband out on the trail. I also realized I'd rather sleep on the cold, hard ground with my Dave than in a soft, warm bed all alone. I knew that my home wasn't this building; it was wherever Dave was. Right then, my home was out there in the dark somewhere. Still, I had a few beloved cats to comfort me. We have never gone looking for a pet; they've always managed to find us, and as I was drifting off to sleep I wondered how and when the good Lord would provide the next pet. We've had cats, dogs, ferrets, guinea pigs, hamsters, rabbits, birds, even a mink. What kind would the next one be?

Back on the trail, Asa had had enough and wanted to leave, which left Dave and me alone on the trail again. It was good to be home where I belonged. We spent the next week climbing some of the most grueling hills I've ever had the privilege to hike—in 95-degree weather. But once we were on top, near Three Corner Rock, it was an easy cruise down to Oregon. We camped our last night between Table Mountain and Gillette Lake.

The next day, as we neared the lake, four of Dave's relatives approached us, carrying their cute little Chihuahua and an adorable, tiny, black and white kitten. I thought, "How cute, they brought their kitten hiking." As they approached, Dave's niece handed me the kitten saying, "Here, Lynn, this is for you."

"Wow! You got me a kitten!? And what good timing! How did you know?" Then they told me the rest of the story.

That skinny little scratched-up kitten had found our relatives on the PCT, in the middle of nowhere. They had parked at Icehouse Lake near the Bridge of the Gods and hiked up to meet us. When they were nowhere near any houses, the little kitty began crying after them and following them down the trail. At first, they tried to shoo it away, but she was persistent; she followed the hikers for two miles. Then Dave's niece picked her up and carried her the remaining half mile to us. They named her PCT.

My heart nearly broke as I tried to imagine how she ended up where she was. The best scenario I could come up with was that someone had brought her home to a house with an established cat that didn't welcome her. Perhaps she fought with the cat (hence the scratches) but was finally driven off. She must have spent a few days foraging (thus the boney figure). The saddest part was picturing her crying after every hiker who passed by in hopes that someone would feed and love her.

We took turns swimming in Gillette Lake so someone could keep an eye on the kitten and dog. For one panicky moment, I thought I'd lost her. I feared she had wandered off into the brush, but we found her resting in the shade of my pack. I was already in love with her and wasn't going to lose her again. All we had to feed her was a little jerky, but I knew it would have to do till I could get her home and give her a real meal. She was amazingly trusting right from the start, and we discovered that the notch between a backpack and the back of a person's head makes a perfect place for a kitten to rest. She was happy to sleep there all the way back to the car. For the first year of her life with us, she slept draped across my neck. Our little "trail angel" has healed up and filled out nicely. And since PCT is her official name, whenever I take her to the vet, they ask me what PCT stands for and I get to tell the story.

BEAR BAGGING

By Kim Todd

Every Pacific Crest Trail hiker knows about the prevalence of bears along the trail and the precautions hikers should take to protect both their food and their hairy, charismatic neighbors. Because, as bad as it is for the hungry hiker who has lost food to a marauding prowler, it is even worse for the bear. Habituation to human food, in most cases, ultimately leads to the death of the habituated bear, prompting the familiar phrase, "A fed bear, is a dead bear." In this piece, Kim Todd humorously describes the two most common methods of "bear bagging"—or protecting food from bears—used along the trail. Although neither method is perfect, and both have their frustrating difficulties, many hikers are fiercely loyal to their preferred method. Of course, in some areas along the trail, agency officials have settled all such squabbles by requiring the lockable bear canister. While Kim and her partner manage to keep their food away from any ursine thieves, in the California volume of the Trailside Reader *Krystal Rogers describes a successful raid on her camp and the aftermath that ensues when the bear bag fails and the bear wins.*

If we'd been more skilled at interpreting omens, we would have turned back the first day. From the moment my friend Karen and I set foot on the Pacific Crest Trail, planning to hike the length of Washington State, rain pelted us, tree roots barricaded the trail, and our packs proved too heavy to carry without significant pain. But eventually, near dark, we reached our mud-puddle campsite. All we had to do before shedding our wet clothes and crawling into our sleeping bags was hang our food in a tree to keep it safe from bears.

Rain running down the inside of our jackets, pooling in our boots, we flung the rope over the bough again and again as the rock tied to the end as a weight slipped loose or a loop snagged on a branch. The branch tilted downward, shrugging off our attempts to harness it. My throwing arm weakened, and the rock whistled short or long or, in a rare moment of precision, bounced off the branch and hurtled back at my head. Finally, the stone arced over and we hauled the stuff sack, soaked and muddy, up into the crown of the tree. I moved to the trunk to tie the rope secure. Then, with a groan and a crack, the limb snapped, and the bag plummeted to our feet in a shower of bark and pine needles.

Over the course of the next week, dreams of reaching the Canadian border after five hundred miles of striding over mountain tops receded, replaced by a persistent fantasy of finding the perfect bear bag branch. In my mind, the tree loomed tall and stately. The branches were few and far between. In the midst of them, twenty-four feet off the ground, a bough reached out perpendicular to the trunk. Only as thick as my two hands could circle, but sturdy, it stretched for a good twelve feet before any twigs or leaves marred its surface.

But day after day we were thwarted by slope-shouldered subalpine fir, shrubby mountain hemlock, and crooked whitebark pine. Bear bags resting against the trunk, bear bags tangled in the canopy, bear bags bobbing inches above the forest floor marked our travels. We examined specimen after specimen, all unique, all flawed.

Every night as light leached from the sky, and we packed our food into stuff sacks and unwound our ropes, Karen and I pondered the same question: smart bears or tall bears? We couldn't agree which to believe in. After a season working in Glacier National Park, where the grizzlies can reach up fourteen feet to claw down a Snickers bar or a trembling nature enthusiast, I preferred the traditional method. To hang a conventional bear bag, a camper ties one end of a string to the top of the sack of food, ties the other end to a rock, throws the rock over a branch, hoists the bag up, and secures the rope to the trunk of a nearby tree. When the food was hanging high over our heads, gently bouncing in the breeze, I slept easy.

But Karen would have none of this. She had spent a summer as counselor at a camp just outside Yosemite National Park, where campers woke in the middle of the night to find bears licking off their strawberry lip gloss. The black bears in Yosemite were bold and too wily for the standard bear bag rig. They had learned to slash the line and wait for the food to tumble to the ground like a care package dropped from a plane. Karen only felt comfortable with the elegant alternative method: the counterbalance.

With this hang, the camper divides the provisions into two bags of equal weight. Then she hoists the first sack the same way as with the traditional method, but loops a second rope through the bag, which dangles free as the food is raised. When the bag is as high as it can go, the camper ties the second bag to the free end of the rope and lets go. Voilá! The bags counterbalance one another. The looped string can only be pulled down by humans with opposable thumbs, so the bears remain hungry and out of luck.

Unfortunately, this method cuts the height of the hang in half. While the Park Service confidently recommends selecting a branch approximately 20 feet high, the most suitable ones we found were 12 to 14 feet off the ground, leaving our bags swinging a good foot or 2 above our heads, well within the reach of almost any self-respecting megafauna.

When we left our food in a low-slung counterbalance, bears paced through my dreams, batting the bags down with heavy paws, sucking down a week's supply of dried pears and apricots in long gulps. Just as my nightmare *Ursus arctos horribilis* hungered for meat protein, I would start out of sleep, anticipating the noise of ripping tent nylon and the smell of hot breath laced with putrid salmon.

So Karen and I alternated, one night traditional, one night counterbalance, each sticking resolutely to our preferred technique. The only thing we could agree on was to call it "the food bag," rather than "the bear bag," because neither of us liked to say the word bear after dark.

Like so many aspects of backpacking—purifying water and donning clothes that breathe while warding off evil weather—hanging the bear bag seems ritual as much as rational. Methods, born of luck and hearsay, are passed down through generations. Some hoist their whole packs. Others use bear wires rigged by the Park Service. My father, an engineer, designed a bear bag rig of breathtaking complexity under a towering hemlock in the Olympic rain forest. I went to bed before he was done, with eye strain from peering up at the crown in the dark for two hours and a headache from trying to visualize the network of interlacing ropes he planned.

A week later, after Karen and I lost the PCT in snow drifts, left the trail, bushwhacked for miles to intercept the friend making a food drop along the road, missed the food drop, and were contemplating hitchhiking to the nearest phone, we found it: the branch. Tall, moss-covered trees lined our campground at Placid Lake near Bird Mountain in the Indian Heaven Wilderness. From one of them, a long, brawny limb pointed toward the water. Although the lowest branch on the trunk, it still arced high above our heads. No tangles of twigs distracted from the smooth bark. When we finally hoisted our stuff sacks up twenty-five feet above the ground and counterbalanced them, the bags swung free, dangling gaily like birthday party piñatas.

Lying in the tent that night, I listened as frogs croaked their boasts on the shore, the birds settled down at the water's edge, and I strained to hear heavy footsteps in the grass or low growls and the crackle of underbrush. When I woke in the dawn half light and saw no claw marks circling the tree, no huck-leberry-filled scat near our camp, I breathed in a bit of disappointment with the morning air.

Maybe it was still early enough for the hills to be bountiful and the bears reluctant to pad down to campsites. Maybe our Top Ramen and powdered lemonade didn't loom as large in their imaginations as their claws and teeth did in ours. In my heart, I knew that the bears were both smart and big, and our food-hanging ritual served as much as an act of faith as a practical deterrent. If we do everything right, maybe they won't bother us, argued our superstitious souls. But at times, just like the most faithful, I wanted a sign of the value of our offering. I wanted the elegance of our efforts to draw them in.

A VERY WARM MOUNTAIN

By Ursula K. Le Guin

The eruption of Mount St. Helens in May 1980 was a cataclysmic event that killed fifty-seven people, diminished the height of the volcano more than 1300 feet, and distributed an estimated 540 million tons of ash over more than 22,000 square miles. Although the Pacific Crest Trail was relatively unaffected by the force of the blast (the PCT is about twenty miles away from Mount St. Helens at its closest point), it was directly in the path of the massive ash plume blown to the east by the prevailing winds.

In early July 1981, Rees, Howard Shapiro, and Jim Peacock hiked the PCT through southern Washington. Shortly after they crossed Killen Creek on the picturesque north face of Mount Adams and began the long descent to Lava Spring, the ash became noticeably thicker. As Rees observed in his trip journal, "Soon a gray pall was obvious in the forest. The ash covered downed trees so that we often saw just mounds; although a few flowers had pushed through, most greenery had succumbed to the ash. The lack of foliage had also reduced the presence of animal life. It seemed a place of death." It was an eerie, muffled silence with the few sounds swallowed by the ash. The ponds that speckled the terrain north of Potato Hill, with their gray bottoms, had been smothered as with the rest of the forest. "The walking became more arduous," Rees continued. "It was much like walking through sand." They estimated the layer to be between four and six inches, with many drifts blown much higher. Each step resulted in a puff of ash that permeated everything. They each dampened a handkerchief

SOURCES: "A Very Warm Mountain," copyright © 1980 by Ursula K. Le Guin, first appeared in *Parabola*. Edited with the author's permission for this anthology, from the author's collection *In the Red Zone*. Reprinted by permission of the author and the author's agents, the Virginia Kidd Agency Inc.

and tied it around their noses and mouths. It took them a day and a half
to cross the swath. It was hard not to take it personally.

An enormous region extending from north-central Washington to north-eastern California and including most of Oregon east of the Cascades is covered by basalt lava flows ... The unending cliffs of basalt along the Columbia River ... 74 volcanoes in the Portland area ... A blanket of pumice that averages about 50 feet thick ...
—*Roadside Geology of Oregon*, Alt and Hyndman, 1978

Everybody takes it personally. Some get mad. Damn stupid mountain went and dumped all that dirty gritty glassy gray ash that flies like flour and lies like cement all over their roofs, roads, and rhododendrons. Now they have to clean it up. And the scientists are a real big help, all they'll say is we don't know, we can't tell, she might dump another load of ash on you just when you've got it all cleaned up. It's an outrage.

Some take it ethically. She lay and watched her forests being cut and her elk being hunted and her lakes being fished and fouled and her ecology being tampered with and the smoky, snarling suburbs creeping close to her skirts, until she saw it was time to teach the White Man's Children a lesson. And she did. In the process of the lesson, she blew her forests to matchsticks, fried her elk, boiled her fish, wrecked her ecosystem, and did very little damage to the cities: so that the lesson taught to the White Man's Children would seem, at best, equivocal.

But everybody takes it personally. We try to reduce it to human scale. To make a molehill out of the mountain.

Some got very anxious, especially during the dreary white weather that hung around the area after May 18 (the first great eruption, when she blew 1300 feet of her summit all over Washington, Idaho, and points east). [...] Everybody read in the newspapers everywhere that the [...] eruption was "five hundred times greater than the bomb dropped on Hiroshima." Some reflected that we have bombs much more than five hundred times more powerful than the 1945 bombs. But these are never mentioned in the comparisons. Perhaps it would upset people in Moscow, Idaho or Missoula, Montana, who got a lot of volcanic ash dumped on them, and don't want to have to think, what if that stuff had been radioactive? It really isn't nice to talk about, is it. I mean, what if something went off in New Jersey, say, and was radioactive—Oh, stop it. That volcano's way out west there somewhere anyhow.

Everybody takes it personally. [...]

For the first couple of hours there was a lot of confusion and contradiction [in news coverage], but no panic, then or later. Late in the morning a man who had been about twenty miles from the blast described it: "Pumice-balls and mud-balls began falling for about a quarter of an hour, then the stuff got smaller, and by nine it was completely and totally black dark. You couldn't see ten feet in front of you!" He spoke with energy and admiration. Falling mud-balls, what next? The main West Coast artery, I-5, was soon closed because of the mud and wreckage rushing down the Toutle River towards the highway bridges. Walla Walla, 160 miles east, reported in to say their street lights had come on automatically at about ten in the morning. The Spokane–Seattle highway, far to the north, was closed, said an official expressionless voice, "on account of darkness."

At one-thirty that afternoon, I wrote:

It has been warm with a white high haze all morning, since six AM, when I saw the top of the mountain floating dark against yellow-rose sunrise sky above the haze.

That was, of course, the last time I saw or will ever see that peak.

Now we can see the mountain from the base to near the summit. The mountain itself is whitish in the haze. All morning there has been this long cobalt-bluish drift to the east from where the summit would be. And about ten o'clock there began to be visible clots, like cottage cheese curds, above the summit. Now the eruption cloud is visible from the summit of the mountain till obscured by a cloud layer at about twice the height of the mountain, i.e., 25–30,000 feet. The eruption cloud is very solid-looking, like marble, a beautiful blue in the deep relief of baroque curls, sworls, curled-cloud-shapes—darkening towards the top—a wonderful color. One is aware of motion, but (being shaky, and looking through shaky binoculars) I don't actually see the carven-blue-sworl-shapes move. Like the shadow on a sundial. It is enormous. Forty-five miles away. It is so much bigger than the mountain itself. It is silent, from this distance. Enormous, silent. It looks not like anything earthy, from the earth, but it does not look like anything atmospheric, a natural cloud, either. The blue of it is storm-cloud blue but the shapes are far more delicate, complex, and immense than storm-cloud shapes, and it has this solid look; weightiness, like the capital of some unimaginable column—which in a way indeed it is, the pillar of fire being underground.

On the 19th, I wrote down from the radio, "A helicopter picked the logger up while he was sitting on a log surrounded by a mud flow." This rescue was filmed and shown on television: the tiny figure crouching hopeless in the huge abomination of ash and mud. I don't know if this man was one of the loggers who later died in the Emanuel Hospital burn center, or if he survived. They were already beginning to talk about the "killer eruption," as if the mountain had murdered with intent. Taking it personally...Of course she killed. Or did they kill themselves? Old Harry who wouldn't leave his lodge and his whiskey and his eighteen cats at Spirit Lake, and quite right too, at eighty-three; and the young cameraman and the young geologist, both up there on the north side on the job of their lives; and the loggers who went back to work because logging was their living; and the tourists who thought a volcano is like Channel Six, if you don't like the show you turn it off, and took their RVs and their kids up past the roadblocks and the reasonable warnings and the weary county sheriffs sick of arguing: they were all there to keep the appointment. Who made the appointment?

A firefighter pilot that day said to the radio interviewer, "We do what the mountain says. It's not ready for us to go in."

On the 21st I wrote:

Last night a long, strange, glowing twilight; but no ash has yet fallen west of the mountain. Today, fine, gray, mild, dense Oregon rain. Yesterday afternoon we could see her vaguely through the glasses. Looking appallingly lessened—short, flat—That is painful. She was so beautiful. She hurled her beauty in dust clear to the Atlantic shore, she made sunsets and sunrises of it, she gave it to the western wind. I hope she erupts magma and begins to build herself again. But I guess she is still unbuilding. The Pres. of the U.S. came today to see her. I wonder if he thinks he is on her level. Of course he could destroy much more than she has destroyed if he took a mind to.

On June 4 I wrote:

Could see her through the glasses for the first time in two weeks or so. It's been dreary white weather with a couple of hours sun in the afternoons.—Not the new summit, yet; that's always in the roil of cloud/plume. But both her long lovely flanks. A good deal of new snow has fallen on her (while we had rain), and her SW face is white, black, and gray, much seamed, in unfamiliar patterns.

"As changeless as the hills—"

Part of the glory of it is being included in an event on the geologic scale. Being enlarged. "I shall lift up mine eyes unto the hills," yes: "whence cometh my help."

In all the Indian legends dug out by newspaper writers for the occasion, the mountain is female. Told in the Dick-and-Jane style considered appropriate for popular reportage of Indian myth, with all the syllables hyphenated, the stories seem even more naïve and trivial than myths out of context generally do. But the theme of the mountain as woman—first ugly, then beautiful, but always a woman—is consistent. The mapmaking whites of course named the peak after a man, an Englishman who took his title, Baron St. Helens, from a town in the North Country: but the name is obstinately feminine. The Baron is forgotten, Helen remains. The whites who lived on and near the mountain called it The Lady. Called her The Lady. It seems impossible not to take her personally. In twenty years of living through a window from her I guess I have never really thought of her as "it."

She made weather, like all single peaks. She put on hats of cloud, and took them off again, and tried a different shape, and sent them all skimming off across the sky. She wore veils: around the neck, across the breast: white, silver, silver-gray, gray-blue. Her taste was impeccable. She knew the weathers that became her, and how to wear the snow.

Part of my satisfaction and exultation at each eruption was unmistakably feminist solidarity. You men think you're the only ones can make a really nasty mess? You think you got all the firepower, and God's on your side? You think you run things? Watch this, gents. Watch the Lady act like a woman.

For that's what she did. The well-behaved, quiet, pretty, serene, domestic creature peaceably yielding herself to the uses of man all of a sudden said NO. And she spat dirt and smoke and steam. She blackened half her face, in those first March days, like an angry brat. She fouled herself like a mad old harridan. She swore and belched and farted, threatened and shook and swelled, and then she spoke. They heard her voice two hundred miles away. Here I go, she said. I'm doing my thing now. Old Nobodaddy you better JUMP!

Her thing turns out to be more like childbirth than anything else, to my way of thinking. But not on our scale, not in our terms. Why should she speak in our terms or stoop to our scale? Why should she bear any birth that we can recognize? To us it is cataclysm and destruction and deformity. To her—well, for the language for it one must go to the scientists or to the poets. To the geologists. St. Helens is doing exactly what she "ought" to do—playing her part in the great pattern of events perceived by that noble discipline. Geology provides the only time-scale large enough to include the behavior of a volcano without deforming it. Geology, or poetry, which can see a mountain and a cloud as, after all, very similar phenomena. Shelley's cloud can speak for St. Helens:

I silently laugh
At my own cenotaph ...
And arise, and unbuild it again.

So many mornings waking I have seen her from the window before any other thing: dark against red daybreak, silvery in summer light, faint above river-valley fog. So many times I have watched her at evening, the faintest outline in mist, immense, remote, serene: the center, the central stone. A self across the air, a sister self, a stone. "The stone is at the center," I wrote in a poem about her years ago. But the poem is impertinent. All I can say is impertinent. [...]

How long may her labor be? A year, ten years, ten thousand? We cannot predict what she may or might or will do, now, or next, or for the rest of our lives, or ever. A threat: a terror: a fulfillment. This is what serenity is built on. This unmakes the metaphors. This is beyond us, and we must take it personally. This is the ground we walk on.

A PACIFIC CREST ODYSSEY

By David Green

In David Green's account of his 1977 thru hike, he comes to consider himself a pawn in the battle between the strengthening Storm King and the weakening Sol as he passes through Washington in September. Walking over the Bridge of the Gods leads Green to start seeing the elemental forces of nature as deities ruling the vast and wild sky—thoughts familiar to many Pacific Crest Trail hikers. As the gods seem to turn on him, and the weather dampens his expectations, Green finds his emotions falling and his spirits tested. But, just when Green finds himself feeling as if he is participating in a forced march to complete his goal, he regains his perspective. Although he encounters abundant rain and snow and even a shattered tooth before he reaches the border, his love of the trail prevails.

Now, nearly thirty-five years later, Green's challenges revolve more around raising his twin twelve-year-old boys. He confesses that he doesn't "think of the trip much these days, although I did become an assistant scoutmaster of our town's Boy Scout troop . . . but I can't remember the last time I backpacked." But like all of us who have touched the trail, especially those who have walked long sections, it will, as Green concludes, forever be one of life's "benchmarks."

The record high temperatures of early and mid-August were being washed away by record rainfalls. As I walked across the Bridge of the Gods over the Columbia River on the last Sunday evening of August, I was escorted by a rare misty lull in the nearly continuous rains.

Source: Excerpted from *A Pacific Crest Odyssey*, by David Green (Wilderness Press, 1979). Reprinted by permission of the author.

Although I did not suffer the same despondency that had accompanied the conclusion of the High Sierra, I was again the victim of my expectations. Washington was betraying me. I had envisioned the bracing chill of frosted mornings warming to shirtless afternoons, the hillsides aflame with the colors of aging vine maple and huckleberry bush, the long shadows and golden tones of the autumn sun. Washington was supposed to be gravy, an idle stroll through a fir-lined Eden. Instead, it was the Flood. My second morning, after several hours of torrential rains, I woke to find myself lost in a fog . . . inside my tent! The dampness was all-pervasive. Even clothing that had been sheltered began to cling with a galling clamminess. Each day found down bag and clothing less lofty, straining less vigorously at the confines of their stuff sacks. It was ugly weather, graceless and without charm.

For nearly five months, the Pacific Crest had been weather-blessed. For the mountain traveler, drought conditions provide a benign environment. Except for the early May storms in the Sierra and, to a lesser degree, the early June storms, the trek had suffered only a very occasional sprinkle. And I had been doubly blessed. I seemed always to walk the edges of the weather. When the High Sierra received two feet of snow and more, I was in the Piutes where less than a foot fell. Although others walked through the customary oppressive, near-100 degree temperatures in the northern California lowlands, I met only the breezy days of a momentary lapse in the norm. I almost felt like I was cheating.

The Northwest, however, was returning to form, playing proctor on my Pacific Crest exam. I had lived five years in Oregon and was well aware of the stamina and stability of its rains. When Mt. Adams peeked coyly from behind a veil of disintegrating clouds, I knew it was only a ruse. Even as I walked a second day alongside Adams, the horizon bristling with the spires of Mts. Rainier, St. Helens and Hood, I could not completely shake the undercurrent of urgency that had joined my journey. I no longer trusted in the powers of Sol; I had entered the kingdom of the Storm King. Washington was an impressive display of his ascendancy.

From deep within the forest I can see the mass of brilliant white cutting into the backdrop of cirrus-ed blue. No form or delineation, just a gleaming promise to start the blood perking. As I climb up through the thinner growths, the mass begins to take shape, teasing me with partial exposures of the summit crown. Awww, Mother E, it feels so good to be excited again. From timberline, Mt. Adams stands to reveal itself. What a massive, overwhelming presence! With what broad strokes the Master Artist created this work!

Under shredded greys and splotches of summer we walk, through fields heavy with the most plump, luscious huckleberries that the trail has yet offered. As we climb into the high country, the clouds climb with us, revealing the magnificent sweep of glaciated Klickitat Canyon, the ancient rubble of the Goat Rocks. Mid-afternoon, and we huddle inside the Yelverton Shelter on the slopes of Old Snowy, the clouds coming back down to us, hustling before a growing wind. The word yesterday was of a front moving in from Alaska; the thought of negotiating the extreme exposures of the Goat Rocks in the weather it would bring is not an appealing one. We push on, the inclemency of the weather growing in proportion to the sublime beauty of the country. Snow Creek Canyon falls away 3000 feet below us as we traverse above the gaping crevasses of the Packwood Glacier, encountering a party of horsepackers who had nearly lost an animal to this tightrope of a trail. We creep along a knife-edge ridge, the wind accelerating, its gusts transforming one's rhythmic pace into the herkyjerk of puppets. The clouds lower still more, enfolding us in storm, flaying us with a stinging rain. The shelter of McCall Basin rises to meet us, and the beauty and savagery of the day are steeped in the warmth of evening reflection.

The rain continues unabated through the night. I wake in the morning, a Pooh with his provisions at sea in the flood: an ill-conceived choice of campsite has set my tent in the middle of an overnight pond.

Midday, and a cheerful "howdy-do" to a backcountry ranger brings the response, "you must be hiking the Crest Trail from Mexico." His ambiguous "There's a certain look about you" couldn't have referred to the three of us hiking the rainswept, wind-whipped, open slopes in our shorts, could it?

❧

The Cascades of Washington seem at first to be a continuation of the Oregon range: trail winding through the understory of huckleberry beneath the conifer canopy, meeting the sky only at a cluster of woodland lakes or the occasional patch of clearcut, rolling up through the hill country to the subalpine meadows at the foot of an Adams or a St. Helens. The Goat Rocks provide the first evidence that, though geologically mated with the Cascades of Oregon, the

Washington Cascades are a breed apart. Remnant of an ancient stratovolcano that has suffered the ravages of nature's forces over the past two million years of its dormancy, the Goat Rocks area is a country of sinuous alpine ridges rising above severely glaciated canyons.

Mt. Rainier appears in princely garments, crown of lenticular cloud, robes of silver icefall. I am a pilgrim come before the mountain that was God. My devotions are a peaceful practice, a brimming of quiet joy.

Excitement is a chameleon, changing its colors to fit the mood. Morning greets me with the first snow of the fall and my excitement has a crazyquilt of emotions to ride: relief that this latest storm came and went in the night that I spent in the sheltering confines of one of the infrequent trail cabins. Through lichened forest, an elk family leads me down to a golden meadow, where I stay the morning to watch the earth's vaporous breath rise, a devotion to the sun.

⋙

The day began innocently enough: a skyful of sun, frosted mummybag, a cluster of elk ushering me onto the morning trail. [...] But my eyes were turned ever outward, taking my passion for granted, never looking inside myself. So I did not see how Washington was eating away at my heart. How my steps had become hurried, forced, trudging along a map, no longer caressing the land. How my trail journal had become an obligation, no longer a plaything, carrying odes to my sweet. I did not sense the hollowness beneath my joy. I was in love, damn it, nothing could ever be wrong. And the shadows of depression grew silently longer.

I could not get a handle on the cause of my malady—perhaps it was a fear of the Storm King. Perhaps it was anxiety about the nearing Journey's End and the unknown that lay beyond—but the symptoms were obvious: I was trying to escape. Speed was an escape; I didn't have to live with myself when I was pushing a ridgetop, straining to make one more lake before dark. People were an escape, for I would take myself out of the wilderness to enter the social milieu. Books were an escape; Gail Sheehy's *Passages*, bought in Portland, was the first non-trail-related book I had carried. Evenings found me entangled in the theories of mid-life crisis, ignoring the riot of color in the celebration of Sol's farewell.

I had to get back in touch. Take time to watch a tribe of Clark's nutcrackers exercise an indecipherable pecking order while scavenging sardines from an open tin in a lakeside firepit. Take the time to let my emotions flow like the wild river. I mailed Sheehy back to Portland, installed a governor on my engine. The confrontation had succeeded and my demons seemed vanquished. Despite the Storm King's return, I could hardly sleep that night with my eagerness to return to my lover.

The mountains are a carnival with the hillsides dipped in cotton candy, elves tap dancing on the shelter roof. I whisper smoke signals to the gods—I am well, but be kind. Sol searches out the weak spot in the Storm King's armor to send down a ray of morning. There's even an occasional chink of blue, like a penny lying lone in the gutter. But the Storm King comes to sweep clean the streets, brushing the blues away. The Storm King raises his voice, spittle flying from his mouth, but I am not moved. The storm fades, clouds cracking with age; no pennies of blue this time, but bills of large denomination and Sol setting the stage for starry-eyed night.

The moment I bite into the supposedly pitted date and hear the grinding crunch, I know the odds have caught up with me. Throughout the journey, my timing had been perfection and I brushed up against only the fringes of misfortune. Now, as I spit out my mouthful of date to examine the damage, I feel the fear of failure for the first time. Tongue and compass mirror tell the story: a lower molar is fractured, gum to crown.

❦

I had set only one measurable goal for myself prior to the start of the trek: to walk the length of the Pacific Crest Trail in one hiking season. It was an unobtrusive target, however, no carrot before my donkey-nose. Perhaps this was due to the extraordinary scope of the undertaking—how does one comprehend the notion of hiking 2500 miles; what is there to hold in one's hand, where the tangibility? Perhaps it got lost in the experience of the moment—after plunging through knee-deep snow or ripping through clinging chaparral, one does not immediately reward oneself with the thought, "I am 13 miles closer to Canada." Canada was a goal only on a grimy, tattered sheet of paper that I carried with my identification papers.

As the months of miles slipped easily by, however, I began to take the accomplishment of the goal for granted, began building dreams of the future on the foundation of its achievement. Then, in one terrifying moment, I saw my future lying crushed in the wreckage of a tooth. I had not realized how important the gaining of the border was to me until after its achievement was threatened. As it happened, the fractured tooth did not stand in the way of my completing the trail; it became only one more incident among many, one more anecdote to share with friends. But it was an enlightening and humbling experience. I left that moment with a somewhat firmer grasp on my humanity.

EDITORS ON THE EDGE

By Tom "Bullfrog" Griffin

It has been said that what makes the wilderness so sublime is the absolute congruity between beauty and death, the pairing of opposites, like pleasure and pain. Oftentimes a hike on the Pacific Crest Trail will do that for us, bringing us both hardships and obstacles to overcome as well as the intense euphoria of having succeeded and persevered. In this story Tom "Bullfrog" Griffin returns to the beauty of the PCT after surviving a potentially deadly disease and, fittingly, he chooses to hike one of the most picturesque and dangerous sections of the trail. The Knife's Edge (also known as Egg Butte), as it is called, is a perfect example of this stunning union of beauty and death, a slender crest trail carved literally on the edge of a knifelike escarpment, where the eye dances from one distant horizon to the other and the foot fears even the smallest of missteps, which would lead to certain death.

The challenging, almost mystical nature of the Knife's Edge and Goat Rocks have made this area the subject of many stories. It is a treacherous landscape with abundant precipitous drops. We once heard a fireside story of a seasoned backpacker who ended up navigating his way through the area on the darkest of nights aided only by a walking stick. The stick, which he tapped cautiously in front of him as he proceeded, gave him information about the terrain. He came to a point where the probing stick failed to make contact with the ground in front of him. He tested the space to his left and right. No contact. Had he inadvertently found his way to a point with steep drop-offs on three sides? Horrified at his mistake, the hiker turned in retreat only to find no place around him where the walking stick made contact with the ground. How could that be? Not willing to risk a fatal misstep, the hiker wrapped himself in his sleeping bag and waited for first light. After a long and uncomfortable bivouac, dawn revealed him to be sitting in the middle of the trail with the bottom two feet of his walking stick broken off from the original, now substantially shorter stub.

As corny as it sounds, the darkest hour is just before the dawn. If you haven't learned that lesson yet, take a hike on the Pacific Crest Trail.

My story takes place in 2003, but first I have to rewind to 2001—a bad year for America and a bad year for me. I was diagnosed with a relatively rare disease. At one point, I thought it had spread throughout my body, and I was certain that I was going to die. Anguish doesn't even begin to describe the mental pain one suffers as a torturously slow medical machine scans the body looking for death.

I was lucky. After a modest-but-painful operation, the prognosis was good. But an encounter with death shakes you up. I decided that my "someday" goals needed to be tackled right away. I had been backpacking for twenty years and had always thought about doing the Pacific Crest Trail in sections. I couldn't wait any longer; I decided to hike the PCT bit by bit through my home state of Washington.

Due to the operation and its aftermath, I had to wait. Two years later, it was finally time to take the first step. I planned a journey from the Bridge of the Gods to the heights of the Goat Rocks and on to White Pass. This is 147 miles—the longest PCT section in the state without a town stop or major highway crossing. My cousin would walk the first part with me, and some fellow magazine editors I knew—Chuck, Beth, and Kevin—would join me for the second week. We would rendezvous where the PCT crosses a forest service road near Mount Adams.

The first week went as planned, with sunny skies and easy trails. But at the rendezvous, my editor friends told me some disturbing news: The weather forecast wasn't good. Rain was expected for the coming week.

For many PCT thru hikers, rain doesn't start until they reach Washington in September. It's never fun to hike in the rain, and, frankly, thru hikers are pretty spoiled by the dry conditions in California and Oregon. Their trail journals are full of laments and curses once they come to my state. Having hiked in Washington for more than twenty years, I'm used to the rainy weather, although I don't like it. It can be dangerous if all your gear gets soaked. But maybe the forecast was wrong? Or, perhaps it was right.

On the fourth straight day of rain, we entered the Goat Rocks Wilderness. The weather got worse and worse. Our shoes and socks were wet, our packs were wet, our clothes were wet. When we made it to Sheep Lake, we knew we had to stop.

That night the skies opened up. Rain pounded the tent like never before. The deluge was of biblical proportions. It felt like it had been raining for forty days and forty nights. Of course the inside of the tent got damp along the edges. Nothing was going to keep this torrent out. The tent floor was wet, and the bottom of my sleeping pad was wet. I had to curl up in a fetal position to keep my feet off the soaked floor. Somehow I made it through that long night.

The next morning, just when we were considering giving up, there was hope. Another backpacking party told us the weather was supposed to improve— "dry by tomorrow." Instead of leaving, we decided to take a rest day, build a bonfire, and try to dry as much of our gear as we could.

With a pile of wet wood and a twenty-foot downed log (and a tube of fire-starter), I tried to start the fire. The tinder caught but was in danger of going out in the rain. Beth and Kevin took turns holding an umbrella over it as I continued to slowly coax the fire along. It would have been funny if we were not so desperate—an umbrella over a smoldering fire? The whole process was like trying to get a colicky baby to go to sleep. Everything had to be done slowly and deliberately. One false move and the whole effort would be doomed. But it worked.

The rain finally stopped, and our bonfire consumed everything we fed it. As we dried off our gear, we obsessed about the weather. Even though the skies were solid gray, we could hear the wind briskly moving over the ridge. This was a sign that the front was passing. The sky even teased us with a few patches of blue, and we could see the lake, finally, about fifty yards from our campsite. Before, it had been socked in by the fog. We might just make it after all.

I've met some legendary long-distance hikers over the years. Scott Williamson hiked from Mexico to Canada and then back to Mexico again on the PCT in one year (what hikers call a yo-yo). Brian Robinson completed all three US long-distance trails (the Appalachian, Continental Divide, and Pacific Crest Trails, —a.k.a. the Triple Crown) in one calendar year. Both told me that the Knife's Edge in the Goat Rocks is one of their favorite sections of the entire PCT. When the US Postal Service put the PCT on a stamp, it used a view of the trail on the Knife's Edge. It is the epitome of a crest walk: stark, exposed, yet magnificent. At times the ridge falls a thousand feet to the left and to the right of the narrow ledge hewn from a rock backbone. The perspective is breathtaking but the consequences of a misstep terrifying. I had been telling my hiking partners about the beauty of the Knife's Edge since we began planning this trip. But if the weather didn't improve, my friends wouldn't even be able to see it. If by some miracle the clouds lifted, could it live up to its hype?

We woke up to cloudy skies again, but Kevin was optimistic. "I think it will clear," he declared. It seemed as if, by a force of will, he was going to part the clouds and let the sun in. And his willpower worked. As we were packing up, patches of sunshine broke through the cloud cover. After five days of rain, we left our camp in a much brighter mood.

As we climbed up to 6400-foot Cispus Pass, more clouds dissipated. Suddenly a huge wall of the Goat Rocks and Gilbert Peak came into view. The morning sun hit it sharply, with air so clear we seemed to be living in hyperreality.

The climb over the pass was tough, but the gardens on the other side were divine. A feast of little streamlets poured down the sides of the ridges to form the headwaters of the Cispus River. No photograph could capture the intensity of this green hillside. Feeling the warm sun on our faces as we stepped across the gurgling brooks was heavenly. No one really wanted to leave this paradise. We called it God's Garden. After five days of suffering, we deserved this. And even more wonders were coming.

I hiked ahead of the rest for a few miles, but I was determined we would cross the Knife's Edge together. So at the top of the final approach, I dropped my pack and waited. It was cold but sunny. Clouds swiftly moved in and out of the valleys. From my vantage point, I could see the white, mystical pyramid of Mount Rainier and a high mountain lake called, what else, Goat Lake.

While I waited, I decided to check out the Packwood Glacier crossing. The trail crosses an icy patch on the side of a steep bowl; one slip and you could be headed for rocks below. Trail journals warned it could be dangerous. But when I got to it, I found the hot summer had melted most of the snow away.

The remnants had rocks poking through except for about ten to fifteen feet of snow and ice.

I turned back and strolled to the ridgetop. Soon Kevin appeared and then came Chuck and Beth. Everyone gasped when they got to the ridge crest—and not because they were out of breath. Everywhere there were unimaginable views—mountains, glaciers, valleys, rivers, lakes, clouds, sky, snow. We could see the challenge of the Knife's Edge ahead. All the agony of five days of hiking and camping in the rain dropped away at that moment. We were on the top of the world.

Now came the long traverse to the glacier crossing. I shared the good news: the crossing would be much easier than expected. I scampered across first. Then came Kevin, who posed for my camera as he hit the most difficult spot. Beth was not certain she wanted to try it. She thought about hiking below the glacier in some rock fields. But just starting off in that direction dissuaded her. It was rough going, and the rocks were too loose. It was not long before we were all successfully across and set for the next adventure.

The Knife's Edge trail is carved from the top of a sharp ridgeline, with steep drop-offs on both sides of the trail. When you are not directly on the crest, you always seem to be on the edge of the mountain. A bad slip and you could get killed tumbling down the side. It is certainly no place for someone with vertigo or acrophobia.

We traded cameras to take shots of the group and the scenery. At one point we saw a mountain goat hike down McCall Glacier. After all the talk, the Knife's Edge exceeded its reputation. "You feel like you are on the edge of the earth," Kevin said.

I didn't want to leave, yet hiking in these conditions is intense. You want to be gazing at the view, but you can't. Every step requires a certain amount of concentration. You spend a lot of time looking down to make sure your footing is secure. It was already late afternoon and the guidebook said the best campsite was still a few miles away.

Slowly we made it to Elk Pass, the end of the Knife's Edge section of the PCT. We took more photos to celebrate and then I told our crew that we had to march on. We needed to get to that campsite before it got too dark to dry out our tents.

When we finally arrived at the campsite, we were all tired and crabby. Our gas canisters were cold, and the stove wasn't working very well. We had to warm up the canisters with our body heat to get them to start. This was our last night on the trail. We should have wanted to sit by the campfire and tell each other stories about the trip. But everyone was too tired for that. We crept into our sleeping bags and got ready for the coldest night of the week.

We woke up to our last day full of sunshine and good vibrations. Our success had been a combination of planning, luck, and perseverance. In the dark days of the deluge, it could all have turned out much worse. If the "trail telegraph" hadn't promised better weather ahead, we might have bailed out at Sheep Lake and never seen God's Garden and the Knife's Edge. If we hadn't planned for slow going and a possible rest day, we might not have had enough food or fuel to wait out the rain. And, if we had not been a bunch of stubborn editors who insist on meeting our deadlines—maybe we wouldn't have overcome the adversity. Our dark hours did end in the most extraordinary dawn.

GROWING UP ON THE TRAIL

By Barbara Egbert

Gary Chambers's wedding present to his new wife, Barbara Egbert, was a pair of hiking boots and convertible pants. Not surprisingly, their daughter Mary, born four years later, was weaned on backcountry outings. Mary had been a part of six backpacking trips by the end of her first year. Each year, the family challenged itself to tackle increasingly ambitious goals. When Mary was in first grade, Barbara and Gary kept her out of school to backpack the Pacific Crest Trail from Sonora Pass to Tuolumne Meadows, a stretch of trail that includes some of the most difficult terrain along the entire Pacific Crest. As Barbara observed, "That's when we realized that Mary had it in her to tackle a really long hike." In 2004, Gary, Barbara, and then ten-year-old Mary took on the entirety of the PCT, which Barbara subsequently documented in Zero Days: The Real-Life Adventure of Captain Bligh, Nellie Bly, and 10-Year Old Scrambler on the Pacific Crest Trail *(Wilderness Press, 2008). But, as Barbara readily admits, Scrambler was not the only one who matured on their thru hike.*

I did a lot of growing up on the Pacific Crest Trail.

People who saw the three of us—me, my husband, and our daughter—trekking along the PCT in 2004 probably thought it was the little kid who was doing the growing up. Scrambler was only ten years old, the youngest person to thru hike the entire trail in one season. But with 20/20 hindsight, I can see that while a thru hike was definitely a maturing experience for little Scrambler, finishing the PCT was that way for me too...even if it did take me five years instead of six months.

When we left the monument at the Mexican border in April 2004, we began introducing ourselves to people we met by our trail names—and they often asked how we acquired them. At that time, I was fifty-two and at the peak of my career in newspaper journalism, hence my chosen trail name Nellie Bly, borrowed from a pioneering nineteenth-century female investigative reporter. My husband, Gary, fifty-one, was a stay-at-home dad. One night he and Mary were packing resupply boxes and Gary was directing Mary: "Put that roll of toilet paper in this box! Count out the vitamins and put them in that other box!" Tired of being bossed around, Mary told him, "You're just like Captain Bligh!" That became his trail name, based on the outstanding navigator but also the famously tyrannical captain from *Mutiny on the Bounty*. Mary earned her trail name Scrambler for the ease with which she scrambled over the rocky trail between Aloha Lake and Echo Lake on the Tahoe Rim Trail during our second thru hike of the 165-mile route around Lake Tahoe in 2003.

At home, Mary was an independent-minded youngster, but during backpacking trips we necessarily functioned as a unit. On the trail, I was all mom, Gary was all dad, and—at first—Mary was all child. On steep slopes we often took some of the weight from her pack. We fussed over her, encouraging her to eat when she felt too tired. I told endless stories as we walked along to occupy her mind so her feet could keep moving. But by the time we entered Oregon, Scrambler had not only improved her strength and her backpacking skills, she had perfected the perseverance and willingness to endure hardship that characterize the true thru hiker. After we reached Cascade Locks on the Oregon–Washington state line, I returned home to California for a week to deal with shin splints and an abscessed tooth, while Mary and Gary continued on. When we met up at White Pass, they were making good speed through worsening weather and rough terrain. Scrambler had taken over many of the camp chores that had earlier been mine. As I performed my new role as mobile trail angel for two weeks, I realized that my planning had to include Mary as a true partner in the enterprise, not just a particularly tough and knowledgeable ten-year-old.

With my shin splints healed, I resumed hiking with the Captain and Scrambler at Rainy Pass, seventy trail miles from the border, but stormy weather and deep snow thwarted our efforts to punch through to Canada. When Gary and I were both on the verge of giving up, Mary gave us the pep talk we needed to try once more to reach the border. Why was I taking advice in a potentially life-or-death situation from someone who still used a booster seat in the car?

Because I had come to realize that Mary's willingness to tackle a challenge was an example for me. We did take her advice and we did succeed.

Two years later, in 2006, we returned to the Bridge of the Gods so that I could hike some of the sections of the trail I had missed. Captain Bligh and Scrambler just weren't going to let me give up. Mary was in many ways a typical twelve-year-old, but on this backpacking trip she became my mentor. Since she and her dad had been through this section before, under far worse conditions, Mary took me under her wing, especially through steep, narrow areas where my fear of heights was a problem. When we reached the Katwalk (also known as Egg Butte and sometimes called the Knife's Edge), Scrambler talked me across, cheerfully admiring the scenery and assuring me that the narrow trail with the tremendous drop-off wasn't as dangerous as it looked. In 2004, I had made up stories to entertain Mary. In 2006, she made up stories to entertain me.

The low point of the 2006 trip occurred a few miles from Snoqualmie Pass. I tripped on a rock, plummeted over the edge of the trail, and slid screaming down a steep slope until I could grab onto the damp vegetation. It was Gary who climbed down the slope, took my pack, and spotted me while I crept back onto the trail. It was Mary who cheered me up that evening at the Summit Inn and helped me deal with the fright of the fall and the pain of my bruised ribs and thighs. We don't have a TV set at home, so nights in motel rooms always involve some exploration of the world of broadcast entertainment. Scrambler found a show about extreme makeovers of women's wardrobes. Soon, the two of us were camped on one of the beds and laughing hysterically, just like teenagers at a sleepover. Captain Bligh couldn't figure out why we were glued to the tube when we so obviously needed to sleep. But truly, laughter was the best medicine that night.

Scrambler was fourteen in 2008 when we hiked the final 117 miles from Stevens Pass to Rainy Pass. During one evening we spent with Andrea and Jerry Dinsmore in Skykomish, three southbound hikers from a college in New England—two men and a woman—were also staying the night. Mary had always been able to hold up her end of the conversation with adults, from trail angels to Triple Crowners, but a puppy or another child would always take precedence. That evening I realized Mary was not only much closer in age to the trio—in many ways she had more in common with them than Gary and I did. The torch was passing to a younger generation of backpackers, and Mary was a part of it.

That was my hardest hike ever. My feet and knees hurt and my old problem with shin splints reappeared. I seemed to grow weaker as we headed north.

Mary, on the other hand, started out strong and just got stronger. By the end, she was carrying a lot of what had originally been in my pack. She was especially helpful when we crossed the Chiwawa River north of Stevens Pass near the Glacier Peak Wilderness. During the 2004 expedition, our stream-crossing protocol focused on keeping our petite daughter safe from drowning. Luckily, we never had any problems getting Scrambler across streams. The closest we came to disaster was when my foot slipped while crossing Whitney Creek during a side trip to Mount Whitney. I fell in and got soaked to the knees. By 2008, Mary had shot up several inches and was a member of her high school cross-country team. At the Chiwawa, Captain Bligh and Scrambler waded across first, wearing our two pairs of water shoes. Then Mary returned with my pair (which Gary had borrowed) and made a second crossing with me. So she crossed the river three times in about thirty minutes. A video Gary took shows us walking through the cold, swift water. Mary is focused but confident. I look downright decrepit in comparison.

My ego received a gratifying boost several days later, on our last evening on the trail. Mary wanted to learn how to build a campfire—a very rare treat, since we almost never built fires while backpacking. But our campsite had a fire pit and a supply of kindling, and the day's rain had soaked the forest to the point that fire danger was almost nonexistent. I enjoyed demonstrating my skill at building a fire, especially in light of Mary's eagerness to learn and appreciate my talents.

I learned a lot from hiking the PCT, but the most important lesson was one I learned from my daughter: Never shy away from a challenge. Grab it with both hands. She knew that even before our PCT expedition, and as we grew up on the trail, I learned it too.

OF MEN AND MOUNTAINS

By William O. Douglas

For thirty-six years William O. Douglas served as a US Supreme Court justice. A devoted civil libertarian and enthusiastic outdoorsman, Douglas was profoundly influenced by the years he spent growing up in Yakima, Washington. From the family home at the eastern foot of the Cascades, Douglas roamed extensively through the wild country nearby. As James Newbill observed in the July 1988 issue of Pacific Northwest Quarterly, *"Douglas was often didactic, usually evangelistic, and always passionate when discussing this love of the outdoors and his hope of preserving nature. From his earliest years, he used nature both as his personal testing ground and his refuge. He took great pride in walking long and fast, climbing dangerous precipices, and, by sheer grit and determination, achieving physical goals. And, throughout his life, quiet nature was his haven, his source of philosophical healing, and his channel of communion with eternal verities."*

Douglas served on the Sierra Club board of directors in the early 1960s. His deep devotion to environmental stewardship was often in evidence, although nowhere more so than in his dissenting opinion in the landmark environmental law case Sierra Club v. Morton *(1972). Justice Douglas argued that "inanimate objects" should have standing to sue in court:*

> *Inanimate objects are sometimes parties in litigation. A ship has a legal personality, a fiction found useful for maritime purposes. The corporation sole—a creature of ecclesiastical law—is an acceptable adversary and large fortunes ride on its cases . . . . So it should be as*

*respects valleys, alpine meadows, rivers, lakes, estuaries, beaches,
ridges, groves of trees, swampland, or even air that feels the destruc-
tive pressures of modern technology and modern life. The river, for
example, is the living symbol of all the life it sustains or nourishes—
fish, aquatic insects, water ouzels, otter, fisher, deer, elk, bear, and
all other animals, including man, who are dependent on it or who
enjoy it for its sight, its sound, or its life. The river as plaintiff speaks
for the ecological unit of life that is part of it.*

*What follows is an excerpt from Douglas's autobiographical book about
his youth,* Of Men and Mountains, *which was published in 1950. This
account begins with a philosophical perspective on his beloved Cascades and
concludes with the story of an intrepid Douglas and his younger brother, ages
sixteen and twelve, respectively, on an amazing trip into the mountains.*

The mountains of the Pacific Northwest are tangled, wild, remote, and
high. They have the roar of torrents and avalanches in their throats.

Rock cliffs such as Koochman rise as straight in the air as the Washington
Monument and two or three times as high. Snow-capped peaks with aprons of
eternal glaciers command the skyline—giant sentinels 11,000, 12,000, 14,000
feet high, such as Hood, Adams, and Rainier.

There are no slow-moving, sluggish rivers in these mountains. The streams
run clear, cold, and fast.

There are remote valleys and canyons where man has never been. The meadows and lakes are not placid, idyllic spots. The sternness of the mountains has
been imparted to them.

There are cougar to scout the camp at night. Deer and elk bed down in
stands of mountain ash, snowbrush, and mountain-mahogany. Bears patrol
streams looking for salmon. Mountain goats work their way along cliffs at dizzy
heights, searching for moss and lichens.

The blights of forest fires, overgrazing, avalanches, and excessive lumbering
have touched parts of this vast domain. But civilization has left the total scene
in strange degree alone.

These tangled masses of thickets, ridges, cliffs, and peaks are a vast wilderness area. Here man can find deep solitude, and under conditions of grandeur
that are startling he can come to know both himself and God. [...]

I learned early that the richness of life is found in adventure. Adventure calls on all the faculties of mind and spirit. It develops self-reliance and independence. Life then teems with excitement. But man is not ready for adventure unless he is rid of fear. For fear confines him and limits his scope. He stays tethered by strings of doubt and indecision and has only a small narrow world to explore. [...]

They—if they are among the uninitiated—may be inspired to search out the high alpine basins and fragile flowers that flourish there. They may come to know the exhilaration of wind blowing through them on rocky pinnacles. They may recognize the music of the conifers when it comes both in whispered melodies and in the fullness of the wind instruments. They may discover the glory of a blade of grass and find their own relationship to the universe in the song of the willow thrush at dusk. They may learn to worship God where pointed spires of balsam fir turn a mountain meadow into a cathedral.

Discovery is adventure. There is an eagerness, touched at times with tenseness, as man moves ahead into the unknown. Walking the wilderness is indeed like living. The horizon drops away, bringing new sights, sounds, and smells from the earth. When one moves through the forests, his sense of discovery is quickened. Man is back in the environment from which he emerged to build factories, churches, and schools. He is primitive again, matching his wits against the earth and sky. He is free of the restraints of society and free of its safeguards too.

Boys, perhaps more deeply than men, know this experience. [...] The boy makes a deep imprint on the man. My young experiences in the high Cascades have placed the heavy mark of the mountains on me. And so the excitement that alpine meadows and high peaks created in me comes flooding back to make each adult trip an adventure. As the years have passed I have found in these experiences a spiritual significance that I could not fully sense before. [...]

᛭᛭

It was late afternoon on a clear August day. My brother Art and I were walking with packs on our backs on the high ridge west of Cougar Lake. We were en route from Fish Lake to Dewey Lake. We were on what is now known as the Pacific Crest Trail that runs from Canada to Mexico.

We had camped the night before at Fish Lake, which is the head of the Bumping River. There we made our beds of white fir boughs on a patch of white clover next to a prospector's log cabin that had stood for years on the northern shore of the lake. We had slept late and had a leisurely breakfast. We aimed to make Dewey Lake the next night, which by our reckoning was only 11 or 12 miles distant. So there was no need for hurry.

Fish Lake is about a quarter of a mile long and perhaps not over 75 yards wide. Beavers have built dams at the lower end and turned a part of the meadow into marshland. Fish Lake, like Bumping Lake, lies close to the divide of the Cascades; hence it's a damp place. There is usually a drizzle for a few hours if one stays as long as a week end. As a result the mosquito thrives there and lingers longer in the summer than in the lower lakes in the Cascades. But there are compensations for those discomfitures.

Fish Lake lies in a valley not much wider than the lake itself. It's a small place, a one-party campground. Rich grass fills the meadow. Three kinds of fir surround the lake—red, white, and balsam; and there is a scattering of cedar among the fir. There are cutthroat trout in the lake, and rainbow in Bumping River that runs out of it. The cutthroat we caught on this trip were 10- and 12-inchers, black spotted. They were as brilliant as a sunset when we slipped a forefinger through the gills and lifted them from the water. They were fighting fish, next to the rainbow in the will to live. Fish Lake was a fertile and productive mother. It was rich in algae and insect life.

There has long been a stand of tall snags around the lake. They were killed by fire years ago and rise as giant skeletons of supple trees that once bowed gracefully before the strong northwest wind. Today their beauty is gone. They have none of the moisture that marks all life. They absorb none from the earth, and hence they offer a good supply of dry wood for the camp.

At dusk, deer and elk step noiselessly through the woods, scan the meadow for their enemies, then tiptoe to the marshy land for food and water.

I have seen the meadow a mass of wild flowers in July. Cinquefoil or fivefingers, buttercups, dwarf dandelions, and monkeyflowers for yellow; lupine, violets, and asters for blue; strawberry, a species of penstemon, and snapdragon for pink; cover and cottongrass for white. An abundance of cottongrass has indeed made the marshy land on the far side of the lake look like a miniature cotton field transplanted from some rich Texas bottom land.

This morning the charm of Fish Lake detained us until mid-morning.

Art and I had been at Fish Lake before. But the country beyond it to the west was unknown. We were exploring. From the contour map we knew that the trail out of Fish Lake climbed a ridge, but we had no notion how steep it was.

It's an old sheepherder's trail that takes the shortest route to the top. There are no switchbacks with an easy grade of 10 or 15 degrees on which one can hold a steady pace. The grade of this old trail must be around 40 degrees. It rises for 1500 feet or more. That puts the ridge which the trail finally reaches around 6000 feet, for Fish Lake lies at an elevation of 4650.

On this August morning it was slow going up the steep pitch. Our horseshoe packs that we carried over our shoulders weighed 30 pounds. We had been out a week [...] so we were hardened to the trail. But the rise out of Fish Lake slowed us.

The basic secret on such climbs is the breathing. The professional mountaineer is an expert. The lungs are the carburetor. As the air thins out, and the oxygen decreases and the carbon dioxide accumulates, inhalations and exhalations must increase unless the motor is to drop to an idling speed. Above 10,000 feet some breathe five times or more for every step they take. The increase in respiration varies with the individual. Once the required rate is discovered, co-ordination between breathing and walking is possible. This takes time, patience, and practice. But it turns out the mileage under pressure.

At this time I had not mastered the technique. I climbed the hard way. I suspect I practically lunged at the hillside; at least I went in spurts, taking a dozen steps or so and then stopping to pant. In this way Art and I took almost two hours to master the ridge.

It was a clear August day with no wind. The horseshoe pack hung over my shoulder like a weight of lead. The sweat welled up under it and rolled down my spine. I saw it dripping from Art's nose. Our shirts were wet through. When we stopped to get our breath, we bent over and leaned forward toward the hillside, silent and bowed like beasts of burden. Thus we dropped our sweat in the trail's dust and expended ourselves on the mountainside, expecting each small shelf above us to be the top. We were exhausted at the true top. There, beside a spring under an ancient western hemlock, we dropped our packs and rested. I was proud of my legs. They had given me no particular trouble.

The bearberry or kinnikinnick was scattered along the ridge in thick carpets that held the soil in place. This low shrub, with its reddish bark and pink urn-shaped berries, seemed in place here. Perhaps its leathery leaves, which the Indians used for smoking, tanning, and dyeing, gave it a hardier appearance. But whatever the reason, it, like all other species of the heather family, seemed at home on these rugged ridges.

Art and I lay perhaps a half-hour in our amateur botanical study while we rested from the climb. Then we moved along to the west toward Dewey Lake. It's easy going. Since there is no substantial gain or loss of elevation, a steady pace can be maintained. The trail winds in and out along the base of high cliffs that form the backbone of the ridge. The sheer cliffs, the towering hemlock, and the balsam fir, pointed like spires to the sky, give this ridge a cathedral's majesty. That feeling is accentuated by the numerous basins that lie on each side of the trail and from whose edges the mountainside drops off 1000 or even 2000 feet into grim canyons.

We had gone only a few yards along the top when Mount Rainier burst into view, so close it seemed to tower over us. Then the trail swung to the eastern slope of the ridge, cutting Rainier from sight. In the distance to the east was Bumping Lake.

We stopped again and again to pick the low-bush huckleberries that were at their peak. We had been out a week and craved sweets above all else. So from time to time we sat in the midst of one of these huckleberry patches and gorged ourselves with the sweet fruit.

The ridge abounds with springs and creeks, at every one of which we saw signs of deer. And once we saw fresh bear tracks, six inches or more across. Every time the trail swung across the ridge to the west so that Mount Rainier came into sight, we stopped to look as if we could not get enough. The result was that it was soon late afternoon and we were still about two and a half or three miles from Dewey Lake. The magic charm of the ridge had such a hold on us that we decided to look along its narrow backbone for a place to camp; and presently we saw a small open shelf a short way below us. We descended to explore it. We found a spring with clear, cold water. The shelf had a carpet made of alpine bunchgrass, heather, and moss. Balsam fir, with its needlelike spires, rimmed its edge. There was a scattering of dry wood for a campfire. The western rim of the shelf dropped off 1000 feet or more in a steep incline to a tangle of wilderness. Mount Rainier rose over us. We commanded the whole scene as if we were on the roof of a cathedral. No more perfect place to camp on a clear August night could ever be found. Here we threw off our packs.

We dug out the spring so that it would be wide and deep enough for dipping, knowing that the roily water would settle by the time camp was made and we were ready to start supper. We went above the trail and dragged down branches and logs for our fire. Only then did we unroll our packs.

We took great pride in these packs. We did not know about rucksacks or pack baskets, so we never used them. Once I tried the pack board with the forehead strap, and once the Nelson pack. But I found the horseshoe roll more to my liking. Each would take one-half of a canvas pup tent which would serve as the outside cover of the roll. Inside would be the blankets (two in each pack) and the food. And we designed a method for carrying food that suited our needs. We took the inside white cotton bag of a sugar sack, washed it, and then had mother, by stitching lengthwise, make three bags out of one. We'd fill these long, narrow white bags with our food supplies. The sacks, when filled, would roll neatly up with the blankets. Each end of the roll would be tied with the rope, later to be used for pitching the pup tent. Then the roll could be slipped over the head onto the shoulder.

We could not pack fresh meat, not only because of its weight but because it wouldn't keep. Canned goods, ham, and bacon were too heavy to carry. We would, however, take along some bacon rind for grease. We'd substitute a vial of saccharin for sugar and thus save several pounds. Into one white sack we would put powdered milk, into another, beans. We'd fill one with flour already mixed with salt and baking powder and ready for hot cakes or bread. In another we would put oatmeal, cream of wheat, or corn meal. One sack would be filled with dried fruit—prunes or apples. Another would contain packages of coffee, salt, and pepper. Usually we would take along some powdered eggs.

On the outside of our packs would be tied a frying pan, coffee pot, and kettle. One of us usually would strap on a revolver; the other would carry a hatchet. Each would have a fishing rod and matches. Thus equipped, each pack would weigh between 30 and 60 pounds, depending on the length of the trip planned.

We also took along a haversack which we alternated in carrying. In it were our plates, knives, forks, spoons, lunch, and other items we wished to keep readily available. It hung by a shoulder strap on the hip opposite from the horseshoe pack. The one who carried it was indeed well loaded.

Art and I had oatmeal, scrambled eggs, bread, and coffee for supper, and ended up gnawing on dried prunes for dessert. We did not pitch the pup tent that night. There were no trees on the small shelf between which we could stretch the ridge rope; and there was no threat of inclement weather.

The sun was setting when supper was over and dishes were done. I walked to the edge of the shelf to watch the last light leave the cold shoulder of Rainier. The mountain seemed close enough to put out my hand and touch. Up, up, up it rose, eight or nine thousand feet above me. Its eternal ice fields looked down, threatening and ominous because of their intimacy. The great, dark shoulders of lava rock that crop out among its ice and snow stood stark and naked in all their detail—mightier than any fortress, bigger than any dam or monument that the hands of man could erect.

Alongside that view I felt as if I were no more than the pint of ashes to which some day every man will be reduced. That dust, I thought, when scattered on the gargantuan shoulders of Rainier would be as insignificant as a handful of sand in an endless ocean.

It is easy to see the delicate handiwork of the Creator in any meadow. But perhaps it takes these startling views to remind us of His omnipotence. Perhaps it takes such a view to make us realize that vain, cocky, aggressive, selfish man never conquers the mountains in spite of all his boasting and bustling and exertion. He conquers only himself.

The sun, which had sprayed the ice and snow of Rainier with the colors of the spectrum, had now set. Rainier stood alone in silhouette, bleak and gray in the dusk. The mood of the mountain took hold of me.

Why was this peak called Rainier? Its Indian name was Takhoma, for one of two wives of an Indian chief. The other wife, Metlako, gave birth to a son. Takhoma remained barren. Jealousy grew in Takhoma's heart. She resolved to kill the boy. Metlako, learning of the plot, left the lodge with her son, like Hagar of old, and would not return. The Spirit Chief stepped in and settled the affair by turning Takhoma into a mountain. He threw around her shoulders a white, cold mantle so that the fires of jealousy would not burst forth from her breast.

There may have been some reason to name Mount Adams after John Adams. But he did not in my view have as much claim to it as Klickitat, who, indeed, had been transformed into the mountain. Teddy Roosevelt's name would be more fitting than Adams, since Roosevelt represented some of the daring and adventure of the west. But Rainier seems greatly out of place. Captain George Vancouver chose the name in 1792. It is the name of a British admiral, Rear Admiral Peter Rainier. Vancouver did the same for Mount St. Helens. That peak bears the name of the British Ambassador to Spain in 1792. And later in the same year Lt. Broughton of Vancouver's expedition named Mount Hood for a British admiral.

None of these men, so honored, ever saw the mountains that bear their names. None of them ever set foot on the Cascades. They never perspired on these slopes or slept in the high basins on beds of fir boughs. They never fished for cutthroat or rainbow in the streams or lakes or stalked a deer on the ridges. They never saw the delicate Sidalcea on the slopes of Darling Mountain or the fields of squawgrass in Blankenship Meadows. These men were total strangers to the Cascades and to America as well.

The Indians had for thousands of years hunted their slopes, drunk their ice-cold waters, and lived in their shadows. Yet of all the major peaks in the northwest range of the Cascades, only one has retained its Indian name. That is Shuksan, the Place of the Storm Wind, which is near the Canadian border.

There were no white fir boughs for our bed that night. They are the best for mountain mattresses, because their needles grow out from opposite sides only and thus produce flat branches. Jack Nelson of Bumping Lake always called them "mule feathers." Once I asked him the reason.

"Well," he said, "the best mattresses are stuffed with feathers, aren't they? A mattress of white fir boughs is the best in the mountains, isn't it? Well, can you think of any animal that would grow feathers like those fir boughs except a mule?"

The night we were camped on the little shelf looking on Rainier we did not seek boughs for our bed. The meadow seemed soft enough, and for two tired lads of twelve and sixteen, the ground is not so hard as to ruin rest. By the time we turned in, the wind was blowing on us from the ice and snow fields of Takhoma. It would be a cold night and the heat of a bonfire would be dissipated. So we let the campfire die and put rocks and branches on the edges of our blankets, throwing the two pieces of the tent over us as a windbreak.

I slept fitfully. I had thought my legs had stood up well the day before. But this night they twitched behind the knees. Moreover, the wind never died; and the bed got draughty no matter how we arranged the blankets. During the dark hours I was sitting up a dozen times, it seemed, tucking them in. Each time, before I settled down again, I looked once more at Takhoma—a sentinel of the night, a mother watching over her brood.

A MAGNIFICENT DIGRESSION

By Greg "Strider" Hummel

There is no more iconic landmark in the Evergreen State than Mount Rainier, a feature visible from much of the Pacific Crest Trail as it follows the Washington Cascades. Although the trail passes along the eastern flank of the massive mountain, the technical nature of the summit climb is a sufficient deterrent for most PCT hikers. With twenty-six major glaciers, significant permanent snowfields, and a temperamental climate, Mount Rainier is as daunting as it is picturesque. Not so for thru hikers Greg Hummel, Paul Hacker, and Jeff Zimmerman, who took a side trip from the PCT to ascend this famous peak.

For many years the mountain's name was the subject of serious dispute. In fact, the question of whether it should be Mount Rainier or Mount Tacoma went before the arbiters at the US Board of Geographic Names in 1890, 1917, and again in 1924. The issue was debated in Congress, with even Presidents Taft and Roosevelt weighing in. On the one hand, it was argued that Tacoma *was closer to the Indian name for the mountain; the mountain's name was variously recorded as* Takhoma, Tahoma, Taco-bet, Tuwouk, and Tacoba, *but* Tacoma *was popularized by influential travel author Theodore Winthrop in his 1862 book* The Canoe and Saddle. *After all, Peter Rainier, the man after whom Captain George Vancouver named the mountain in 1792, never visited the Pacific Northwest let alone the mountain. But, ultimately, the board declared that since the mountain's name had been Rainier for 125 years it was firmly established and there was no good reason to change it.*

On the southern California portion of the PCT in 1977, several of us ran into a fellow named Duane Wyman, who said he was section hiking the southern portion and then would be working at the Paradise Lodge on Mount Rainier the rest of the summer. He suggested that, should we make it that far, we should hitchhike over from White Pass and look him up. He would outfit and school us on how to climb the mountain.

So, 2000 miles later, Paul Hacker, Jeff Zimmerman, and I found our way from White Pass and walked into Paradise Lodge with our huge external frame packs and the stringent smell of thru hiking. We asked for Duane at the front desk and within a few minutes out he walked, totally flabbergasted at seeing us. He quickly ushered us down the hall to a dormitory-like room with single bunks and hardly any space. We laid out our gear—packs, sleeping bags, food, and dirty clothes everywhere—and soon the stench was almost unbearable. Duane ran off down the hall and reappeared loaded with headlamps, climbing harnesses, ropes, crampons, and carabiners, borrowed from his coworkers. We loaded some food, a first-aid kit, and sleeping bags into a single pack and began to divide up the technical gear.

That night we stayed up late going over the strategy of climbing the mountain and recounting some of the adventures of our hike so far. Being young and in fantastic shape, we thought nothing of loading up on beer and tequila in preparation for the physical challenge the next day.

The next morning we packed and headed up a snowfield to Camp Muir. Duane had suggested that we get there early so that we could secure our bunks in the shelter. The walk up on steep snow was easy for us, and we reached the shelter around noon to find brilliant sun, ice, rock, towering buttresses, and snow. We donned shorts and added to our tans through the afternoon.

A dirty trail in the snow wandered up from the shelter past a sign that warned, "Dangerous Area, experienced parties beyond this point only!" A short distance beyond this sign, the trail disappeared into a crevasse that looked too wide to jump across. But the trail continued on the other side toward an incredible and intimidating field of interlaced crevasses, winding around some, across others, disappearing here, reappearing there, until we could see it in the distance climbing a steep, dark ridge of loose volcanic rock. We would be crossing that in the dark.

When the sun went down the temperature followed. We tried to sleep early, but our adrenaline kept up the chatter of nervousness for hours. Parties of seven to ten people filled the shelter and packed it tight with gear strewn all around.

Midnight came soon and Jeff, Paul, and I had our gear on and ready before any-one else. We waited for another group to head out first, as Duane had instructed, and followed the line of headlamps off across the crevasse field. Our little party of three trudged on, each wearing a climbing harness, roped together, each with an ice ax, crampons, and headlamp. The stars, brilliant in the clear, moonless sky, contrasted against the dark silhouette of the mountain.

Our rope team moved like an inchworm across the crevasses: two of us would dig in with our ice axes and give the third just enough rope to get across each dark, gaping crack in the ice. In this way, should one fall, the other two would be ready to catch his weight and minimize the consequences. Our head-lamps shined down 75 to 150 feet into each crevasse, illuminating the ice and showing it to change from pure white near the surface to deeper and deeper blue, until it disappeared into the black depths of the glacier. Starting at mid-night ensured that ice bridges were stronger, in the cold of the night, and still safe enough to cross on the return trip down, later in the morning.

We climbed the dark ridge, following the first party, up and over and down onto the Ingraham Glacier, which presented us with even larger crevasses to negotiate. The first party began to go down the glacier and we, in our ignorance and faith that this party was far more experienced, followed them. After twenty to thirty minutes we looked back to find that two more parties had crossed the dark ridge and headed *up* the glacier! We quickly realized that the party we were following was most likely heading to climb a different route, and so we back-tracked and headed up into "the ice fall" of seracs, where the Ingraham Glacier flows off the steep side of the mountain. We had been instructed not to hesitate or rest here, as the ice blocks are almost always in motion. We followed a faint trail, sometimes coming to a vertical wall only to discover a side trail heading off in a new direction. The ominous, black-silhouetted blocks leaned in over our heads, some fifty feet high. We heard deep shuddering groans, pops, and loud explosions of ice shifting under huge strain. We hightailed it and made our way up the steep glacier, where we could see the three teams ahead of us.

Partway up, front-pointing with our crampons, my legs felt great but my lungs were having trouble maintaining the pace that my fully conditioned legs wanted to keep. The route was rather simple, just straight up, hardly any obsta-cles. The three of us powered up in the dark and passed the third team, then an hour later the second team, and then later the leading team. One of the lead team hailed us to hold up and said, "I've tried to climb this mountain eight times—I've succeeded four times, been blown off of my feet twice, snowed out twice, and I've never seen anyone on this mountain move as fast as you guys! We saw you follow that other group down the glacier, then you turned around and followed us up. Now you've passed us all and I have just one question: what in the hell did you do to get into such incredible shape that enables you to climb like this?"

Paul and Jeff looked at me with big grins and said, "He won't believe us if we tell him."

"Try me," the group leader said.

We told him that we'd all walked from the Mexican border, two thousand miles on foot to get here.

"Bullshit," he exclaimed, but then the wheels began to turn in his head and he got it. "You, you're hiking that Pacific Coast, uh, Pacific Crest, uh . . ."

All three of us together said, "Pacific Crest Trail."

By that time, the sun was casting a deep orange glow across the white ice, filtered through the layers of smoke from the many forest fires that year. Details of our surroundings began to emerge, and slowly the view below clarified. We turned our headlamps off and turned our backs on the darkness of night to embrace the brilliant orange illuminated mountain ahead.

The angle of the glacier gradually diminished and we sensed we were close, but we couldn't yet see the summit. We came to a massive crevasse—the bergschrund—and had to search for a narrow spot to cross. This time, though, the jump was not only across but also up. Intimidation haunted us and we prepared better than ever for a fall; however, we succeeded without incident. The trail now wound between two walls of ice. This, in fact, was the uppermost bergschrund and we were literally walking along inside the filled crack.

We rounded a small serac . . . and there was the summit crater. Two hundred feet to go and my adrenalin surged: my legs said "GO!" my lungs said "SLOW!" I unclipped from the rope and leaped out ahead to the top. It was a success rivaling all others in my short life. Paul and Jeff joined me on the summit and we collectively celebrated.

The forest fire smoke obscured all but the highest volcanoes. Mount St. Helens (pre-eruption), Hood, and Adams stood proudly above the clouds, striking a dominant stance. We thought we could even see Mount Jefferson through the haze to the south. The immediate valleys around Mount Rainier were fairly clear—they were lush, deep in green and rich with texture. Steam wisped from the ice caves on the lower edge of the small crater and I recalled the story of several of the earliest climbers seeking shelter there during storms, alternating between steam and cold throughout the night. The interiors of these caves were beautiful, sculpted by the steam that issued from the depth of the volcano.

It was 6:30 AM. We took pictures, gazed a last time from the top of the world, and then began the race back down, as the sun was rising and the ice and snow would be softening soon. As the sun warms the glaciers they begin to move, opening new crevasses, pushing up new seracs, knocking over others. Duane had instructed us to move quickly and safely down, to not hesitate, especially in the ice fall, which becomes even more dangerous during the day.

Coming down was easy. The surface of the glacier, hard on the way up, was now softening and getting slippery, even with crampons on. Slipping and sliding we dropped all the way to the ice fall in just an hour. We found it moving! The movement of these huge blocks of ice was perceptible and deeply audible. Now we understood Duane's instructions, and we hustled through. A couple hours later we came into Camp Muir and found the temperature to be a comfortable 70 degrees or so.

We slipped and slid down the snowfield to Paradise Lodge, where we landed with a celebratory air. But it was not long before my thoughts returned to the trail. We had spent two years planning, preparing, and walking the PCT, and we had only one goal—reaching Manning Park. We were really close now.

We stayed one more night in the lodge and then hitched back to White Pass and went onward, northward, to Canada. The trail was good—soft and moist with abundant ferns, spruce, moss, and signs of plentiful, life-giving water. And soon it came, a bit of rain here, some fog and mist a day later, then rain ... more rain ... and it rained all day and all night. We had nine straight days of rain north of Mount Rainier. We barely caught a glimpse of the mountain after conquering the summit. She had seemingly disappeared into the fog and mist. But our memories remain sharp and clear to this day.

THE 1853–54 NACHES PASS WAGON ROAD

By Dennis Larsen

For many Pacific Crest Trail hikers today, it is easy to take our well-built and maintained backcountry trails for granted. From paved highways complete with rest stops and gas stations, to trailhead parking lots with bathrooms, to seasonally maintained hiking trails and their associated guidebooks, our travels lack many of the trials and tribulations that were so common for our historical counterparts. In addition to the difficulty of not knowing the best routes over the rugged western mountains, earlier travelers, in many cases, had to construct sections of their trails themselves, often while transporting all their worldly possessions.

Similar stories exist along the length of the PCT—from the pioneers crossing the arid mountains of southern California to the early settlers who navigated the Carson Wagon Road, the Nobles or Applegate Trails, or the Barlow Road. In this story Dennis Larsen captures the harsh conditions and daunting obstacles faced by the first emigrants who followed the Naches Pass Wagon Road, just north of Mount Rainier. Often using their own words, Larsen describes the grueling effort required to build ramps of brush and logs to drive cattle, horses, and wagons over fallen trees, as well as the heart-stopping thrill of lowering stock and supplies by rope down a sheer cliff face. Although many PCT hikers enjoy "roughing it," stories like this one make us cherish our GPS, atlases, trail guidebooks, and trail crews with new appreciation.

Just north of Mount Rainier the PCT winds its way down from Arch Rock to Louisiana Saddle and shortly thereafter reaches Government Meadow. Continuing north from the meadow, the PCT crosses a jeep road. This rutted track is the Naches Pass Wagon Road made famous by the deeds done here in the 1850s by the pioneers of the future state of Washington. PCT hikers might pause here and reflect, for they are standing on historic ground.

The Naches Trail was well known to Northwest pioneers. Native Americans had worn a horse trail over the Cascade Mountains and had used it for years. In the 1830s, employees of the British Hudson's Bay Company used the trail as a trade route from the Pacific coast to the interior. In 1841 Lieutenant Robert E. Johnson of the Wilkes United States Exploring Expedition traveled over Naches Pass (4920 feet) following the old Indian trail. In 1850 M. T. Simmons of the fledgling village of Tumwater, the first settlement on Puget Sound, made an attempt to create a wagon road here but was defeated by the geography of thick forests and steep ridges. The trail's lasting fame came in the fall of 1853 after the Longmire-Biles pioneer wagon train became the first to follow the new "road" over the Cascades.

In 1852 the number of American settlements on Puget Sound could be counted on one hand. The future city of Seattle was just a handful of cabins and Tacoma did not yet exist. The citizens of "northern Oregon," as the territory north of the Columbia River was then called, badly needed an influx of settlers. Congress responded by appropriating $20,000 to build a military road from Fort Steilacoom on Puget Sound over the Cascades, creating a shortcut that would bypass Portland, in Oregon Territory, and take the immigrants directly from Wallula (the junction of the Walla Walla River with the Columbia) into the Puget Sound basin.

As the wagon trains began working their way west from the Missouri River in the spring of 1853, it became a matter of serious concern among Puget Sounders to bring at least part of that year's migration north, away from Oregon. However, it was also clear to the settlers of the future Washington Territory that the wheels of government would move too slowly to get a road built by fall for the wagons that were already on their way. If there was going to be a road, the settlers would have to build it themselves, and build it quickly. In May and July 1853, meetings were held in the village of Olympia (which became the capital of Washington Territory and later of Washington State), and a plan for this wagon road was discussed. Sixty-nine subscribers pledged $1,195 to fund construction that summer. It was hoped, but not guaranteed, that the subscribers would eventually be reimbursed by the federal government. Lafayette Balch, the founder of Steilacoom, the largest village on the Sound at the time, sweetened the pot with an offer of free town lots for the road builders.

A scouting party of four men—John Edgar, Whitfield Kirtley, Edward J. Allen, and George Shazer—was dispatched to determine the feasibility of using the Naches Trail as a wagon road. With the aid of Indian guides, the scouts followed the old route into and over the mountains, marking the way with blazes, occasionally veering off the Indian trail where it was deemed too difficult for wagons. Rain, lingering snow, and thick timber made the scouting difficult. When the scouts broke out into the open country along the Yakima River, Allen wrote, "Our journey was now at an end! our mission finished. We had ascertained, from personal observation, the practicability of cutting a road thro the Cascade Range, which had hitherto been doubted" ("Letters from the Oregon Trail," newspaper clippings in Yale's Beinecke Rare Book and Manuscript Library). Allen and Shazer raced back to Olympia with their report, while Edgar and Kirtley followed at a more leisurely pace, thoroughly blazing out the route.

With this news in hand, but before any construction had actually begun, the following advertisement was sent out to forts and supply stations along the Oregon Trail:

NOTICE TO EMIGRANTS DESIROUS OF SETTLING IN WASHINGTON TERRITORY.—By the united exertions of the citizens of Washington Territory, a road is being opened across the Cascade mountains from Puget Sound to Fort Walla-walla through which emigrants may pass without taxation—incurring no expense after leaving Grande Ronde, except ferriage at Columbia river. This road is being opened by those who entered Washington through Oregon Territory, and having experienced the expense and time lost by so doing, now throw open this avenue to that portion of the emigration of 1853, who design to make their homes in Washington Territory. The whole distance from Fort Walla-walla to the Sound is about 225 miles, and the road across the mountains will be the best one crossing the Cascade range.—There is no scarcity of grass or water on the whole route. Emigrants are particularly cautioned against sacrificing their cattle and horses, as they will, if brought through, command high prices; and if unable to be got farther, most excellent range will be found in the valley of White river, at the base of the mountains after crossing.

Rev. B. Close, Edw. J. Allen,

E. Sylvester, B. F. Yantes,

Jas. Hurd, Whitfield Kirtley,
John Alexander, Wm. Packwood
B. F. Shaw
Cascade Road Committee, Washington Territory, July 13th, 1853.

On July 30 two construction crews departed Olympia. Allen, leading twenty men, was to work from the west. Kirtley, leading a smaller group, was to work from the east. They were aided in their work by two Nisqually Indians. Queimuth went along as a guide and packer, and his brother, Leschi, supplied the workers with many of the needed horses.

Their biggest obstacle was the forest and the downed trees. Allen measured some that had fallen and found them to be "268 feet long, and 35 feet in circumference, many of them being clear of branches for 150 feet! They stood so high it was impossible to see over and beyond them, even on horse-back" ("Letters from the Oregon Trail"). Getting the high-clearance wagons over the smaller downed trees involved cutting three notches in the tree, two for the wheels and one for the wagon's center coupling pole. Ezra Meeker, pioneer of 1852, describes how these trees were negotiated: "In such places the oxen would be taken to the opposite side, a chain or rope run to the end of the tongue, a man to drive and one or two to guide the tongue, others to help at the wheels, and so with infinite labor and great care the wagons would gradually be worked down the mountain." (All Meeker observations are taken from his *Pioneer Reminiscences of Puget Sound*, 1905.) The monster trees Allen described were dealt with by building ramps of small logs and brush up to and over them. Amazingly, by the end of September the western half of the route was pretty well finished, although, as Allen wrote to Meeker, "Assuredly the road was not sandpapered" (Meeker Papers, Washington State Historical Society, Tacoma).

On August 1, 1853, Nelson Sargent started east from Naches Pass to meet the Longmire-Biles wagon train at Grand Ronde on the Oregon Trail in eastern Oregon. Sargent had family among the immigrants. He informed the travelers that all the good lands in the Willamette Valley were already taken and urged them to follow him over the new Naches Pass Wagon Road to Puget Sound, where there was an abundance of available unclaimed land. About 140 people in thirty wagons decided to follow Sargent, who assumed the road had been completed.

When the wagon train reached the Columbia River at Wallula they found no ferry in operation. Using driftwood and crosscut saws, they fashioned lumber on the spot and built a flatboat to ferry their wagons across the river. Once across, the wagon train followed the Yakima River into the mountains, crossing it eight times, and then turned up the Naches River. They would eventually cross the Naches River sixty-eight times before reaching Naches Pass. On September 15 the wagon train reached the end of the open prairie and entered the timber. They found no sign of Kirtley's track but, committed, they plunged on, cutting their own way through the forest.

Ezra Meeker later wrote that Kirtley's crew did little work that summer on the eastern portion of the wagon road: first, because the work party spent one-third of their allotted time simply traveling to and from the assigned work area, and second, because the men "fell out among themselves." Allen's crew, on the other hand, actually worked their way to the summit and a few miles beyond.

On October 8 the wagon train finally reached Naches Pass and Government Meadow. It had taken them three weeks to cut their way through twenty-five miles of forest. The exhausted pioneers rested their stock for two days at the meadows, but with the threat of winter coming on they then hurried down Allen's road for five miles until they encountered a hill so steep it could justifiably be called a cliff. The story of the "cliff" and the two-day struggle to get the wagons down it (losing only one in the process) has become the stuff of Northwest legend. Meeker tells the tale.

> Go around this hill they could not; go down it with logs trailed to the wagons, as they had done before they could not, as the hill was so steep the logs would go end over end and be a danger instead of a help. So the rope they had was run down the hill and found to be too short to reach the bottom. One of the leader's of the party turned to his men and said "Kill a steer"; and they killed a steer, cut his hide into strips and spliced it to the rope. It was found yet to be too short to reach the bottom. The order went out: "Kill two more steers!" And two more steers were killed, their hides cut into strips and spliced into the rope, which then reached the bottom of the hill; and by aid of that rope and strips of the hides of those three steers, twenty-nine wagons were lowered down the mountainside to the bottom of the steep hill:

Quite a tale indeed, but did the killing of the oxen really happen? It seems that George Himes, who was nine years old when he crossed the mountains with his parents, was the first to tell this version many years later as an adult.

Contemporary accounts do not mention it at all. And while some descendants of those pioneers adamantly stand by this version of events, many historians find the story too improbable to believe. Does it matter? Probably not. It is the stuff of legend after all, a riveting evocation of the spirit of hardships met and overcome—ingenuity, heroics, and all the larger-than-life doings that comprised the pioneer experience.

On October 17, 1853, the wagon train camped six miles outside of Steilacoom. The Longmire, Himes, Woolery, Kincaid, Light, Biles, Downey, Wright, Baker, Judson, and Van Ogle families had arrived at their new home. The impact of these families on the history of Washington Territory would be huge.

A second, lesser-known wagon train came over the trail three weeks later, and the next year, more trains followed. In September 1854, Ezra Meeker traveled out over the trail from Steilacoom to meet his parents and siblings in eastern Oregon and to guide them to Puget Sound. Meeker, going east, met many immigrants struggling along the route. He helped them as best he could, found his family, and brought them safely to Puget Sound.

The outbreak of the Northwest Indian wars in 1856–58 ended use of the Naches route by the pioneers, although it was well used by both Indians and the military during the hostilities. The Naches Pass Wagon Road thereafter fell into disuse and eventually was superseded by the opening of the lower and more easily traveled Snoqualmie Pass route, which the northbound PCT hiker encounters a few days after Naches Pass.

Hikers with time on their hands can easily explore Government Meadow, where the immigrants of 1853 camped, and might also consider side trips to Naches Pass or the cliff that nearly did in the Longmire party. To visit the "pass" go east on the jeep road for about a mile. To see the "cliff" follow the jeep trail five miles west.

MAN V. NATURE: CHANGING THE
WAY WE LOOK AT THE LAND

By George Marsh and Judge William L. Dwyer

Along the length of the Pacific Crest Trail, the route crosses or detours around aggressively cut areas of forest. Perhaps most infamous are significant stretches of Section O in California and Section I in Washington State. Although the implementation of the Pacific Northwest Forest Plan in 1994 began a new era in forest management, the scars of past practices are slow to heal.

This story began long ago but accelerated significantly in the Pacific Northwest in the years following World War II. Forest management philosophy emphasized timber productivity and economic efficiency and promoted techniques such as clear-cutting, slash burning, and planting of single species stands on harvested land. The result, according to the 1994 Northwest Forest Plan, was a "highly fragmented mosaic" of recent clear-cuts, thinned stands, and young plantations interspersed with uncut old growth.

As our understanding of ancient forests improved, the importance of the biodiversity present in late-successional forests was recognized. The call to reconsider high-yield, short-rotation forestry practices increased in intensity. However, such a change in social policy is not made without controversy; jobs, lifestyles, timber practices, even the way people interact with the natural world are affected. By 1992, there were over a dozen lawsuits and three court injunctions that had created gridlock in the public forests of the Northwest.

This entry in the Trailside Reader *combines a seminal environmental perspective on forestry written in 1864 with excerpts from the landmark*

Sources: *Man and Nature*, by George Perkins Marsh (Charles Scribner, 1864); Seattle Audubon Society et al. v. John L. Evans (US Forest Service) et al., 771 F.Supp. 1081 (W.D. Wash. 1991).

court ruling from 1991 that finally gave Western forests some of the protections long called for by many. George Perkins Marsh's prophetic book, Man and Nature, *was penned nearly 150 years ago and warned of the consequences of the destruction of American forests. A native of Vermont, Marsh witnessed the indiscriminate clearing of woodlands and the resulting change that he characterized as "too striking to have escaped the attention of any observing person." It seemed appropriate to partner Marsh with Judge William Dwyer's injunction, which set the stage for policy that heeded Marsh's cautionary words—the Northwest Forest Plan.*

Although logging is hardly the only battle line in the conflict between man and nature that one experiences on the trail (there is also grazing, mining, skiing, hydropower, etc.), it certainly is the most omnipresent as one passes through the fecund mountains of northern California, Oregon, and Washington.

PCT hikers who wander through these areas may ponder these and similar questions: How do we find the proper balance between the needs and desires of people and the environment? What is our responsibility as PCT hikers to minimize our impact and how can we give back to the places that have given us so much? How can we meet our needs today, while ensuring that future generations will have the natural resources to meet their needs?

Man and Nature, by George Perkins Marsh

Here, Marsh gives an accurate and telling overview of the impact of deforestation on the landscapes that support and sustain us, warning prophetically that we endanger ourselves when we destroy our vital forests.

As soon as multiplying man had filled the open grounds along the margins of the rivers, the lakes, and the sea, and sufficiently peopled the natural meadows and savannas of the interior, where such existed, he could find room for expansion and further growth, only by the removal of a portion of the forest that hemmed him in. The destruction of the woods, then, was man's first physical conquest, his first violation of the harmonies of inanimate nature. [...]

With the disappearance of the forest, all is changed. At one season, the earth parts with its warmth by radiation to an open sky—receives, at another, an immoderate heat from the unobstructed rays of the sun. Hence the climate becomes excessive, and the soil is alternately parched by the fervors of summer, and seared by the rigors of winter. Bleak winds sweep un-resisted over its surface, drift away the snow that sheltered it from the frost, and dry up its scanty moisture. The precipitation becomes as regular as the temperature; the melting snows and vernal rains, no longer absorbed by a loose and bibulous vegetable mould, rush over the frozen surface, and pour down the valleys seaward, instead of filling a retentive bed of absorbent earth, and storing up a supply of moisture to feed perennial springs. The soil is bared of its covering of leaves, broken and loosened by the plough, deprived of the fibrous rootlets which held it together, dried and pulverized by sun and wind, and at last exhausted by new combinations. The face of the earth is no longer a sponge, but a dust heap, and the floods which the waters of the sky pour over it hurry swiftly along its slopes, carrying in suspension vast quantities of earthy particles which increase the abrading power and mechanical force of the current, and, augmented by the sand and gravel of falling banks, fill the beds of the streams, divert them into new channels and obstruct their outlets. The rivulets, wanting their former regularity of supply and deprived of the protecting shade of the woods, are heated, evaporated, and thus reduced in their summer currents, but swollen to raging torrents in autumn and in spring. From these causes, there is a constant degradation of the uplands, and a consequent elevation of the beds of watercourses and of lakes by the deposition of the mineral and vegetable matter carried down by the waters. The channels of great rivers become unnavigable, their estuaries are choked up, and harbors which once sheltered large navies are shoaled by dangerous sandbars. The earth, stripped of its vegetable glebe, grows less and less productive, and consequently, less able to protect itself by weaving a new carpeting of turf to shield it from wind and sun and scouring rain. Gradually it becomes altogether barren. The washing of the soil from the mountains leaves bare ridges of sterile rock, and the rich organic mould which covered them, now swept down into the dank low grounds, promotes a luxuriance of aquatic vegetation that breeds fever, and more insidious forms of mortal disease, by its decay, and thus the earth is rendered no longer fit for the habitation of man.

Seattle Audubon Society et al. v. John L. Evans (US Forest Service) et al., ruling by Judge William L. Dwyer

From April 30 until May 9, 1991, Judge William L. Dwyer heard evidence "of high quality from biologists, economists, and others." Based on that information, Dwyer ultimately granted the logging injunction requested by the Seattle Audubon Society. The injunction, which paralyzed timber harvests on federal forest land in the range of the northern spotted owl, was lifted as a result of the work of a Forest Conference convened in Portland, Oregon, in early 1993. In attendance were President Clinton, Vice President Gore, and five cabinet-level officials.

The new president directed his secretaries of agriculture and the interior to work together on a strategy that would enable the agencies to fulfill the terms of the injunction. The strategy was to satisfy five foundational principles, which included providing for a stable and sustainable supply of timber and meeting the agencies' conservation obligations toward the owl and other protected species at the same time. The Northwest Forest Plan grew out of the impasse and affects much of the area in Washington, Oregon, and northern California through which the PCT passes.

These excerpted passages from Dwyer's decision provide a glimpse into the evidence, the findings, and the judge's strong statement about the importance of rebalancing environmental and economic interests. Almost 150 years after George Perkins Marsh's call to value and conserve our western forests, with Dwyer's decision Marsh's ideas made the leap from environmental philosophy to environmental policy.

FINDINGS OF FACT

A. Background Findings

1. The fate of the spotted owl has become a battleground largely because the species is a symbol of the remaining old growth forest. As stated in the ISC (Interagency Scientific Committee to Address the Conservation of the Northern Spotted Owl) Report:

> Why all the fuss about the status and welfare of this particular bird? The numbers, distribution, and welfare of spotted owls are widely believed to be inextricably tied to mature and old-growth forests. Such forests have been significantly reduced since 1850 (mostly since 1950) by clearing for agriculture, urban development, natural events such as fire and windstorms, and most significantly, by logging in recent decades. Nearly all old growth has been removed on private lands. Most of the remainder is under the management of the BLM, FS, and NPS on Federal lands. As its habitat has declined, the owl has virtually disappeared from some areas and its numbers are decreasing in others.

2. An old growth forest consists not just of ancient standing trees, but of fallen trees, snags, massive decaying vegetation, and numerous resident plant and animal species, many of which live nowhere else.

3. A great conifer forest originally covered the western parts of Washington, Oregon, and northern California, from the Cascade and Coast mountains to the sea. Perhaps ten percent of it remains. The spaces protected as parks or wilderness areas are not enough for the survival of the northern spotted owl.

4. The old growth forest sustains a biological community far richer than those of managed forests or tree farms. As testified by Dr. William Ferrell, a forest ecologist:

The most significant implication from our new knowledge regarding old-growth forest ecology is that logging these forests destroys not just trees, but a complex, distinctive, and unique ecosystem.

5. The remaining old growth stands are valued also for their effects on climate, air, and migratory fish runs, and for their beauty. A 1984 Forest Service document summed up the controversy:

There are at least three main reasons cited for maintaining old growth: wildlife and plant habitat, ecosystem diversity, and preservation of aesthetic qualities. Those opposed to the retention of old growth are primarily concerned with economic factors and urge rapid conversion of the existing old growth to managed forests of productive, young age classes.

6. Through most of the country's history there was little or no logging in the national forests. Intensive logging began with World War II and has accelerated.

7. NFMA (National Forest Management Act) was adopted in 1976, after three decades of heavy logging, in the hope of serving both wilderness and industry values. Senator Humphrey of Minnesota, a sponsor of the act, stated:

The days have ended when the forest may be viewed only as trees and trees viewed only as timber. The soil and the water, the grasses and the shrubs, the fish and the wildlife, and the beauty that is the forest must become integral parts of resource managers' thinking and actions.

8. Despite increasing concern over the environment, logging sales by the Forest Service have continued on a large scale.

9. Some major firms in the Pacific Northwest have extensive private forests and need little or no wood from public sources. Many small mills and logging companies depend in whole or in part on federal timber.

10. Mill owners and loggers, and their employees, especially in small towns, have developed since World War II an expectation that federal timber will be available indefinitely, and a way of life that cannot be duplicated elsewhere.

11. The region's timber industry has been going through fundamental changes. The most important is modernization which increases productivity and reduces the demand for labor (i.e., the jobs available). There have also been recent changes in product demand, in competition from other parts of the country and the world, and in the export of raw logs for processing in the Far East. The painful results for many workers, and their families and communities, will continue regardless of whether owl habitat in the national forests is protected.

B. Statutory Violations

12. The records of this case show a remarkable series of violations of the environmental laws [by the Forest Service and the Fish and Wildlife Service].

13. The reasons for this pattern of behavior were made clear at the evidentiary hearing.

Dr. Eric Forsman, a research wildlife biologist with the Forest Service, testified, in regard to the 1988 ROD [record of decision] and other Forest Service plans for the spotted owl that preceded the ISC Report:

Q. Were you satisfied at the time with the results of those previous works?

A. No. On all of those plans, I had considerable reservations for a variety of reasons. But primarily because in every instance, there was a considerable—I would emphasize considerable—amount of political pressure to create a plan which was an absolute minimum. That is, which had a very low probability of success and which had a minimum impact on timber harvest.

George M. Leonard, associate chief of the Forest Service, testified that the agency experts began in early 1990 the work [...] Congress mandated. But the Secretaries of Agriculture and Interior [Clayton Yeutter and Manuel Lujan Jr.] decided to drop the effort. The public was not told of this decision to ignore what the law required.

15. [...] This is not the doing of the scientists, foresters, rangers, and others at the working levels of these agencies. It reflects decisions made by higher authorities in the executive branch of government.

D. *Probability of Irreparable Harm*

22. The northern spotted owl is now threatened with extinction. The ISC Report states:

We have concluded that the owl is imperiled over significant portions of its range because of continuing losses of habitat from logging and natural disturbances. Current management strategies are inadequate to ensure its viability. Moreover, in some portions of the owl's range, few options for managing habitat remain open, and available alternatives are steadily declining throughout the bird's range. For these reasons, delay in implementing a conservation strategy cannot be justified on the basis of inadequate knowledge.

The FWS [Fish and Wildlife Service] has found that the owl is threatened *throughout* its range.

23. The population of northern spotted owls continues to decline.

25. The Forest Service estimates that an additional 66,000 acres of spotted owl habitat would be destroyed if logging went forward to the extent permitted by the ISC Report over the next sixteen months. That would be in addition to about 400,000 acres of habitat logged in the seven years since the agency began preparing these guidelines, all without having a lawful plan for the owl's management in place.

26. The ISC Report recommends standards and guidelines aimed at assuring the owl's long-term viability. The strategy contains seven major components: four categories of habitat conservation areas ("HCAs"), two different spacing requirements between HCAs, and the 50:11:40 rule (50 percent of Forest

Service and BLM lands outside HCAs would be in stands of trees measuring at least 11 inches in diameter with at least 40 percent canopy closure).

27. No timber management activities may take place in HCAs.

32. To log tens of thousands of additional acres of spotted owl habitat before a plan is adopted would foreclose options that might later prove to have been necessary.

33. Mr. Leonard of the Forest Service has testified that the agency will consider the alternative of preserving the remaining spotted owl habitat in the national forests. That alternative would be lost if extensive logging of habitat were to go forward now.

35. The logging of 66,000 acres of owl habitat, in the absence of a conservation plan, would itself constitute a form of irreparable harm. Old growth forests are lost for generations. No amount of money can replace the environmental loss.

36. There is a substantial risk that logging another 66,000 acres, before a plan is adopted, would push the species past a population threshold from which it could not recover.

E. *Economic and Social Consequences*

37. The testimony on economic impact assumed a sixteen-month injunction. The Forest Service would sell between 1.734 and 1.423 billion board feet of timber in fiscal year 1991 from the seventeen "spotted owl" national forests, if permitted to sell timber consistent with the ISC Report. The sale levels if owl habitat were protected in the interim would be about 0.394 billion board feet in 1991. The difference between protecting and not protecting habitat until the Forest Service develops its plan would thus be between 1.03 and 1.34 billion board feet during fiscal year 1991.

42. To the extent that Pacific Northwest mills have had supply shortages, the problem has been exacerbated by the export of raw logs. About thirty percent of the timber harvested in Washington and eleven percent of that harvested in Oregon is exported. Exports from private lands in Washington,

Oregon, and northern California during 1989 totaled 3.637 billion board feet. The exported logs produce no mill jobs or added value in the United States. A ban on exports would not automatically shift every raw log to domestic buyers, but would provide a major source of additional supply.

44. Over the past decade many timber jobs have been lost and mills closed in the Pacific Northwest. The main reasons have been modernization of physical plants, changes in product demand, and competition from elsewhere. Supply shortages have also played a part. Those least able to adapt and modernize, and those who have not gained alternative supplies, have been hardest hit by the changes.

45. Job losses in the wood products industry will continue regardless of whether the northern spotted owl is protected. A credible estimate is that over the next twenty years more than 30,000 jobs will be lost to worker-productivity increases alone.

46. A social cost is paid whenever an economic transformation of this nature takes place, all the more so when a largely rural industry loses sizeable numbers of jobs.

48. The timber industry no longer drives the Pacific Northwest's economy. In Oregon, for example, the level of employment in lumber and wood products declined by seventeen percent between 1979 and 1989. In the same period, Oregon's total employment increased by twenty-three percent.

49. The wood products industry now employs about four percent of all workers in Western Oregon, two percent in Western Washington, and six percent in northern California. Even if some jobs in wood products were affected by protecting owl habitat in the short term, any effect on the regional economy probably would be small.

50. The remaining wilderness contributes to the desirability of this region as a site for new industries and their employees. The resulting economic gains, while hard to measure, are genuine and substantial. The FWS has recently noted that preservation of old growth brings economic benefits and amenities "of extremely high value."

THE PUBLIC INTEREST AND THE BALANCE OF EQUITIES

The court must weigh and consider the public interest in deciding whether to issue an injunction in an environmental case. It must also consider the balance of equities among the parties.

The problem here has not been any shortcoming in the laws, but simply a refusal of administrative agencies to comply with them. This invokes a public interest of the highest order: the interest in having government officials act in accordance with law.

The public also "has a manifest interest in the preservation of old growth trees."

The loss of an additional 66,000 acres of spotted owl habitat, without a conservation plan being in place, and with no agency having committed itself to the ISC strategy, would constitute irreparable harm, and would risk pushing the species beyond a threshold from which it could not recover.

Any reduction in federal timber sales will have adverse effects on some timber industry firms and their employees, and a suspension of owl habitat sales in the national forests is no exception.

To bypass the environmental laws, either briefly or permanently, would not fend off the changes transforming the timber industry. The argument that the mightiest economy on earth cannot afford to preserve old growth forests for a short time, while it reaches an overdue decision on how to manage them, is not convincing today. It would be even less so a year or a century from now.

INJUNCTION

On the basis of the foregoing findings and conclusions, it is ordered and adjudged that:

A. The Forest Service is enjoined to proceed diligently in compliance with NFMA, as required by the order entered on April 1, 1991, and to submit to the court and have in effect by March 5, 1992, revised standards and guidelines to ensure the northern spotted owl's viability, together with an environmental impact statement.

B. The Forest Service is further enjoined from auctioning or awarding any additional timber sales from Regions Five and Six that would log suitable habitat for the northern spotted owl until the said standards and guidelines are adopted and in effect.

MILES MISSED

By Dawn "Garbanzo" Hanseder

It takes an intense amount of fortitude and dedication to complete a thru hike of all 2650 miles of the Pacific Crest Trail. A single-minded focus and a persevering spirit are required to overcome the thousands of miles and hundreds of obstacles standing in the way. From illness to injury, weather delays to equipment failures, a host of potential problems wait to beset the beleaguered thru hiker on her journey. Few people who have not thru hiked the PCT can imagine the desperate way the mind and spirit will cling to a goal when it is within sight, especially if it is slowly slipping out of reach. Dawn Hanseder's account captures this intent and focused frame of mind and shows how easy it is to take it too far—how, when we are burning with desire to reach that destination, and surging with adrenaline, we can lose sight of the journey itself. Fortunately, she also shows how successfully laughter, lightness of heart, and good trail companions can bring us back to embrace the present moment and find our meaning all along the trail, rather than just at its end.

I was inconsolable. Alone in the parking lot at Snoqualmie Pass, I dialed number after number, but not a soul answered. A few scattered patrons walked between the pancake house and hotel, looking with pity at me in my tattered skirt and long face, accompanied only by a dirty pack and my wet dog huddled in a small sunspot on the cement next to me. I would welcome their pity—in fact, I was feeling quite sorry for myself—but their pity was slightly misguided; I wasn't lost, or homeless, or here by accident, and this was the finest weather Stink and I had seen in four days.

I'd left my hiking partner Dak for the first time in 2194 miles at a trashy little gas station in Whistling Jack, with an extensive menu of made-to-order fried food that compensated for its otherwise sparse rations. We'd hitched to town with a couple of camouflaged hunters, sloshing around anchorless in the open bed of their double cab. The pain in Dak's knee had slowed him to a crawl and persisted through all of the standard thru-hiker treatments, including high doses of vitamin I and long pulls of whiskey at bedtime. I'd nearly plowed into him several times that morning as I thundered down the trail, Stink panting at my heels, trying to make up for a frustratingly late start to the day. Dak ambled along, still preferring to enjoy the walk despite the pain. I fumed in silence, madly driving him toward Canada.

The days were getting short now, on the inside of October in the northern Cascade Range, with Dak and me still more than three hundred miles from the Canadian border. The fine powder of our first snowfall dusting the handsome oranges and reds of the turning huckleberry bushes gave me reverent pause— momentarily. It was quaint at first: the tiny footprints of birds on a puffy white canvas, the vacuous silence endemic to a wilderness snowfall, the white ribbon of virgin tread sidewinding along under the sleepy eye of Mount Rainier, fading into the descending fog. More of the nuance of each passing moment was regrettably lost on me, as I failed to witness the inherent beauty in the unique and irretrievable snapshot of each step, instead seeing only obstacles and reminders of a ticking clock. As melted snow seeped into my shoes, and the winds hardened the soft powder into a driving sleet, I lamented the passing of autumn. To finish in Canada this late in the season, when early snowstorms could come fast and hard without warning, we would need to hike at least 25 miles a day, rumored to be a remarkably ambitious goal in the wild, remote peaks of the Washington Cascades, even for seasoned thru hikers for whom 30-mile days were typical on rolling hills back in sunny southern Oregon. Clearly, Dak's knee, most likely suffering an overuse injury, would prohibit 25-mile days, and the approaching winter would prohibit anything less. Dak and I teetered at a crossroads.

Dak and I had forged a partnership back at mile 178, where he'd agreed, for all of our safety, to hike with Stink and me over Fuller Ridge, notorious among thru hikers for its late-season deep snow and reputation for sending hikers wandering aimlessly trying to recover buried tread. In the more than two thousand miles we'd hiked together since, Dak had made it clear that he had no intention of hiking into Canada. I'm just going to hike until it's not fun anymore, he'd told me. I couldn't understand that. How could someone start something without the intention of finishing it? Wasn't that failure? I needed something to show for my six months out of the workforce and mounting credit card debt. Didn't six months of trailside daydreaming and lavish breakfasts in small-town diners need to be a part of something greater? Now, with Dak's injured knee, the plummeting temperatures, and waning hours of sunshine draining the last of the fun from his hike, he was ready to leave the trail. For hundreds of miles I'd dreaded the moment I'd have to choose between my loyalty to my own aspirations and my loyalty to an unexpected friendship. I could hike on alone, or we could fail together.

Stink and I would hike on alone.

After a heaping basket of jojos and mayo at the barely-gas-station, Dak and I prepared to part ways. I climbed into a big diesel 4x4 with the cashier and her husband and headed back up to the trailhead. I met Dak's eye as he came out the back door with the cook, who'd agreed to give Dak a ride forty miles to Yakima. Turning to leave, Dak remembered something, dug into his pockets, and handed me the crumpled mass of his waterproof mitten shells. I took them without a word. I watched with guilt as Dak—who'd stayed steadily by my side for 153 days—ducked into the rusty hatchback without looking back.

For three lonely days Stink and I toiled on in abruptly alternating rainy, snowy, and vaguely dry but exceedingly dreary weather. We negotiated mile after mile of the narrow trail corridor, dense brush overhanging and dripping with icy slush. If he were here, Dak would have had us stop to pull on our raingear, probably back at the trailhead, reasoning that wet clothes would never dry in this soggy weather, which could put us in real danger of hypothermia. But I was so frustrated with the seemingly endless stops and starts of retrieving and stowing, layering up and layering down, consulting maps and checking my elevation, that I—finally free to act completely on my own—instead blazed doggedly on, sponging up snow and dew, sights fixed on the finish line. I stuffed my pockets with energy bars, granola, and candy bars to eat on the move. I drank dangerously little water to avoid as much as possible the monumentally inconvenient task of stopping to pee. I was exhausted and reckless, and my feet struggled to keep pace with my pounding heart. I ignored the nips of pain from rolled ankles and twisted knees, and the resultant bursts of adrenaline forestalled the mental clarity that would eventually lay bare this lunacy.

At night, dense swirls of my breath caught the light of my headlamp as I wriggled into my sleeping bag. Gritting my teeth, I undressed completely to prevent my wet clothes from fouling my dry downy refuge, lest I compromise the integrity of my most critical piece of safety equipment. Every morning, I pulled a cold, soggy shirt over my bare skin with a squeal. I carefully stowed my last remaining dry layer in a double-wrapped trash bag in the middle of my pack and crossed my fingers. It took a hot breakfast and a firm tug on the scruff to cajole Stink out from the warm nest of her upturned fleece jacket in the corner of the tent. I broke camp with painfully numbed fingers and packed up a slimy tent stuck with pine needles, dirt, and gravel, under a sky that oscillated only between sunless gray dawn and sunless gray dusk. Two-hundred and sixty-seven more miles—just twelve more days, I thought. I can do anything for twelve days.

On the fourth day, Stink and I awoke tightly enveloped in my bag, shivering—because of my late-night resignation, too exhausted to take another step, I'd made camp in a lake basin, where the heavier cold air and moisture settled overnight. I stumbled through the heinous routine of morning chores and set out on the trail, still sleepy-eyed and numb, with only two short miles to town. Thin shards of sunlight sliced through the fog as we ascended out of the basin. As we finally rounded the top of the ridge, my breath caught in my throat. Under a vibrant blue sky, the warm glow of late-morning sunshine poured down the grassy hill before me and drenched the length of the valley as far as I could see. At the bottom of the hill, shimmering like the Emerald City, stood a little gas station, hotel, and restaurant, aflutter with activity. North, beyond Snoqualmie Pass, steep crags shot skyward thousands of feet above me. Under yesterday's dreary sky, the peaks might have looked menacing, as sharp and tragic as they were, but here in the bright sunlight and calm breeze they were ravishing, draped in glistening pearls of delicate snowfields and trailing scarves of autumn huckleberry.

I bounced gleefully down the hill and across the highway, imagining an omelet with sautéed mushrooms and Swiss cheese, perfect golden hash browns smattered with hot sauce, rye toast sodden with butter, and strong dark coffee with two creams. From the gas station, I obtained a promising forecast of blue skies and collected my food drop, mailed from home. Elated again, for the millionth time I imagined myself eleven days from now rounding a corner in the trail to catch my first glimpse of the northern trail terminus in Canada and running wildly toward it to embrace it lovingly. I called the Dinsmores, trail angels up in Skykomish where Dak would be waiting for me, to check in and see if his knee would permit him to rejoin Stink and me when we arrived there in four days.

"Ah, yes, the girl with the dog!" Andrea Dinsmore had been expecting my call.

"The trail is all snowed in," she reported. "You're not going anywhere." She listened respectfully to my protests, but firmly reiterated, "The trail is impassable.

Three guys went out a couple of days ago, hiked thirty miles out, and turned back to Snoqualmie. You're not going out there alone."

"Which three guys?" I asked, skeptical of their credentials.

"Even if you make it to Skykomish," she continued, "the trail north out of here is snowed in too. I have some hikers stranded here at the house. You sit tight," she said, "I'm coming to pick you up." I thanked her but told her I needed some time to process. I snapped my phone shut and sank to the ground, stunned. Eventually I picked myself up and headed into the hotel to find these other three hikers.

"Are you Garbanzo?" An unfamiliar hiker approached me coming through the door. "Andrea said we're not supposed to leave without you. Rocketman's renting a car to bounce us all up to Chelan. From there we'll take the ferry to Stehekin." He gestured to two other thru hikers milling around the leather lobby furniture, laughing and carrying on. *Stehekin*?! Bouncing up to the last resupply stop on the trail, after a 162-mile illegal skip, rendered the trophy meaningless to me. Everyone had to have some reason to be on the trail; otherwise, when the going got tough, it'd be too easy to give up. To each his own, but I'd come to hike the entire trail in one season, come what may. With that trophy apparently slipping away, what would keep me on the trail?

"I might still try to hike out," I told him. He called over to the others.

"Canadoug! Grab that video and show Garbanzo what the trail was like yesterday!"

My heart sank. A wobbly account of hikers wading through hip-deep snow on the vast, sheer edge of a steep ridge confirmed what I'd been dreading for weeks: we were too late. Loose snow cascaded freely off the side and out of the field of view. The only discernable sound through the howling wind and crunching snow was the strained panting of the cameraman trudging on through the faint path left by the other two hikers. It was over. Winter had descended into the high Cascades. After all the years of dreaming about the PCT, the months of planning, the guidebooks, spreadsheets, resupply boxes, and gear; after five and a half months of slogging across scorching deserts and soaring mountains, fording swift creeks and postholing through heavy snow—it was all for naught. I'd failed, twelve days short of the prize. I berated myself for all the zero days I'd wasted gorging on fried food and coffee, all the pale ales I gulped with other hikers at the taverns, and all the hours I whiled away, tucked in the tent idly listening to morning birdsong. I excused myself from the hotel lobby and dropped down on the cement outside next to Stink. With Canada now out of my grasp, my focus shifted to my loneliness. I frantically dialed number after number, desperate for comfort from home, but not a soul answered the phone. Sinking in the depths of failure and desolation, I sobbed inconsolably, attracting the sympathies of pancake-house patrons and passers-by.

It was late when we finally pulled into the motel in Chelan. Rocketman parked the overstuffed SUV in front of two rooms with the doors wide open, spilling light and laughter out into the parking lot. Two men emerged from one of the rooms in a cloud of raucous laughter. One of them was wearing rainpants and flip-flops and the other wore a towel around his waist and a knit hat crooked on his head.

"Rocketman!" they exclaimed at once.

"Waffle! Oz!" Rocketman laughed and embraced them one at a time. Drawn to the commotion, more thru hikers poured out of the rooms.

"Meghan! Whiskey!" I jumped out of the car to hug them both at once. I hadn't seen them since a raucous night of pickled eggs and beer nearly 795 miles ago at a dark tavern in Etna, crowded with thru hikers celebrating the last stop in California.

"Garbanzo … STINK!"

"Hey, Not-a-Chance! Rocketman!"

"Skywalker!"

"Canadoug?!"

"Lil Buddha! Stinky!"

"Backtrack! Giggles!"

"DAK!!"

"Stink!"

We hugged and laughed and carried on about all the adventures we'd had since we'd all last seen each other. There were fourteen of us altogether, between our carload, the hikers stranded in Skykomish, and Dak, who'd managed a nearly unbelievable hitchhike up from Yakima. With 96 miles of trail left before us, the evening's conversations inevitably turned to the 2562 miles behind us. Curiously, the off-trail swimming holes and luxurious naps in the shade, the backwoods taverns and Laundromats, and the long breakfasts and hilarious impromptu grocery store resupply outings were as prominent in our nostalgic chatter as were the summits, pristine glacial lakes, and miles and miles and miles of trail. Canada didn't come up. All those zero days now seemed well spent, if not altogether too sparse. I looked around at all the faces in the room, complete strangers in separate corners of the country a short six months ago, now my most intimate friends. Here we were, reunited and about to embark upon the last four days of the adventure of our lives, together. Suddenly, those last 96 miles seemed like far too few.

A FINE AND PLEASANT MISERY:
THE BACKPACKER

By Patrick F. McManus

Whether they are day hikers, section hikers, or committed thru hikers, most PCT travelers are familiar with the go-ultralight philosophy first popularized by Ray Jardine, a name mentioned regularly throughout both volumes of the Trailside Reader. *A famed rock climber, Jardine is best known in the climbing world for inventing the spring-loaded cam. But in the world of backpacking and long-trail hiking, he is most noted for launching the go-light revolution that has dropped pack weight from sixty pounds to twenty-five (or less) in some cases. He first discussed these ideas in his 1996 book* The Pacific Crest Trail Hiker's Handbook, *which was revised and republished as* Beyond Backpacking *(Adventurelore, 1999). With his focus on lighter gear, less gear, and more miles, Jardine has become a veritable guru for the thru hiker and has helped launch an entire industry of specialized lightweight backpacking gear. From superlight alcohol stoves and fiber-fill bags to Gore-Tex tarps, the modern backpacker often rivals the astronaut in terms of sheer technological sophistication. In "The Backpacker," Patrick McManus—a fervent supporter of the old-school hiking style—takes a whimsical poke at the dramatic changes that have overtaken backpacking in the last few decades. Despite being written more than thirty years ago, McManus's insights hold up amazingly well today.*

Strange, the things that suddenly become fashionable. Take backpacking for instance.

I know people who five years ago had never climbed anything higher than a barstool. Now you can scarcely name a mountain within three hundred miles they haven't hoofed up in their Swiss-made waffle-stompers.

They used to complain about the price of sirloin steak. Now they complain about the price of beef jerky (which is about three times that of Maine lobster).

Their backpacking is a refined sport, noted for lightness. The gear consists of such things as silk packs, magnesium frames, dainty camp stoves. Their sleeping bags are filled with the down of unborn goose, their tents made of waterproof smoke. They carry two little packets from which they can spread out a nine-course meal. One packet contains the food and the other the freeze-dried French chef.

Well, it wasn't like that back in the old days, before backpacking became fashionable. These latecomers don't know what real backpacking was like.

The rule of thumb for the old backpacking was that the weight of your pack should equal the weight of yourself and the kitchen range combined. Just a casual glance at a full pack sitting on the floor could give you a double hernia and fuse four vertebrae. After carrying the pack all day, you had to remember to tie one leg to a tree before you dropped it. Otherwise, you would float off into space. The pack eliminated the need for any kind of special kind of ground-gripping shoes, because your feet would sink a foot and a half into hard-packed earth, two inches into solid rock. Some of the new breed of backpackers occasionally wonder what caused a swath of fallen trees on the side of a mountain. That is where one of the old backpackers slipped off the trail with a full pack.

My packboard alone met the minimum weight requirement. It was a canvas and plywood model, surplus from the Second World War. These packboards were apparently designed with the idea that a number of them could be hooked together to make an emergency bridge for Sherman tanks. The first time you picked one up you thought maybe someone had forgotten to remove his tank.

My sleeping bag looked like a rolled up mattress salvaged from a fire in a skid row hotel. Its filling was sawdust, horsehair, and No. 6 bird shot. Some of today's backpackers tell me their sleeping bags are so light they scarcely know they're there. The only time I scarcely knew my sleeping bag was there was when I was in it at 2:00 AM on a cold night. It was freckled from one end to the other with spark holes, a result of my efforts to stay close enough to the fire to keep warm. The only time I was halfway comfortable was when it was ablaze. It was the only sleeping bag I ever heard of which you could climb into in the evening with scarcely a mark on you and wake up in the morning bruised from head to toe. That was because two or three times a night my companions would take it upon themselves to jump up and stomp out my sleeping-bag fires—in their haste neglecting to first evacuate the occupant. Since I was the camp cook, I never knew whether they were attempting to save me from immolation or getting in a few licks for what they thought might be terminal indigestion.

Our provisions were not distinguished by variety. Dehydrated foods were considered effeminate. A man could ruin his reputation for life by getting caught on a pack trip with a dried apple. If you wanted apples, brother, you carried them with the water still in them. No one could afford such delicacies as commercial beef jerky. What you carried was a huge slab of bacon. It was so big that if the butcher had left on the legs, it could have walked behind you on a leash.

A typical meal consisted of fried bacon, potatoes and onions fried in bacon grease, a pan of beans heated in bacon grease, bacon grease gravy, some bread fried in bacon grease, and cowboy coffee (made by boiling an old cowboy in bacon grease). After meals, indigestion went through our camp like a sow grizzly with a toothache. During the night coyotes sat in nervous silence on surrounding hills and listened to the mournful wailing from our camp.

There were a few bad things, too, about backpacking the old style, but I loved all of it. I probably would never have thought of quitting if it hadn't been for all those geophysical changes that took place in the Western Hemisphere a few years ago.

The first thing I noticed was a distinct hardening of the earth. This occurred wherever I happened to spread out my sleeping bag, so I knew that the condition was widespread. (Interestingly enough, my children, lacking their father's scientific training, were unable to detect the phenomenon.)

A short while later it became apparent to me that the nights in the mountains had become much colder than any I could remember in the past. The chill would sink its fangs into my bones in the pre-dawn hours and hang on like a terrier until the sun was high. I thought possibly that the drop in temperature was heralding a new ice age.

Well, I could put up with the hard and the cold but then the air started getting thinner. The only way you could get sufficient oxygen to lug a pack the size of an adolescent pachyderm was by gasping and wheezing. (Some of my wheezes were sufficient to strip small pine trees bare of their needles.) My trail speed became so slow it posed a dangerous threat to my person. If we were in fact at the onset of a new ice age, there was a good chance I might be overtaken and crushed by a glacier.

The final straw was the discovery that a trail I had traveled easily and often in my youth had undergone a remarkable transformation. In the intervening years since I had last hiked it, the damn thing had nearly doubled in length. I must admit that I was puzzled, since I didn't know that trails could stretch or grow. The fact that it now took me twice as long to hike it, however, simply did not allow for any other explanation. I asked a couple of older friends about it, and they said that they had seen the same thing happen. They said probably the earth shifted on its axis every once in a while and caused trails to stretch. I suggested that maybe that was also the cause for the ground getting harder, the nights colder, and the air thinner. They said that sounded like a plausible theory to them. (My wife had another theory, but it was so wild and farfetched that I won't embarrass her by mentioning it here.)

Anyway, one day last fall while I was sitting at home fretting about the environment, a couple of friends telephoned and invited me along on a pack trip they were taking into the Cascades. Both of them are of the new school of backpacking, and I thought I owed it to them to go along. They could profit considerably by watching an old trail hand in action.

When I saw the packs R. B. and Charley showed up with I almost had to laugh. Neither pack was large enough to carry much more than a cheese sandwich. I carried more bicarbonate of soda than they had food. I didn't know what they planned to sleep in, but it certainly couldn't be in those tidy little tote bags they had perched on top of their packs. Anyway, I didn't say anything. I just smiled and got out my winch and they got a pry pole and before you knew it we had my pack out of the car and on my shoulders. As we headed up the trail I knew it was going to be a rough trip. Already a few flakes of snow had fallen on my eyeballs.

The environment on that trip was even harsher than I had remembered. The trails were steeper, the air thinner, the ground harder, the nights colder. Even my trail speed was slower. Several porcupines shot past me like I was standing still.

R. B. and Charley showed obvious signs of relief when I made it to camp that first night.

"You probably thought I wouldn't make it with all the food," I chided them.

"No," R. B. said. "It was just that for a moment there we didn't recognize you. We thought we were being attacked by a giant snail."

I explained to them that we old-time backpackers made a practice of traveling the last mile or so on our hands and knees in order to give our feet a rest.

It was disgusting to see them sitting there so relaxed and cheerful after a hard day's hike. They didn't seem to have any notion at all what backpacking was about. I could hardly stand it when they whipped out a little stove and boiled up some dried chunks of leather and sponge for supper. It probably would have hurt their feelings if I had got out the slab of bacon, so I didn't mention it. I just smiled and ate their food—four helpings in fact, just to make my act convincing. I never told them, but the Roast Baron Beef was not quite rare enough for my taste and they had forgotten the cream sauce for the asparagus tips. And I have certainly tasted better Baked Alaska in my day, too.

Well, they can have their fashionable new-school backpacking if they want it. I'm sticking with the old way. Oh, I'm making a few concessions to the harsher environment, but that's all. When I got back from that trip, I did order a new pack frame. It was designed by nine aeronautical engineers, three metallurgists, and a witch doctor, and weighs slightly less than the down of a small thistle. My new sleeping bag weighs nine ounces, including the thermostatic controls. If I want to sleep in, my new cook kit gets up and puts on the coffee. Then I bought a few boxes of that dried leather and sponge. But that's all. I'm certainly not going to be swept along on the tides of fashion.

HOW COYOTE HAPPENED TO
MAKE THE BLACK MOSS FOOD

As told by Mourning Dove (Hum-ishu-ma)

The black moss central to this story is one of the six hundred species of Usnea. *Also called old man's beard, beard lichen, or tree moss,* Usnea *is a common hairlike lichen that grows on the trees and bushes along much of the length of the Pacific Crest Trail. This particular species of* Usnea *is nutritious (high in vitamin C) and considered a delicacy by Native Americans. Prepared by cooking in carefully layered pits covered by a hot fire for several days, the black moss is reduced to a jellylike bluish-black substance. This can be sliced and eaten when cooled or it can be dried for future use.*

In "How Coyote Happened to Make the Black Moss Food," the seeming inconsistencies common in a creative tradition like storytelling are very much present, along with humor and hyperbole. You will never again look at Usnea *without thinking of the ill-fated Coyote and little Top'-kan.*

Coyote and *Top'-kan* were traveling. Wherever the trail was rough, little *Top'-kan* rode on his father's back. They came to the lodge of *En-ze'-chen*—Wolf, an old man. He was busy skinning a beaver. After watching old Blood-Curdling Call for awhile, Coyote asked, "*En-ze'-chen*, how do you kill the *stun'-whu* (beaver)?"

"It is at the beaver dam," answered Wolf. "I sit on the dam, with one leg in the water. As a beaver passes over my leg, I strike hard with a big stick. The *stun'-whu* cannot live after a blow like that."

Source: "How Coyote Happened to Make the Black Moss Food," from *Coyote Stories*, by Mourning Dove (University of Nebraska Press, 1990).

"*Ha-ha-eah*!" Coyote laughed. "That is my way of killing the *stun'-whu*!"

Old Wolf said nothing. He knew that *Sin-ka-lip'*, the Imitator, had never killed beavers in that way. He suspected that Coyote soon would be in trouble.

Coyote took a heavy stick and went down to the beaver dam and sat with one leg in the water, as Wolf instructed. The beavers saw him. One of them said, "Look! There is *Sin-ka-lip'*! He is trying to trick someone. Let us walk over his leg, and see what he does."

Two young beavers swam up to the dam. They climbed over Coyote's leg, and he struck hard with the heavy stick. He missed the beavers—they were too quick for him—but he hit his leg a terrific whack. He howled and danced with pain and rage, and then he tore into the beaver dam and threw the sticks and mud right and left. In a little while there was no dam there. He found the two beavers that had fooled him. They appeared to be dead.

"They will make good eating," he remarked, and he carried the beavers to where *Top'-kan* was playing. "You can wear these as ear ornaments while I am getting wood for a fire," Coyote told his son, and he tied the beavers to the little boy's ears, one to each ear.

As soon as Coyote was busy gathering wood, the beavers jumped up and ran, dragging *Top'-kan* behind them. They ran down the bank to the place where the dam had been. There they squirmed into different holes. That stretched *Top'-kan's* ears in opposite directions. *Top'-kan* yelled, for the stretching hurt.

Hearing the cries of his son, Coyote ran to help him. He found poor *Top'-kan* braced between the holes and unable to move. There was nothing to do but to cut the thongs that held the beavers, which Coyote did. The beavers got away. Ever since that time the ears of coyotes have stood long and pointed.

No beaver to roast, Coyote and *Top'-kan* started traveling again. They went along until they came to a large lake. Resting in the water were many *si-mil'-ka-meen* (white swans). Coyote wanted one of those swans to eat, so he swam out into the lake. He kept under water, but the swans were not fooled. They knew he was there.

"Here comes *Sin-ka-lip'*!" they said. "See his tail floating! Let him catch a couple of us, and we will see what he will do."

So two of the younger swans allowed Coyote to catch them. He carried them to shore. They pretended to be dead. He tied them fast to *Top'-kan*. Then he climbed a pine tree to get the pitch-top, where *Kwil-kin* (porcupine) had gnawed. He wanted the pitch-top for fire-kindling.

Just as he got to the top of the tree, Coyote heard his son crying. He looked down and saw the swans flapping their wings. They were starting to fly. Coyote jumped, but his long hair braid caught on a branch of the pine tree and did not come loose. Coyote swung there, helpless. He could not untangle his hair.

The swans flew past the tree, past Coyote, and up into the sky. Dangling beneath them, tied to them by the thongs, was little *Top'-kan*. When the swans were high in the air they cut the thongs, and *Top'-kan* fell to the ground and was killed. Then Coyote took his flint knife and chopped off his hair braid, and dropped to the earth. He looked up at his hair hanging from the branch.

"You shall not be wasted, my valuable hair. After this you shall be gathered by the people. The old women will make you into food," he said.

That was Coyote's ruling near the Beginning. That is why his hair, the long black timber-hair, hangs from trees in the mountains. It is called *squil-lip*. It is the black moss that the people cook in pit-ovens.

Top'-kan did not stay dead. Coyote restored him to life by stepping over his body three times. Then they returned to their own country.

THE NORTH CASCADES
THE GREAT WHITE NORTH

Covering Section J–Section L

Snoqualmie Pass—Stevens Pass—Glacier Peak
Rainy Pass—Manning Provincial Park

TWO ON THE TRAIL

By Ann Marshall

Why is it that we focus on the dramatic rain-drenched day or the early-season snowstorm rather than including stories of the crisp but spectacular autumn morning or the leisurely afternoon spent lazing in a flower-filled meadow? Ann Marshall and Lee McKee began at the California-Oregon border in mid-July and recorded their adjustments to the trail, to the mosquitoes, and to each other in Two on the Trail. *Although they "did have many, many nice camps and beautiful views" (Ann's words), we selected their account of an absolutely miserable day in the Alpine Lakes south of Stevens Pass.*

As anyone who has backpacked extensively in the Washington Cascades comes to recognize, you can only get 100 percent wet. As moisture permeates every layer of protective gear during endless days of rain or a torrential downpour, there comes a point where you cease to care. Why bother with rock hopping to navigate a tricky stream crossing? So what if the moisture-laden chest-high underbrush rakes across you as you pass? There is a certain freedom that comes with the knowledge that it is impossible to get any wetter.

SEPTEMBER 10

Log: 12.1 miles from Waptus Lake to Cathedral Rock. Flood.

Ann's journal: This has been the most miserable day I have ever spent hiking, except for tomorrow, which probably will be worse. If we survive to reach Stevens Pass we shall be fortunate.

SOURCE: Excerpted from *Two on the Trail: A Thousand Miles on the PCT,* by Ann Marshall. Copyright © 1985. Reprinted by permission of the author and the Washington Trails Association.

Lee's journal: Rain began in the wee hours of the morning and has continued ever since. What a disappointment to awake to rain and foul weather after such a nice afternoon and evening.

All the while hoping the rain would quit, we didn't get started until 9 AM We set out with poor attitudes. Ann especially was unhappy.

Ann's journal: This was not the kind of rain that comes in showers; no—it has been a steady, hard rain, occasionally increasing to a downpour. All day. The trails were absolutely running with water, the brush was sopping, and mud holes were frequent. Miles and miles of this we did, climbing to Deep Lake.

After only a few hours, the creeks had swollen to rushing torrents. Footlogs and stepping stones had disappeared. Below Deep Lake, I tried inching across a branch of Spinola Creek on a spindly, swaying pole. I slipped and fell in. Sat right down in the creek, pack and all.

Lee came to my rescue, although he was not happy about coming halfway back across the creek to reach me as he had already crossed safely by a different route. That I was doused with creek water didn't matter by now, since my coated nylon rain gear was completely inadequate for these conditions; it had "failed" and I was soaked to the skin anyway. Lee's Gore-Tex coat had also "failed" and he was as wet as I.

Lee's journal: When we reached Deep Lake I was in the lead and followed what I thought was the trail. It went along the wrong side of the lake through swamp and marsh and I didn't realize the mistake until we were halfway around the lake. Hauling out the map, we discovered we had gone wrong; then we had to go back over that miserable trail.

Ann's journal: We had to figure out how to cross the Deep Lake outlet, normally an easy rock-hop. But with the flood waters rising, we crossed with difficulty on the few rocks that were left.

We met six people on the trail—two horsemen heading out; a man and a woman ready to cut their trip short and head out; and two gals at Deep Lake, heading out. We can't "head out;" we just keep "heading north!"

We climbed to Cathedral Pass in the downpour, hiking along a trail which itself had turned to a streambed. Water sloshed in my boots and ran down my neck. We were warm only as long as we kept moving. For "lunch" we gobbled one of Lee's energy bars, washing it down with a swallow of water as we stood in the trail.

We called it a day after twelve miles in the storm, and set up camp at 2:30 PM by a stream on the north side of Cathedral Rock. As soon as we stopped hiking we both were cold and shivering. We were aware that this was a dangerous time—both of us wet, both cold, and perfect hypothermia weather. In our urgency to set up a protective camp, we had little patience with each other.

Lee's journal: I tried to set up Ann's extra poncho to protect our packs while we unloaded them, but I got upset by the weird size of it—too narrow to do much good.

Ann's journal: Stringing up the poncho started out as a good idea, but Lee ended up shouting at me, which I didn't appreciate.

Shelter was a priority, and we set up the main tarp as quickly as possible. Next was getting out of wet clothes and into "less-wet" garments. We had to start from the skin out, as even our underwear was drenched. We then pulled on a warming, if not-quite dry, layer of wool.

The little stream by our camp was now a nearly uncrossable torrent. Its one footlog was awash and looked as though it would be swept away any minute. A little gully near our camp that had been dry when we arrived suddenly became a raging watercourse. As the afternoon passed and the rainstorm continued, we watched in amazement as every little ditch and hollow became a running creek. Waterfalls appeared from the cliffs on Cathedral Rock above us, and thundered down into the basin. We hoped we were on high enough ground to escape the flood.

With camp finally set up, warm clothes on, and ruffled feathers smoothed, we took shelter in our tarp and had an official lunch with hot drinks. The next day we planned to face the crossing of the infamous Mount Daniel glacier stream. Fed by ice fields high on Mount Daniel, the stream was said to be dangerous to cross. In such a storm, we discussed the possibility that we would not be able to ford it.

Lee's journal: It looks like tomorrow we will back-track and take the alternative route to avoid the glacier stream. It will be longer and will cost us time, but it's too unsafe to try to ford an already questionable stream.

My rain jacket and pants are wet inside and out. My wool shirt and pants are damp and my pack is sopping! We've been very careful, but it has rained so much—more than I have ever experienced out hiking. The rain is coming down even harder now! This is unbelievable. We can't continue in this weather. Either the sun has to come out, or we have to head out by the shortest route to seek shelter.

Not long after we finished lunch, we decided it was time for dinner. Spaghetti was on the menu. We boiled the noodles, washed the dishes, and cooked our tea by collecting rain water from the edge of the tarp. The run-off was so heavy that our pot filled in a matter of seconds. After dinner we spread out our bed things.

Ann's journal: Our ground cloths are still wet from last night, but my sleeping bag has only one small wet spot from its dunking in Spinola Creek. Three cheers for plastic bags.

How I wish I were home and warm and dry and safe, but wishing does no good now. It is important to be careful and stay calm.

That evening over tea we looked at the maps, deciding which way the closest road was, which direction we should go the next day to end the hike, to seek civilization and safety.

As dusk fell, a tremendous thunderclap resounded through the little basin, as a giant flash of lightning lit the sky. We looked at each other with wide-eyed concern.

Lee's journal: Might be a long night.

THE KINGDOM

By Elizabeth Dodd

Pacific Crest Trail hikers will be reminded by this story that, although they are in rugged and beautiful wilderness, there is a long history of human presence along virtually every stretch of the trail. From the First Nations people who lived and hunted here and the itinerant explorers and trappers, to emigrants who saw these mountains as a life-threatening obstacle to cross, to the more recent refugees from urban life, there have been many layers of human presence. However, not all of that presence has been friendly. Here, Elizabeth Dodd recounts her own experience with a trailside confrontation and reflects on our long history of conflict in the wilderness. By connecting her own story with the recent archeological discovery of a five-thousand-year-old corpse in the Tyrolean Alps, Dodd suggests that the most dangerous predators in the backcountry might just be human.

Upon hearing about such rare but frightful experiences of conflict along the trail, some PCT hikers may feel, like Marcellus in Hamlet, *that there is something rotten in Denmark, that something is out of place in our wilderness kingdom. In reality, violence remains exceedingly rare along the PCT. But, as Dodd reminds us, although we often praise the solitude of wilderness travel, there is much to be said for sharing that stunning view with our fellow countrymen, and for the companionship and security offered by good hiking companions, dinner fellows, and tent mates.*

It's the first night on the trail. We got a late start—my brother, his girlfriend, and I—and we huffed our way steeply up through an old clear-cut and then through mature forest before crossing some invisible line into designated wilderness. We're hurrying, hardly pausing to admire the wildflowers or taste the berries along the way, sweating to make it before dark to Hope Lake, the first possible campsite along this section of the Pacific Crest Trail. We'll be out a week and the packs are heavy with provisions.

But when we reach the lake, we have to stop and reconnoiter. There are already two parties there. One has pitched a couple of cheap tents right beside the water (not, we note scornfully, the required hundred feet from shore), with an illegal campfire sending surly smoke slowly from its scar in the grass; two hoodlum-looking teenagers slouch in the clearing. The other party, a group of four, isn't camping. They are a middle-aged father, his young son, and two men who look to be in their early twenties; they are having a tense conversation with the scruffy teenagers from, as we say in the language of political struggles, "the other camp." Hudson, Dawn, and I stand still to catch our breath and watch the little drama.

The father and his group have been doing trail restoration work all day, carrying heavy saws and picks and shovels; they evidently left their other gear stashed in the woods by the pond, and now, they say, it's missing. The hoodlums deny knowing anything about it but none of us believes them. They also say a ranger was there earlier in the day and told them their fire was fine so long as they made sure it was out before they left. We don't believe this either.

"Would you mind staying for a few minutes?" the father quietly asks my burly brother. And so we become international observers, there along the Pacific Crest Trail. We stand quietly, the air stiff with tension and our own drying sweat.

One of the hoodlums finally confesses, "My friend took your stuff, okay? I'll try to find it for you," and he plunges theatrically into the underbrush. His initial efforts retrieve a backpack, a flashlight, and not much else. The little boy's pack is missing, as is the father's sleeping bag. Two more hoodlums arrive and mill ineffectually about. A man of perhaps thirty-five or forty appears—he seems to be the leader of their outlaw gang—and declares repeatedly that he had *no idea* what the boys had been up to, he'd just brought them for a fishing trip and to show them the wilderness. I stand beside him and tell him, brightly, that this is a teaching opportunity he can take advantage of, though in truth I wouldn't trust him farther than I can spit—which, after the hot, quick climb, might not be much farther than my own boots. The young men from the father's party also search, and they have greater success than the sullen louts: the father's sleeping bag is located and the son's pack, though a few items are still missing.

"I can't find my Ninja Turtle!" the boy says. (He is perhaps ten.)

"Oh," I say to the Head Hood, as if he will share in my indignation. "For shame, stealing from a child." He sputters a bit, wanting, I suspect, to be mistaken for a better man than he is.

We need to get moving; this peacekeeping mission has taken nearly an hour and the sun is dropping fast. There's no question of our staying here now, bedfellows (or at least shorefellows) with the shamed and surly riffraff, so it's on with the packs and away we go, at an achingly brisk pace. Perhaps another mile and a half along, according to the map, we'll cross a ridge and hit a small stream. That's our new goal, since we don't think we can reach the ominously named Trap Lake by dark, and we've left Hope behind (I can't resist pointing this out, but we're walking too fast for anyone else to chuckle at the pun much).

It turns out to be more than a mile and a half to the stream—and it's a very, very small stream. We set up tents in the day's last light, while dried vegetables soak in a water bottle. We're all a little snappish, hungry and unhappy to have arrived right on the verge of dark, and of course out of sorts about our brush with delinquency. The backpacking stove sputters and gasps and uses too much air, blackening my lightweight cookware with fuel-smelling soot.

But dinner is wonderful. It's alpine stew, with vegetables I blanched and dehydrated back home: carrots, peas, potatoes, mushrooms. A powdered cream sauce. A miniature can of chicken. And biscuits, hot and delicious, if unevenly browned because of the disreputable—indeed, delinquent—behavior of the stove. I turn to Hudson and Dawn and quote Steinbeck to them. "Now each of you kids get a nice flat stick," I say, but this joke falls flat too, even to my ears. Ma Joad is out of place here, and we want to have left the struggle of the social world behind. Hudson and Dawn wash dishes in the dark, scrubbing the soot with wet pine cones; we hang the bear bag, dangling our food high out of reach, and we feel sheltered by the old-growth trees. The air chills quickly with the sun down, and the ground smells moist, fungal, and rich.

We talk briefly about tomorrow—where we'll go, what we might see, what we'll eat. I suggest, "We could have pasta with salmon and nettles. Or pasta with morels." Hudson has packed in a water bottle of chardonnay as well; we'll set it to chill in some high-elevation lake, and the wild mushrooms, brought all the way from a riparian woods in eastern Kansas, will plump up in the cold water. We feel communally self-sufficient, with gear and food and excellent company.

Lately, I have been reading an account of the discovery and study of Ötzi, the 5300-year-old mummified corpse found frozen in the Tyrolean Alps. He was found by energetic, athletic hikers where he poked out of the rapidly melting ice of retreating glaciers; they assumed Ötzi was a recent corpse, something only decades old, or maybe from the last century. Then, after they ripped and chiseled him out of the ice, they realized they were looking at someone who died long before the rise of nation-states and bungling governments.

Ötzi is a deeply appealing character in his multimillennial drama. He lived—and died—at the cusp of two eras: most of his tools are stone and bone but he also carried an ax cast of nearly pure copper.

The archaeologist Konrad Spindler has suggested a disaster narrative, in which the long-dead man was an Alpine shepherd who had come down from his usual pasturage in the high country to his home village in the valley, perhaps to help with an agricultural harvest. There he fell victim to some kind of attack, during which some of his equipment—arrows in his quiver, his bow—as well as a few of his ribs were broken. Perhaps it was a struggle for land, or personal property, or some other *thing* thought worth fighting over. These plot details chime unsettlingly with our own little story, confronting the hoodlums in that alpine clearing by the lake, suggests the frequency with which that particular path has been taken, over rough terrain. In Spindler's story, the man quickly cut wood for a new bow and shafts for twelve new arrows and then fled to the high country, where he could be safe in terrain he knew well; exhausted and injured, however, he never made it off the pass where he was found more than five thousand years later.

Not long after that final meal, the man must have collected his belongings and hiked north into the high-country world of snow and stone. He carried excellent gear: a birchbark container holding embers for firestarting; a leather fanny pack holding flint blades and a drill bit, an awl of bone, a wood-handled retoucher for sharpening stone blades, and the fungal tinder. He had a quiver with arrows and his new, partially carved bow; a flint-bladed dagger with its own little grass pouch; a wooden backpack frame. He wore leather boots lined with grass, a fur coat or undercloak, leather leggings tucked into his boots, a fur cap with earflaps, and a water-repellent grass cape. I imagine my own backcountry stuff, scrutinized and studied from some vantage point in the hypothetical future. Objects of an era, they will be: high-tech equipment that allowed their owner at least the feeling of stepping off the grid. My poncho: lightweight as a sock and large enough that I've sat within its polymer drape, chin to knees, waiting for wind and rain to pass. My candle lantern: its glass chimney that telescopes out from the red-metal case. My ripstop tent that looks a bit like an oversized grub, dully phosphorescent in the forest's damp shade. But none of them reflects the personal touch of ingenuity. Not one has been fashioned by hand, by individual necessity.

Most interesting to me, Ötzi seems to have had something of a first-aid kit. Two mushrooms, threaded on a leather thong as if for a talisman or ornament, were identified as *Piptoporus betulinus*, commonly known as the razor-strop fungus, a bolete that has antibiotic properties. One should always be prepared, of course, when heading into the backcountry. Don't I carry a doctor's bag of bandages, medicines, and painkillers? The quantities might serve only a few days, but the supplies still might help ensure that someone *would* make it back. And Ötzi wasn't in the flower of youth; he was likely old for his era, in his late forties. There were small tattoos on his lower back, legs, and feet, several corresponding with ancient Chinese acupuncture points; x-rays revealed that he suffered from arthritis, so researchers wondered whether the tattoos were a form of therapy.

I am—I hardly need to say this—no longer young. Maybe that's one reason I feel such tenderness for Ötzi, for his individual humanity—and mortality—wrapped and buried deep within the wonder of his age. Sometimes, though, it's hard to convince myself I've already walked away from my own youth, when I dream of joining my brother among the Pacific Northwest peaks again, even though we may risk unpleasant encounters like that with our lakeside hoodlums. The mountains hide among their jags and folds so many unexpected things; they embody a kind of solitude, but I'm thinking today that it's good not to be traveling alone.

The meal together by the lake.

The shared moment at the pass.

The view—"*Oh*," we say to one another, voices small in the sky's dome that hardly covers us, "*come look*—from here."

NIGHT RISE ON THE PACIFIC CREST TRAIL

By Paul Bogard

Many religious traditions and First Nations people around the world link the solo wilderness experience with mystical insight, enlightenment, and the vision quest or the search for spiritual meaning. These disparate cultural traditions recognize that a confrontation with the unfamiliar lends itself to the creation of new insight, epiphany, and awareness. For those of us living in the twenty-first century, an escape from the ubiquitous presence of electricity that infuses every aspect of our lives represents one of the most unfamiliar experiences possible—the absence of light, the reexperiencing of true night, of organic darkness that has not, and cannot, be beaten back with the easy flick of a switch and the rising halo of halogen, fluorescent, or incandescent light. In fact, as Paul Bogard observes, many children and young adults born and raised in America's bright and shining cities have never seen the star-studded night sky in all its glory, much less the sweeping and sparkling Milky Way. Of the many wild and rare experiences to be had along the Pacific Crest Trail, the true experience of earthly night must be included among them. How strange it is that this nightly experience, once such a common part of our lives, is now so rare that some of us only experience it a few times in our lives, while others know it not at all. In the following essay, Bogard reflects on the value and beauty of night and the importance of preserving it for ourselves and for future generations. As he notes, we are indeed lucky to have such a long and dark corridor in the West, stretching from Mexico to Canada, a single, wavering line of darkness with countless opportunities for us to reconnect with our own beautiful night.

For me, the best sections of the Pacific Crest Trail are those that travel through the dark. Talk about a place where few people tread. Estimates are that 90 percent of people living in North America and western Europe live in places polluted by light, that two-thirds of Americans live where they no longer experience real night (that is, real darkness), and that children born in the United States today have only a one in ten chance of seeing the Milky Way during their lifetime. While most of us hike our PCT hours accompanied by the sun, one of the trail's most wonderful gifts is a previously common experience that has become all too rare: the darkness of a night unblemished by artificial light.

I used to be so afraid of darkness. I grew up in the suburbs of Minneapolis, and my parents were not campers. Instead, we spent the summers going to a cabin in northern Minnesota, which was great for seeing the stars but didn't do anything for my fear of the dark. The woods were often dark enough that I couldn't see my outstretched hand, and there was no way you could get me to walk through them. I would stand out on the dock and wonder at the great sweeps and swirls of stars overhead, and then I'd turn and head directly back into the house's brightly lit interior. But as the years went by and I learned more about the stars, I learned how important darkness is for seeing them. And from there I learned how important darkness is for animals and birds and insects that make the woods their home; and then, how important darkness is for human health—spiritual, mental, and physical. By the time I moved west and began hiking the mountains and wilderness, my attitude toward darkness had changed—I won't say my fear had disappeared, but that fear had been tempered by respect—and in the years since, I've learned to savor the dark.

One of my favorite things about the trail is the chance to be attuned to the natural rhythms of the earth—from waking at dawn, to watching the sun instead of a clock, to savoring the natural rise of dusk. That's right—we're used to saying that night "falls," but night actually rises in the east to wash over the world. What we call night is actually Earth's shadow cast tens of millions of miles into space. That shadow is our window to the heavens and our ticket to night's wonders. When I'm hiking the trail and therefore outside as the world rotates into this shadow, I adjust to the rising darkness at the same speed my ancestors did. Instead of immediately flipping a light switch and spending my night hours inside, I'm present for the gradual change in the light. Often, that gradual change goes along with the gradual changes in me—a slowing from the pace of the day, a rising sensitivity to senses other than sight. It always feels to me at night as though the world reduces speed and size and I am set back to an earlier time when the planet wasn't so everywhere overrun by people, people, people with their wants and greeds. Just being on the trail gets me away from that world, of course, but at night the effect feels even greater. For most of human history we lived without electric light, and time spent returned to darkness feels natural to me, feels right.

I won't lie—I still can get spooked by darkness more easily than I'd like. But that happens more often than not in the city, or when I come out into darkness from being inside a room filled with lights. I don't fear darkness when I'm out hiking and camping, when I'm part of the day's natural rhythm, when I am part of the night.

When you are part of the night, when you're out in it rather than hidden away in whatever lit box where you spend most of your time, you have a sense of being surrounded by life and by life's creatures. Sometimes you see them (fireflies) or hear them (owls) or even smell them (skunks), but most often you don't. And to me, that feels perfectly all right. Once you learn about all the nocturnal and crepuscular (active at dawn and dusk) birds, mammals, reptiles, insects, and amphibians, you come to appreciate how important darkness is for the wild world and how vital it is that we leave this darkness alone for the sake of lives other than our own.

If you have any affinity for the stars, it only takes one good clear night on the trail away from city lights to understand what a difference darkness makes for what you can see, and to understand as well the ways in which light pollution robs us blind. On a clear, dark night, between two and three thousand individual stars should stand visible to our naked eyes—even upward of seven thousand if you're still a child with perfect vision. A sight like this can stay with you all your life and can keep you wanting to come back to those places still dark enough to return you to that beauty, that time.

And the value of darkness doesn't stop there. Scientists are increasingly finding that darkness is vital to our physical, spiritual, and mental health. Our bodies, souls, and minds have evolved through millennia in bright days and dark nights and they need both for optimal health. Though actually, it doesn't take a scientist to tell you that darkness feeds your spirit. One night lying on your back staring at the Milky Way after a good day's trek will teach you that. We know from mythology and religion and art and science that an intimate knowledge of a dark starry sky has long brought inspiration, awe, and questions to those who've gone before us. For example, think about this the next time you're out on the trail in real darkness: every single star you see (including the whole blended mess of the several billion stars making up the Milky Way) is part of our own Milky Way Galaxy, and scientists now estimate that beyond our galaxy lie many, many more galaxies—like, say, 500 billion more. How are you supposed to make sense of that? I don't know that I can, but I do know that whenever I'm face-to-face with the universe on a starry PCT night, and I'm looking out into that overwhelming space (and I mean huge, wild, unending space—and overwhelming in its numbers and beauty), I just feel even more thankful for the wild beauty we have right here on Earth, wild beauty that every day comes under pressure from our light-drenched, consumption-driven society, wild beauty with which this trail puts me back in touch.

Dark nights are full of this wildness. My friend Kathy Moore, a professor of philosophy at Oregon State University, identifies "a more intimate connection with the natural world" as one of the many gifts of darkness. She tells the story of a friend of hers who took a niece to visit a planetarium: when they exited the show the little girl turned to her aunt and said, "Aunt Susan, did you know that a long time ago, people could see stars like this? Really. Once there were that many stars in the sky, and people could just look up, and there they were!" Moore reasons that "when we protect children from darkness, when we dim or destroy it with artificial light, we shut them off from fully half the human experience of what is wonderful."

It used to be that a dark night was a common human experience. Even as recently as the mid-twentieth century most of rural American was still in the dark. But by the end of the 1950s (and especially thanks to the help of FDR's Rural Electrification Act), most Americans had access to electric light. Since then, that light has continued to spread. Satellite photos of the United States at night from the 1950s, '70s, and '90s show an unrelenting flood of light across the country. The trend is unmistakable. But what's truly chilling is the computer's imagined photo from the year 2025 showing nearly the entire country lit, with the cities white blisters of intense light and even much of the West—areas that today are still dark—clouded by glow and glare. What does that imagined view of the future say about the PCT? What will we have lost from the experience of hiking this trail if this projected image comes true?

For me, the experience wouldn't be the same, and it wouldn't be as good. Being out here would be a diminished experience in a world with all too many such diminished experiences already.

The thing is, that image doesn't have to come true. Light pollution doesn't have to spread beyond its current boundaries. In fact, we could reduce the amount of light pollution in this country (and the world) by more than half simply by insisting on light fixtures that direct the light downward to its task rather than allowing it to spray in every direction. Before we can stop the spread of light pollution, more people need to become aware of darkness and its value. When we walk this trail we have an incredible opportunity to gain this awareness.

I say, take it.

I say, do something not many people do: pay attention to dusk, to night's rise, to the natural rhythm of day into night. I say, savor the light of a fire, or a candle, or better yet the moon and the stars—all lights made beautiful by darkness. I say, get to know the night, home to countless creatures that depend on darkness for their lives, and a place in which we can feel at home as well. I say, walk the PCT as it takes you through some of the darkest parts of our country, recognizing the opportunity, savoring the gifts of darkness, and when you come back to wherever you live the rest of your life, tell your friends about the dark you experienced, the skies you saw, the sights and sounds and scents—tell them about how the trail took you to a night we once knew and could know again.

THE ART OF THE TRAIL: AN AESTHETIC APPRECIATION OF WHAT'S UNDERFOOT

By Robert Birkby

If asked to describe its world, the last thing a fish would tell you about is probably water: the most ubiquitous element of its world. The same holds true, as Robert Birkby notes here, for Pacific Crest Trail hikers: often the last thing we notice, study, and appreciate, is the trail itself. Both a figurative and a literal line drawn across the western American landscape, the PCT should indeed be seen and appreciated as a significant and beautiful artistic production. In much the same way that our appreciation of art can be enhanced with some knowledge of art history, our love for the trail can be deepened by understanding its history, the techniques and tools used to build it, and the artists involved in the ever-changing sculpture that is the PCT. As hikers, and appreciators of the art of the trail, we will find our experience heightened when we stop to carefully study the tread at our feet. And with that appreciation may come, we hope, the conviction to protect and preserve such valuable art, to avoid cutting across the switchback, to allow the newly restored campsite to grow back, and ultimately to become artists ourselves, joining a local trail crew and lending our own hand to this great creation stretching over miles of space and decades of time.

In 1976 the installation artist Christo, who would become famous for wrapping buildings, coastlines, and small islands with brightly colored cloth, directed the construction of a sinuous fabric curtain across the northern California counties of Sonoma and Marin. Bending to match the contours of rolling countryside, *Running Fence*—as it was called—was eighteen feet high and twenty-four miles long, the result of three years of planning and organization. The white nylon fabric shimmered in gentle grassland breezes for two weeks and then was removed, along with the posts, cables, and all other traces that the fence had ever existed.

Critics hailed *Running Fence* as a triumph of man's artistic interaction with the environment. Christo was celebrated for having made the definitive statement of linear landscape art.

What the critics failed to figure into their assessments was that a little farther east, in terrain of far greater complexity, was a linear installation more than a hundred times longer than *Running Fence*, the result of almost a century of work by not just one artist but tens of thousands. And while Christo's gossamer vision was gone almost as soon as it had appeared, the Pacific Crest Trail continues to be refined, renewed, and rediscovered with every passing season.

Carved into mountainsides, unrolling through forests, and stretched across desert sands, the PCT is a graceful ribbon three feet wide and 2600 miles long. A fusion of engineering, architecture, and artistry, it is a vast participatory sculpture playing out on the grandest canvas of all, the sprawling, vertical backdrop of the American West.

Hikers have many reasons for setting off on the PCT. No doubt you have yours. You might be eager to take in spectacular scenery and enjoy sharing time with other backpackers. Perhaps you are intent on escaping the demands and distractions of the world that is not the trail. You could be planning to hoist your ultralight pack, give yourself a long-distance trail nickname, and push the miles as hard as you can, or your goal might be as simple as ambling along to the first lovely spot where you can sit in the sunshine and enjoy the passing of the day.

There is nothing wrong with any of those motives, but what you probably haven't thought about doing is studying the trail itself. Oh, there could be a bridge so visually stunning that you'll pull out your camera and photograph the span as you cross. An airy stretch of trail blasted into a cliff might cause you to wonder just how in the world anybody could have built anything like that. But most miles of Pacific Crest tread will roll beneath your feet all but unseen.

That is as it should be. Those who have helped build and maintain the PCT want you to feast on scenery small and large. They want you to revel in the snowy heights of the Cascades and the rocky expanses of the High Sierra, to sweat your way across the Mojave and, ultimately, to delight in the foot-numbing satisfaction of covering more distance than you had thought possible, one step at a time.

What they don't expect you to do is fixate on what's underfoot. In a paradox that would crack a smile on a Zen master's face, PCT crews have done everything they can to make the trail all but disappear, leaving little to catch your attention but the wild country flowing past. They have worked hard to lay the trail so lightly on the land that it melts into the background, hidden in plain sight.

Begin to notice the craftsmanship of the route, though, and the trail will suddenly snap into focus with such clarity that you will never again simply hike. You'll find yourself slowing your pace to study the tread's location and shape. You will need to peer underneath bridges to decipher their design. A rock retaining wall might delay you many minutes while you examine the way the stone has been laid, where the crew retrieved the rock, and how they managed to move it to the work site.

A place to begin a critical appreciation of the PCT is with the question of whether it should exist at all. Of course we know that crowds of hikers going into an area with no trails would soon trample a web of random paths across mountainsides and meadows. Land managers reason that well-designed trails can protect the terrain by concentrating human activity along narrow corridors. Inviting pathways that encourage people to venture into the backcountry can also help develop new generations of wilderness defenders. We are more likely to celebrate and protect what we understand. At least that's the hope.

Even so, a trail is a paradox. Tread is a sacrifice zone of compacted soil where human activity ensures that no vegetation can grow. Do the math and you'll discover that a three-foot-wide trail represents a dead zone on the land sized at a third of an acre per mile. Philosophically that's the opposite of the leave-no-trace ethic that guides many hikers, but we do it anyway. It's as though we were intentionally laying a thin scratch across the face of the *Mona Lisa* and then pretending it wasn't there.

In our efforts to preserve the wild country threaded by the Pacific Crest Trail, we have chosen to secure it as it would have been around 1880, about the time John Muir was scrambling through the high country with his blanket, dried bread, and little bag of tea. In those days distances in the West were so great and infrastructure so lacking that, for many who wanted to visit the mountains, getting to trailheads could involve long days in the saddle. The precedent was set, and horses are still allowed on the PCT, even though they themselves might reach trailhead parking lots in trailers pulled behind diesel-powered pickup trucks.

Unlike horses, mountain bikes weren't around in 1880. Today you're prohibited from pedaling down the PCT even though the damage bikes might inflict on the tread is probably no greater than that caused by horses' hooves. (Of course, if a photograph ever surfaces of John Muir pedaling into Yosemite Valley, that could change everything.) On the other hand, today's PCT hikers are free to carry digital watches, cellular telephones, battery-powered weather radios, GPS receivers, and clothing and gear made of materials no one in the 1800s could have imagined in their wildest fantasies.

When it comes to the work of the trail, legislation has also frozen at about 1880 the tool selection for crews toiling on the PCT's stretches of designated wilderness. They cannot use chain saws or any other motorized machinery, relying instead on crosscuts, shovels, pulaskis, mattocks, and rock bars. Wheelbarrows are banned in some areas because, like bicycles, they have wheels. Outside of wilderness, a crew removing a boulder from the tread can make quick work of the job by firing up a gasoline-powered rock drill. To blast a similar boulder in designated wilderness, a crew might be required to drive a hand drill with the blows of a single-jack hammer, progressing a few inches an hour until the hole is deep enough to hold a dynamite stick.

Embracing methods and standards that have changed little over the last hundred years, generations of crews have thrown their energies into building and caring for the crestline route from Mexico to Canada. Construction on the John Muir Trail, one of the major links in the eventual PCT, began in earnest in the spring of 1915 as two eight-man crews set out to construct routes near Muir Pass and on the Middle Fork of the Kings River. The men earned two dollars a day, as did each crew's full-time cook. The foremen made a dollar more. They hiked forty to sixty miles to reach their camps. Strings of pack horses brought in provisions, tools, and camping gear, though late snows high in the Sierras kept them at lower elevations well into June.

In forested areas they cut back trees and brush to form a corridor wide enough and high enough to accommodate a rider on horseback; then they marked the trail by chopping into tree trunks the traditional Forest Service blaze of a foot-long vertical ax cut with a smaller cut above it. Above tree line they piled rocks into cairns to show the way. With picks and shovels they grubbed out tread. Boulders and angled slab rock that blocked the trail's progress yielded to explosives.

Days for the crew were long, and camp life became monotonous. At such great distances from the nearest road, going home for a day off was out of the question. They labored until hints of winter forced them to cache their tools and descend from the mountains; yet despite the hardship and isolation, a number of the men signed up to return the following summer.

In the decades since, every foot, even every square inch of the PCT has been dug, shaped, smoothed, reinforced, or repaired by somebody. Among these men and women have been brilliant craftspersons and backcountry technicians and plenty of environmentalists, renegades, mystics, goofballs, lost souls, and romantics. Most of their names, if they were ever written down, are all but forgotten on rosters tucked away in filing cabinets of the Forest Service, Park Service, and Civilian Conservation Corps. Others are in the membership folders of the Sierra Club, Mountaineers, Mazamas, California Conservation Corps, Washington Trails Association, AmeriCorps, Student Conservation Association, and dozens of other groups whose members have found satisfaction in working on a few feet or a few miles of trail. Many have been volunteers contributing an occasional weekend of effort or years of dedication. Of those on salary, most were paid so little they might as well have been donating their time, too.

Christo had plenty of critics telling viewers how best to appreciate *Running Fence*. As a beginner's guide to the artistry of the Pacific Crest Trail, then, here are a few elements to consider in understanding the toolbox of trail work.

Location

The PCT is meant to rest easily upon the landscape, conforming to the contours to become an almost natural part of the environment. Surveyors may spend weeks figuring out the exact route of a relocation or a new section of trail. They begin by identifying *control points*—passes, river crossings, and other landmarks the trail must utilize. Using handheld surveying instruments called clinometers, they shoot the grade and mark a potential route with strips of brightly colored flagging tape to show where the tread should be built to connect one control point to the next. In complicated areas, a survey team might lay out half a dozen different flag lines before settling on the ideal route, fine-tuning the location until they have figured out solutions as detailed as getting beyond a boulder or skirting past the uphill side of a big tree.

GRADE

The steepness of a trail is quantified as *percent of grade*, coming from the equation *rise over run equals percent of grade*, with *rise* being the amount of elevation gained over a certain horizontal distance, or *run*:

rise/run = percent of grade

An easy way to think about grade is that a trail gaining one foot in elevation (the rise) over the course of a hundred feet of travel (the run) yields a tread climbing at a 1 percent grade. Climb ten feet in elevation over a hundred horizontal feet and you've got a prevailing grade of 10 percent.

A 1915 crew foreman's report noted the standards of the day: "Tread, 30 inches minimum width. Plenty of turnouts provided in dangerous places. Grade in no case except under extraordinary conditions exceeding 15 percent."

Almost a hundred years later, the standards guiding work on the PCT remain essentially the same. A trail with a prevailing grade of 10 percent with brief pitches up to 15 percent can be walked without drawing too much attention to itself. It is also ideal for horses and easy on hikers, who would much rather go farther on a trail of reasonable grade than huff up an unforgiving steep pathway, seeing little but the backs of the boots of the hiker ahead.

ROCK WORK

The Sierra Nevada is blessed with magnificent angular granite ideal for building rock staircases, retaining walls, riprap, and bridge abutments. Civilian Conservation Corps crews working in Yosemite during the Great Depression, some led by master stonemasons, set extremely high standards for rock work that is still a matter of fierce pride among today's Sierra crews. Take time to marvel at PCT rock structures fitted together with clean lines and such tight points of contact that you'll find it difficult to slip so much as a knife blade between the stones of many staircases and walls.

TIMBER CONSTRUCTION

Western red cedar and Douglas fir in the Pacific Northwest have lent themselves to generations of crews constructing steps, retaining walls, water bars, and bridges. Crews with expertise in timber joinery use axes, chisels, augers, and saws to shape logs and cut notches for fitting projects together. Milled lumber also comes into play, especially in boardwalks and bridge decking. Bridge stringers—the beams laid across a chasm or over a stream—are sometimes fabricated in the frontcountry and then transported by helicopter and lowered on cables into remote locations. Stringers shaped from trees felled near a bridge site might have been winched into place using wire rope, block and tackle, and innovative leverage techniques borrowed from the world of high-lead logging.

Drainage

Water is the enemy of almost any trail. A reasonable grade helps prevent water flowing down a trail from picking up enough speed to gouge the tread. New construction often includes drain dips—occasional reversals of grade to form natural pitch changes that keep water from going very far down the route. Water bars made of stone or timber can be installed at an angle across existing trails to kick water off the tread.

Restoration

Closing unofficial trails and inappropriate campsites brings together hard work, horticulture, and an artistic eye. Crews can loosen compacted soil with hand tools and sow native seeds or transplant vegetation found nearby. Camouflage in the form of carefully placed rocks, logs, and even stumps installed in abandoned trails and revegetated campsites increases the likelihood that future travelers will stay on designated tread and give repaired areas time to heal.

Switchbacks

Perhaps the most challenging structure for a trail crew to build is a switchback. Location is critical in finding a place for a turn that takes advantage of the shape of a hillside, perhaps with a large tree or boulder to anchor the turn. A retaining wall constructed of rock or timber often lifts the lower leg of the switchback up to a flat turning platform with a radius great enough to accommodate hikers and horses. The trail leading into and away from a switchback is often surveyed to be steeper than the prevailing grade so that the switchback legs diverge quickly from one another. That helps reduce the temptation for novice hikers to cut the switchback by taking a shortcut from the upper to the lower leg without going all the way around the turn.

When he built *Running Fence*, Christo intended for audiences to see the shimmering curtain of fabric wandering over a great expanse of land. If they thought about them at all, the posts, cables, pulleys, and clips that held the thing up were secondary to the artistic vision of the fence itself. By contrast, the Pacific Crest Trail is built to be used. It's a rugged, tough, user-friendly sculpture with cables, posts, and the other underpinnings of its construction in full view if you look for them, but otherwise secondary to the joyous experience of being in motion through landscapes that matter.

"I am an artist, and I have to have courage," Christo declared as he surveyed the transitory glory of *Running Fence*. "I think it takes much greater courage to create things to be gone than to create things that will remain."

He was right as far as giant fabric curtains go, but not visionary enough to grasp the brilliance and durability of the Pacific Crest Trail and the courage of those who see the importance of making certain it goes on. That includes you, for at its heart, the PCT is participatory artwork. Begin to understand how it has been crafted and you may find yourself motivated to find a volunteer trail crew, roll up your sleeves, and get busy caring for a piece of the trail. And that, my fellow hikers, may be the most satisfying form of art appreciation of all.

TRIUMPH AND TRAGEDY AT STEVENS PASS

By David Foscue

*Many places along the Pacific Crest Trail have tales to tell, tales that add
new dimensions to the trail experience. As stories throughout the* Trailside
Reader *illustrate, history has happened all along and around the trail
tread. Often history has left clues along the trail for us to discover. For
example, the PCT takes on a different appearance just north of Stevens
Pass: broad, straight and flat, not what you expect to find in the Cascades.
It takes little imagination to realize that you are on a railroad bed. A railroad bed? Yes, Stevens Pass is a railroad pass. What was once a railroad
has become a trailroad. Time has created layers of stories in this place.
David Foscue recounts the first effort to cross the trackless North Cascades
with a railroad and includes the sad story of one of the worst train disas-
ters in the United States.*

James J. Hill, "the Empire Builder," was head of the Great Northern Railway.
His great ambition was to construct an unsubsidized transcontinental railroad west through the northern states from his railroad base in Minnesota. Hill
selected the right man to survey and engineer the efforts to extend his railroad
to Puget Sound—John F. Stevens. The first mountains Stevens had to puzzle a
track through were the Rockies. In 1889 Stevens found Marias Pass, south of
today's Glacier National Park, giving the Great Northern Railway the lowest
pass across the Continental Divide. According to historian David McCullough
in *The Path between the Seas*, "He had made the discovery on foot and alone,
his Indian guide having given up. At night, with no wood for a fire, and the
temperature at 40 below zero, he had kept from freezing to death by tramping

back and forth in the snow until dawn" (Simon and Shuster, 1977). John Stevens was one tough guy.

In 1890 Stevens undertook an even greater challenge, finding a way through the Cascades. He extensively explored the mountains from the Columbia River north, rejecting all of the known passes. Stevens later wrote, "The process of reconnaissance for a railway line is largely one of elimination—to find out where not to go" (quoted in *The White Cascade*, Holt, 2007). He finally located and explored a creek (Nason Creek) that was associated with a very promising low mountain crest. Although there was no evidence of any prior use of this area as a passage, Stevens favored this newly discovered route. His assistant was so certain that a good railroad pass had been discovered that he carved "Stevens Pass" on a cedar tree. The Great Northern had its pass and the pass had its name.

Stevens immediately began surveying and planning the path of the railroad over the pass. He realized that the steepness of the pass could best be conquered by a tunnel under the summit. However, a tunnel would take time, and time was money. Money was money, too, and Hill let Stevens know that the Great Northern could not afford the expense of digging a tunnel through the granite mountains. (Stevens once described Hill as "penny-wise, pound-wise".) So, while planning a tunnel for the future, as a temporary solution Stevens designed a complex system of eight switchbacks to take the trains over the pass. The route was laid out in the summer of 1891 and construction of track from the east and from the west began toward the pass. The first locomotive crossed Stevens Pass in January 1893, and regular service to Minneapolis began in June.

But the route over the top of the pass merely opened the transcontinental railway; a tunnel was needed to make it truly reliable and competitive. Hill soon approved the construction and work began in 1897. Because of Stevens's foresight, none of the original track had to be realigned—it had been designed with the tunnel in mind. Small settlements marked each end of the tunnel. The camp on the east side of the tunnel bore the unimaginative name Cascade Tunnel; the larger settlement at the western portal was named Wellington, perhaps after Hill's county of birth in Canada. Tunneling began from each end. The arduous work at the top of the Cascades employed hundreds of men, and the monthly turnover at times reached 50 percent. Progress on the tunnel averaged 350 feet per month. Excavated portions were lined with 2–3.5 feet of concrete. Although by today's standards the surveying equipment Stevens used was primitive, when the two teams met in the middle the alignment of the two sections was less than an inch off.

The 2.5-mile Cascade Tunnel was completed in 1900, and the sinuous route over the top of the pass was abandoned. Tunneling under the mountain eliminated 8.5 miles of track and 2332 degrees of track curvature. The track elevation was reduced by 675 feet. Compared to the switchback route, the tunnel saved an hour and a quarter on good days and dozens of hours on blizzardy days.

Over the years railway traffic increased. As trains became longer and loads heavier, the Cascade Tunnel proved inadequate. Although the tunnel eliminated the eight switchbacks at the top of the pass, the route still depended on other switchbacks and steep grades and was vulnerable to avalanches. Furthermore, the tunnel had ventilation problems. Eventually the Great Northern leadership saw the need for a new tunnel. In 1925, before embarking on a new tunnel project, the Great Northern again consulted with one of the world's most heralded engineers—John Stevens. Stevens recommended a route for a new eight-mile tunnel under the crest of the Cascades. When it was opened in January 1929, the new Cascade Tunnel would be the longest tunnel in the Western Hemisphere. It is still the longest railway tunnel in the United States and is in use today. The PCT crosses above this tunnel less than a mile before you reach Stevens Pass coming from the south.

Who was the man who left his name and legacy at Stevens Pass? Largely self-taught, John Stevens became one of the most respected engineers of his time. By the time he extended the Great Northern to Puget Sound, Stevens had built as many miles of railroad "as any man in the world," according to David McCullough. In 1905 President Theodore Roosevelt called on Stevens to be chief engineer in charge of the construction of the Panama Canal. Later, on the recommendation of President Wilson, Stevens went to Russia to reorganize the Trans-Siberian Railroad. Eventually Stevens retired in Snohomish, Washington, located not far from the Great Northern line he engineered and not far from the pass that bears his name.

What became of the railroad switchback grades that originally conquered the Cascades? In the late 1930s part of the abandoned railroad grade over Stevens Pass was used for Washington's Cascade Crest Trail, a foundation trail of the PCT. Today the first 1.5 miles of the PCT north of Stevens Pass are on John Stevens's railway bed.

Today, the adventurous PCT hiker who wants to truly touch history can take a short excursion under the earth and back in time. By following the PCT that 1.5 miles north on the old railway grade from Stevens Pass, the modern hiker will veer left, to the west. After a few dozen steps more, the trail crosses above the first Cascade Tunnel. To the right, through the trees, not far below, is a minor paved road: Yodlin Place, lined with seasonal cabins and contouring for several blocks on the hillside. From Yodlin Place, there is a gravel road leading downhill (National Forest Development Road 6989, but it is probably unmarked). By following the gravel road downhill several hundred feet to where it doglegs left, and then turning right into the brush, the intrepid explorer can look to the right and see the east entrance of the abandoned Great Northern Cascade Tunnel.

There, the adventurous hiker will perhaps be transported back in time to February 23, 1910. On that day, a westbound Great Northern passenger train and a mail train pulled to a stop near the tunnel entrance but were barely visible through the raging blizzard. The trains could not continue because a slide had blocked the track on the west side of Wellington, on the other side of the tunnel. Up the hill was a railway cookshack, the only amenity at the east portal. Two cooks at the shack served meals to the stranded train passengers. Three feet of snow fell while the trains were at the east portal. The following day the trains proceeded 2.5 miles through the tunnel to the little settlement of Wellington to wait out the storm on a siding.

Rotary plow trains worked furiously to clear the tracks on both sides of the pass, but they could not keep up with the record snowfall. The blizzard brought occasional avalanches, which further burdened the rotary plows. At times the plows themselves became stuck in the snow and railroad crews had to dig them out by hand.

Meanwhile the passengers waited in the train cars at Wellington. On February 25 they heard the shocking news that during the night an avalanche had destroyed the east portal cookshack, killing the two cooks who had fed them. By noon of February 26 it had been snowing heavily for one hundred hours, and no letup was in sight. That day all four rotary plows became stuck in the snow and slides. On February 27 and 28, several groups of crewmen and passengers hiked through deep snow toward the town of Scenic for help—the last two thousand feet of the hike was a terrifying downhill slide. By then, five to six feet of snow had fallen since the trains had reached Wellington.

Then it turned really nasty—it began to rain. Lightening strikes reverberated around Wellington. The passengers, huddled in their train cars, began hearing slide after slide as the sodden snow yielded to gravity. Shortly after

1:00 AM on March 1, a massive slide began above Wellington. It rolled down, gathering momentum, striking the trains and tossing them off the tracks and into the canyon of the Tye River, 150 feet below. From above, only part of one coach could be seen in the suffocating blanket of snow.

Ninety-six people were killed in the Wellington avalanche. There were only seventeen survivors. Although rescue and removal efforts began almost immediately, the last body was not removed until July. The Wellington slide remains the worse snow avalanche disaster in the United States and one of the worst railroad tragedies. Even the little settlement, Wellington itself, became a victim of the avalanche. The Great Northern changed the settlement's name to Tye, as if a change of name could erase the horrifying memory.

The adventurous can still walk through this tunnel and under the PCT for a change of scenery. The dark tunnel goes 2.5 miles to Tye (Wellington), which remains only as a historical site. Markers commemorate the settlement's brief existence and its darkest moment. And the trains? Well, the trains still rumble beneath the PCT at Stevens Pass, but now far below the trail. But here, at the old tunnel site, the PCT hiker has a unique opportunity to touch history and feel a little of both the triumph and the tragedy of Stevens Pass.

ZERO DAYS ARE NEVER ZERO

By Howard Shapiro

Zero days—days when no mileage is logged, but rest is had, food stocks are resupplied, gear is replaced, and injuries are nursed—hold a special place in Pacific Crest Trail life and culture. Whether taken out of physical necessity, or simply out of emotional desire, zero days may not add mileage to the trip, but they almost always add significant experiences and memories. While many zero days are logged on the trail, or in the middle of a multiday expedition, Howard Shapiro reflects on one of our most important and often overlooked zero days: the day that the seed of the plan for our own PCT hike first sprouts. In this piece, Shapiro's zero day takes place not at high elevation but rather at high altitude, not on the trail but rather in a plane, as he and his hiking companions cook up their first of many PCT journeys. In much the same way that mathematics is impossible without the humble number zero, even the longest of PCT journeys cannot be made without adding a few zero days into the equation.

Zero days are never zero. The word *zero* as well as the number suggests something empty or lacking, but in reality it is quite the opposite. My very first zero day was nothing but significant. It started and ended in an unplanned and unexpected way. I am told by burnished thru hikers that unplanned and unexpected are not unusual qualities of zero days.

My zero day did not occur on the PCT per se. However, for all practical purposes it was the launch point of what has become a long series of PCT experiences crossing decades and states, and forging bonds that will last forever. My zero day took place on an airliner thirty thousand feet up in the rarified air, where dreams are shaped and can come to life. Since that time, I have learned from many days on the trail to expect the unexpected. However, that zero moment was most unexpected and it caught me like a clap of thunder or a heart-stopping view from a break in the trees.

At the time I was traveling with my friend Rees, who had recently moved to the Northwest, just as I had, and together we were finding our way in this new place we now called home. We were young in so many ways. Young in our careers, young in our relationships . . . young. With this youth, romanticism followed, as it commonly can, and that idealism is one of the key ingredients that emerged on our journey. The idealism present high in the sky made for what would be one of the more profound life-changing experiences for not just us but for our friend Jim, who shared our dream and would become a very big part of this dreamcatcher too. Little did we realize what impact a journey such as this would have on all three of us. Looking back it never fails to raise my spirits when I realize that, since that first zero day, high over the western United States, we would go on to cover more than 1500 miles of the PCT together over the next twenty-nine years. We have shared breathtaking views of Mount Rainier from the flank of Mount Adams, and we have slept on the trail at the feet of Mount Daniel in order to muster enough courage to cross at first light its swollen torrent of meltwater from a high snowfield. We have waged war on mosquitoes in central Oregon (and lost). We have had our breath stolen from diving into frigid mountain ponds. We have laughed long and hard over the trivial and profound as we defined and redefined who we were, both as individuals and collectively. The three of us have had conversations that have given birth to goals sprouting from prior formless ideas, and it seems that this and our undying idealism is what has kept us coming back. That and the loyalty to each other that have been borne out again and again over the miles and years.

This airborne conversation, which would ultimately lead to many trips on the PCT, began with the idea that we should take some time and begin what would become a most lengthy walkabout. Right there in the midst of our journey home to see family, we conjured up another kind of journey. We would walk from the Columbia River to Rainy Pass in the course of a month. We were not sure of a lot, but we were sure we could do it, that we would do it. In fact, we did do it. In those thirty days in the summer of 1981 we hiked four hundred miles. During that time we consumed more gorp than we thought humanly possible, were startled by stampeding elk, feasted on huckleberries, slid down ice sheets in the fog, and in the end felt stronger physically and emotionally by the time Rainy Pass found us.

I knew as we raced down the Agnes Creek drainage to try to make the shuttle to Stehekin that we had gained new strength and confidence on all levels. Nothing could stop us, not even a bear in the trail. Jim had outpaced us slightly only to nearly collide with a large, furry, huckleberry-munching mom of a bear. Even Jim, the bravest of our trio, was not about to convince this bear we had the right of way. Instead he turned on his heels and walked just as quickly back to us singing loudly. As we met up he quickly explained his encounter and soon we were a chorus of three, ever so slightly slower making our way toward our destination. We sang long and loud the one or two lines we knew from twenty different songs and laughed that what we lacked in musical memory we had gained in muscle memory. We had lost the bear and found a new harmony in each other.

Our zero day in the air ignited our imaginations and sparked all sorts of "what ifs." Again youth served us, and the concerns were easily outnumbered by the possibilities. In that brief moment of time, we found ourselves dreaming the same dream ... walking the same walk and talking the same talk. That conversation on that zero day brought us together as kindred spirits and would go on to shape the many questions we have answered for each other as we have gone on to cover minutes, days, and miles on the PCT: "What scares you the most?" "Where do you want to be in the next three years?" "Who are the people that make up your inner circle?" "What if you changed careers, and moved to someplace new, would we keep coming back to each other and the PCT?"

Friendships will either be ground up or will blossom from conversations and interactions on the trail. In our case, at thirty thousand feet, we were suddenly sitting in a field of ideas and possibilities—and even more unknowns—but it didn't matter. It didn't matter because the energy we felt could hardly keep me in my seat. These fertile ideas were set to bloom. How long until summer? How do we organize food and whatever else? How will we get there? Oh yes, and equipment ... we will need to organize that. Despite all of this, our friendship, our idealism, and our trust in ourselves and each other even in that freshest of zero-day moments sent our dreams into the stratosphere. Anything and everything was possible.

Six months later we had the equipment, the food, and each other as we stepped out of the first zero day and into the first thirty days of what has become a life-changing experiential journey. Twenty-nine years later, our hikes aren't as long or as often as we would like—fewer thirty-day hikes and more ten-day trips—but we are still doing it. Most recently we walked from Old Station through Lassen Volcanic National Park. We are older but so much is as it was when we began. We savor the moments together, searching for views, finding flat camp spots, asking questions, and coming up with fresh answers. The packs still feel heavy those first days, and slowly the sweet spot arrives and the miles slide by and the distractions are the attractions. We are outside in the elements and sensing the emancipation of the natural world that is the PCT. We all have wives and kids now, and distance that separates us, but we have not separated from our dream that emerged on that very first zero day at thirty thousand feet. We joke that we will cross into Mexico using walkers and jokingly refer to our trail name as Team Geezer. Maybe we will have walkers, but at least we will be walking together and will find our way to some other zero day to rest, recover, and decide where our friendship will take us next.

Zero days aren't really zero in that they are springboards. Where they send you is different for all of us, but for me that first zero day set a tone and helped define the possibilities. Zero days are never zero. They rumble and quake, stir and resonate with what is and what will be or what we hope will be. Zero days are fertile, refreshing, and rejuvenating but never zero.

WHERE THE PACIFIC CREST TRAIL BEGINS:
IS IT CAMPO? MANNING PARK? NO, IT'S
MONTGOMERY—THE SEARCH FOR MONTGOMERY

By Barney "Scout" Mann

Barney Mann has zealously researched the early history and origins of the Pacific Crest Trail. In addition to his examination of the life and contributions of Catherine Montgomery, Mann has also pursued a more complete understanding of Clinton C. Clarke, the father of the PCT. His search included a review of Clarke's "Atlas of the Pacific Coast Trail" (1941), a collection of old auto club maps and US Geological Survey topos meticulously trimmed, with pasted-on labels and a trail indicated in a thick, colored-pencil line. Mann's work reminds contemporary hikers that the PCT started as the seed of an idea and was nurtured over many years by countless contributors who, in most cases, were never able to walk the trail they had helped to make real.

We have included several other stories in the Trailside Reader *about some of the important early pioneers of the PCT. In addition to Robert Cox's profile of Cyrus Bingham, an early Forest Service ranger who blazed long stretches of the Oregon Skyline Trail, in this volume, see "The Beginnings of the John Muir Trail" in the California volume of the* Trailside Reader.

*A*re You My Mother? In this well-known children's book, a baby bird sets forth on that most primal of quests, asking so many in turn, "Are you my mother?" This question bears asking about the PCT: Who is the

SOURCE: A version of this story was published in the magazine of the Pacific Crest Trail Association, *The Communicator*, 23, no. 1 (March 2011)

Pacific Crest Trail's mother? Does she exist? If today's hikers are the trail's sons and daughters, between the raw blisters and mountain views have they forgotten to ask the question? Have they even known to ask it? *Are you my mother?*

Normally, maternity isn't in question. It's the paternity test that's common, not the other way around. But for the PCT it was reversed: paternity, not maternity, was well established. For decades, Clinton C. Clarke, the PCT's paterfamilias, trumpeted his relationship. In two books and a dozen pamphlets, like a proud papa handing out cigars, Clarke declared: "In March, 1932, Mr. Clinton C. Clarke of Pasadena, California, proposed to the United States Forest and National Park Services the project of a continuous wilderness trail across the United States from Canada to Mexico, passing through the states of Washington, Oregon and California….The project was approved and adopted, and Mr. Clarke was placed in charge."

For half a century, the PCT proceeded with no knowledge of a mother. In 1968, the National Trails Act officially created the PCT, but there is no known contemporary record of anyone asking the baby bird's question. In June 1971, no less a source than *National Geographic* referred solely to "Clinton C. Clarke, the father of the Pacific Crest Trail." In 1973, the first Wilderness Press guidebook heralded it a reverse immaculate conception—man gives birth to trail: "The idea for the PCT came from the mind of Clinton C. Clarke in the 30s."

But lurking in history's backwater, a long out-of-print book was waiting. In 1946, a now-defunct Seattle press published Joseph Hazard's *Pacific Crest Trails*. Even then, it took over thirty years, till 1977, for pioneering guidebook printer Wilderness Press to find Hazard's book and, finally, with it in hand, to include the first mention of Miss Catherine Montgomery in a modern PCT history.

In his book, Hazard recounts a conversation that took place in 1926, a good six years before Clinton Clarke's first PCT efforts. It was a foggy January 13 in Bellingham, Washington, and Hazard—already a well-known Pacific Northwest mountaineer—was dressed in a suit for his then day job as an H. Sanborn & Co. textbook salesman. Hazard was hawking his wares, keeping an appointment at the hillside teachers' college, the Washington State Normal School, which we now know as Western Washington University. Squirreled away in Hazard's book, like a nut waiting to be found at winter's end, is his account of his conversation with the supervisor of primary grades, Catherine Montgomery.

After an hour's talk, at the close of their business, Montgomery asked,
"Do you know what I've been thinking about, Mr. Hazard, for the last
twenty minutes?"

"I had hoped you were considering the merits of my presentation of certain
English texts for adoption!"

"Oh that! Before your call I had considered them the best—I still do! But
why do not you Mountaineers do something big for Western America?"

"Just what have you in mind, Miss Montgomery?"

"A high winding trail down the heights of our western mountains with
mile markers and shelter huts—like these pictures I'll show you of the
'Long Trail of the Appalachians'—from the Canadian Border to the
Mexican Boundary Line!"

Hazard then records that "that very evening I carried the plan to the
Mount Baker Club of Bellingham. Favorable action was taken. The rest
of the mountain clubs of the Pacific Northwest promptly contacted all
other outdoor organizations. All adopted the project with enthusiasm and
organized to promote it."

Does any evidence back up the story? Who was Catherine Montgomery?
Did she really launch the PCT?

In September 2008, some eighty years after Hazard and Montgomery
spoke, and sixty years after Hazard's book was published, I started my
search for Montgomery. I began in Bellingham at Western Washington
University, not aware that soon I'd be on a first-name basis with archivists
Tamara, Marian, Ruth, and Tony, and that at the nearby regional archive,
the Center for Pacific Northwest Studies, I'd soon all but have my own seat
in the reading room.

The basics of Montgomery's life came quickly: Born April 1, 1867, Canada's
Prince Edward Island. Died September 17, 1957, a fifty-eight-year resident of
Bellingham, Washington. Primary grade teacher. Childless. Never married.

Ninety years of life is no shabby run. Look at her life's bookends: the Civil
War and Sputnik. It's staggering. Montgomery was Scotch, no surprise there.
Her parents, William and Janet, crossed the Atlantic from Scotland in the
1840s, part of the same immigrant wave that brought John Muir to Wisconsin. Young Catherine's father was a railroad carpenter and he must have been
a practical man, for what else can you surmise about a groom who marries his
wife on the same day as her birthday? When Catherine was three, the family

moved from Prince Edward Island to Schuyler, Nebraska, and when Catherine was in her twenties she crossed the rest of the continent, landing in Chehalis, Washington, to pursue her career as a teacher. In 1899, at thirty-two, she made her last move, to Bellingham, Washington, as a founding faculty member of New Whatcom Normal School, Washington State's third teachers' college. She taught there for twenty-seven years.

Then the surprises and puzzles started coming. Surprise: "You must know about the Catherine Montgomery Nature Interpretive Center, don't you?" This was an early question from Tamara Belts, archivist. No, I didn't. Montgomery, upon her death, left her entire estate, the equivalent of a million dollars today, to the Foundation Forest State Park near Enumclaw, Washington. They built an expansive nature interpretive center and named it for her. Today, thousands of school children empty out of yellow buses to visit the center on field trips. Each child walks past a two-foot-tall photo of Montgomery. How does a teacher who stopped working in 1926, with an annual salary of $3,200, end up in 1957 with a rich woman's estate?

A most troubling puzzle: I also could find no evidence substantiating her conversation with Hazard. The Mount Baker Club, founded in 1911, has no records predating 1928. What post-1927 records exist give no hint that Hazard and Montgomery talked. In Portland, I examined the early records of the Mazamas, the most prominent Northwest outdoor club in Hazard's day. There, too, no mention. And at the Trails Club of Oregon? The same.

"Will you still be interested in her if she didn't do it?" My truthful answer was no.

After two Bellingham visits, I scheduled a trip to Seattle. Seattle is the home of the Mountaineers, a club founded in 1906 and that, in 1926, rivaled the Mazamas in Northwest outdoor club prominence. The Mountaineers' handwritten original minute books are preserved in a locked, glass-front case. The 1926 minutes showed immediate promise. Hazard's wife Margaret—Hazzie as he called her—was a member of the Mountaineers' board of trustees. And late in 1926, I saw that Joseph Hazard himself was in attendance at a meeting. I turned the pages expectantly. But there was no mention of anything trail related. I prepared for disappointment. I decided to push on through 1927. I'd come straight from the airport, it was nearing 8:00 PM, and I'd skipped two meals. Approaching 1928 in the minute books, I felt I was plodding, like I was hiking trail miles well after sunset, that it was long past time to stop and make camp.

Then I saw this entry for September 6, 1928: "Motion passed that the Trails Committee be revived, and that the matter of a trail all up and down the Pacific Coast be referred to the Trails Committee."

My effort was rewarded! But, aaaghh, it said "Coast," not crest, and what did "all up and down" mean? Regardless, this was it. They were talking about a long trail. It's likely that Catherine Montgomery did have that conversation with Joseph Hazard; that Hazard did act as midwife, passing the trail idea along.

I was rewarded again with the October 4, 1928, records: "The President reported that the committee ... for the trail from the Canadian Border to the Mexican Border ... had not been appointed." This would be a border to border trail.

Soon enough, the Mountaineers committee was formed. Almost as important, the Mountaineers minutes show that members of the committee attended trail events in the Los Angeles area. Why does that matter? These very same events were likely attended by Clinton Clarke, whom we know as the PCT's father. That Montgomery is the trail's mother seemed supported by the evidence.

Who was she, the PCT's mother? Thankfully, in addition to the PCT, Catherine Montgomery left another trail. In faded newsprint and on microfilm, the faint trail of her life can still be made out. She was a hard-bitten nail spitter. She'd stand up to anyone. Her 1957 obituary described her as a "militant crusader." She was a windmill-tilting Joan of Arc who'd fit right in with the thru-hiker crowd, though she'd tell us, "Stand straight and tuck in your shirt, young man." And with a smile, we'd do it.

Who was the PCT's mother? She was a caring, adored teacher. A teacher of teachers. For a quarter century she helped mold a significant percentage of Washington State's elementary school teachers. One year the school newspaper summed her up in one line, "Miss Montgomery—'To know her is to love her,' so say we. For just and true and kind of heart is she." In 1949, at Western Washington University's fifty-year reunion, she was the best remembered of the faculty.

Who was the PCT's mother? She was a dauntless outdoorswomen, sawing fiercely against the grain of an era when a woman's place was near the coal-burning stove. At age fifty-three, in 1921, when she lost her best friend Ida Baker, Montgomery wrote of "tramping" together. She described days of hiking fourteen miles each way into the Mount Baker Forest, "when we slept on cabin floors with wet feet stretched toward a rude fireplace." A fading photo still exists, showing that cabin, a twelve-foot-by-twelve-foot cedar-shake structure. She and Ida Baker were staunch, often stern women, yet at day's end, from Montgomery's memorial, you can picture the two of them wriggling damp, sore toes, giggling before sputtering leaping flames. And Montgomery was a spinster, childless. She once opened a newspaper article with this self-description: "An old Maid, spelled with capital letters." Montgomery's second-best friend in her life, Washington's poet laureate Ella Higginson, once penned a poem, "The Childless Mother's Lullaby," which seems a fitting ode for Montgomery.

Learning about this woman, I wondered, was there a way to give Montgomery her due? On September 27, 2009, a nomination form was submitted to the Northwest Women's Hall of Fame. In February 2010, a vocally grateful committee gave notice that Catherine Montgomery would be the 2010 Legacy Inductee. On March 21, 2010, in front of a large crowd, Catherine Montgomery was inducted into the Northwest Women's Hall of Fame. For thirty minutes her life was lauded. The final paragraph of the Induction Citation reads: "Of her many legacies, perhaps the most enduring is her vision of a hiking trail along the ridges of the Pacific Coast that she began to champion starting in 1926. Others took up the cause and, today, that 2650-mile-long trail that runs from Canada to Mexico attracts thousands of hikers. She is justly called 'The mother of the Pacific Crest Trail.'"

Thanks, Mom.

OUT ON THE CREST TRAIL

By Walkin' Jim Stoltz

Like many who have hiked one of America's long trails, Walkin' Jim Stoltz found himself and his life transformed from his very first experience. Until Walkin' Jim's untimely death from cancer on September 3, 2010, at the age of fifty-seven, he had taken to the backcountry every season since 1974, returning with images, music, and words to share on behalf of these wild, wonderful, and often imperiled places. In the process, he walked the complete lengths of the PCT, the Appalachian and Continental Divide Trails, made an east-to-west cross-continent hike, and did trips from Yellowstone to the Yukon. In total, Walkin' Jim hiked more than 28,000 miles on these long-distance trips.

On April 10, 1996, Jim set out from the Mexican border on the Pacific Crest Trail. Exactly five and a half months later he finished his trek at the Canadian border. The following excerpt begins with lyrics from Walkin' Jim's PCT song "Out on the Crest Trail" and includes an excerpt from his journal written during the third week of September, in the Cascades. In this piece, Walkin' Jim reflects on the rare opportunities we are given on the trail to connect to our wild brethren—the bear, marmot, and other residents of these wild western forests.

May Walkin' Jim and his message never be forgotten.

I'm a walker of the clouds, snow and misty rain,
Mountains of the northwest, anything but tame,
But then the wind will shift, and the clouds will lift,

Source: "Out on the Crest Trail," by Walkin' Jim Stoltz, first published in *Wild Wind* (Fall 1996). Reprinted by permission of the author.

And the peaks stand in the sun,
Out here on the crest, yes, I'm feelin' blessed,
I can't stop now, 'cause I'm almost done.
Out on the crest trail, there's a wind a blowin'
It's a Cascade wind, blowin' way my cares
It's pushing me northward, that's where I'm-a-goin'
I'm bound for the border and I'll soon be there.

I am up and going early this morning. I've gotten used to the rain and snow, but it's dry today. The clouds are hung high, draped over the skies like a wrinkled tarp. They cloak these mountains in a dull, steel grayness, adding a chill to the air just by their somber mood. And the canyon is cold. The ground is frozen solid, the snow patches as hard as granite. Ice coats the log and the rocks I'd planned to cross the creek on. The stream tumbles down from the glaciers above. Ice to water, to ice. It's slick as, well . . . ice. It's quite some time before I find a safe place to cross.

The trail wanders in and about the shoulders of Glacier Peak, traversing one high basin, then another. As I top the first side ridge and scan the open slopes before me, I note a large black object moving slowly across the steep mountainside. It's a black bear. Though nearly half a mile away, the sighting thrills me. I wonder if it'll still be there when I get over to the trail above it.

The ice and snow on the trail crunches and cracks as I make my way around the big bowl, in and out of little pockets of stunted trees. I'm halfway thinking I may frighten the bear away with all this racket, but as I step from the last stand of forest he is still down there, moving steadily over the slope, sniffing at this and pawing at that.

I'm so intent on watching the big bear below me, that it's quite a surprise when I realize someone else is watching from above the trail! It's Mama Bear with two cubs, and she's very much aware of this strange critter with the load on its back. A scant 50 yards separates us, but the cubs are another 40 yards up the slope, chasing and tumbling over each other heading toward the trees.

I stop in my tracks, waiting and watching. Mama Bear peers down at me. A curious look passes in a flash before she goes back to her huckleberries, raking them into her big mouth, catching them adroitly with her smooth tongue. I must say she has her priorities right. My own tongue has been purple for days from chowing on all the tasty berries covering these mountains. Once the cubs are out of sight and Mom has her rump to me, I continue along the trail. Soon she's out of sight as I crest another side ridge and come down into another high basin. For a moment I can't believe what I'm seeing. Another bear! I pass well above it on the trail, stopping to watch it through my telephoto lens. For a time I almost have myself talked into believing it is a grizzly bear. But no, as much as I'd like to see one of the rare Cascade grizz, this is another black bear.

I walk on, higher and higher. The snow gets deeper and the air gets colder. The peak is no longer visible as the clouds have dropped a bit. But I can still see for miles to the north and west. As I approach Fire Creek Pass I'm crunching through six inches of snow and the wind is stinging cold.

I crest the pass and find a place in the rocks to stop. Time to put on some warm clothes and gobble a Thunder Bar. The view is spectacular. The Pacific Crest Trail is often like that in this country. I'd like to linger, but it's too cold. Got to move.

I head down, coming to a narrow ridge separating two more basins. Leaving the trail, I walk over for a better look into the western bowl. I can't believe this! Two more bears! These are both on the smaller side, but clearly enjoying the berry season here in huckleberry heaven. Seven bears in the space of a few hours. I'm a lucky man.

The trail leads me down, down, down, through a boulder filled basin, past Mica Lake, down a few thousand feet to the murky waters of roaring Milk Creek. Then it's back up a couple thousand more feet of elevation to a high ridge and another vast basin. The clouds are hanging ever lower and a few sprinkles are falling, but I've got bears on my mind. I stop every hundred yards to scan the slopes. Dozens of marmots, fat and sassy ones, but no more bears.

To the west a dense wall of clouds is approaching. I know it's more rain. And I accept it. No use fighting the weather. I'm seven miles from the river where I'll camp and nearly 5000 feet of descent. Down I go, humming along, down, down, down, back into the big old growth, the lush mossy forests that radiate a vibrant sense of green and growing.

By the time I reach the Suiattle River the rain is a steady patter on the bill of my hat. I cross the bridge into a dark climax forest. The big firs and cedars offer some protection from the rain, but they also cut out the limited remaining light. I find a window of cleared ground above the bank of the river and set up my tent. Then a hasty dinner and a few camp chores before slipping into my cozy shelter and dry clothes. The welcome warmth creeps into every nook of my chilled bones as the guitar tops off the day and the tent rings with song and images of the trail, the mountains and ... bears.

THE GIFT

By Larry Hillberg

*Anyone who has completed a thru hike of the Pacific Crest Trail knows that
such a Herculean feat cannot be accomplished alone. It takes the support of
dedicated friends and family who provide the time, resources, resupplies,
and encouragement needed to make such a journey. In this story, Lights-
Out Larry recalls the inspirational support his dying father offered to him
during his 2002 thru hike. Like many who have embraced the daunting
challenges, humbling majesty, and uplifting beauty of hiking the PCT,
Larry reminds us of the life-affirming quality of such experiences, the true
gift we have been given when we have the opportunity to walk the trail.
And many readers will be reminded of loved ones, those who have often
helped make these journeys through the high country possible but who
are unable to be there themselves. How wonderful it would have been to
share a majestic panorama, a star-filled night sky, or the burst of color of a
mountain meadow with a missing family member or friend.*

Snow pellets rattle the outhouse walls as I escape inside. In a pinch, I might
sleep here—enveloped in odors and mustiness—right on the floor. But there
is no time. After doing my business in relative luxury, I resolutely return outside.
I cannot do otherwise. Wind slams the door behind me. Snowflakes frost my
cheeks, stirring self-doubt about hiking on alone. But I taste Canada now. So
with my woolen cap stretched below my ears and my backpack cinched tightly, I
stride onto the trail and into the woods. Dense evergreens dampen the blasting
snow as the Rainy Pass trailhead vanishes behind me. My pace quickens.

SOURCE: A version of this story was published in the magazine of the Pacific Crest Trail Association, *The
Communicator* 20, no. 4 (September 2008).

At this very place, three years earlier, I delivered supplies to my wife, Helen, on her thru hike. As she and her dog, Ceilidh, disappeared north toward Canada, I day hiked south for my own taste of the North Cascades. Later, hustling back toward my car through swirling fog and mist, I met thru hiker Jonathan Ley as he headed toward his resupply. In awe, I had pondered what thru hikers feel near trail's end. Now I know—a force.

Five months ago, following the April 29 PCT Annual Day Zero Kickoff event, I started alone from the Mexican border. Initially hiking twelve to fifteen miles daily, I eased into fitness. Four and a half months ago, I celebrated my sixtieth birthday at 8725 feet in southern California's San Jacinto Mountains. With only cognac for company, leaning against a Fuller Ridge boulder, I had nothing to do but enjoy the sunset. Today, heading north alone from Rainy Pass, I have a duty to finish this hike, this privilege, soon. We lose track of outside events in the freedom of a thru hike, but the world beats on—real life intervenes.

Two weeks ago, I detoured from the trail to deal with an ailing tooth and used the opportunity to call home. "Something happened to Dad, Larry. You need to phone your brother Les. Now." Helen's inflection told far more than her words.

Dad is eighty-nine. A native of Michigan's Upper Peninsula, captain of the 1938 University of Michigan hockey team, and a career forester, he worked into his eighties. Living in Wisconsin near my next-younger brother, he has tracked my hike as intently as he tracked Helen's three years ago. Sharp as ever, enjoying life, and in good health, he has seemed immortal. Yet this sounds bad. Filled with foreboding, I make the call.

"Dad had a serious stroke yesterday. He's hospitalized in Oconto Falls, paralyzed on one side, and can't see or speak. The doctors don't know what will happen. Do what you think is right." Les sounds troubled.

Even with well-entrenched thru-hike inertia, the choice is obvious. My hike is over. Worried, disheartened, I reserve the morning bus to Seattle and a red-eye to Green Bay. Even with hiker fatigue and a comfortable bed, I don't sleep much.

When I arrive home, Dad visibly shudders upon first hearing my voice. Paralyzed except for his left arm and leg, he remains conscious and seems to understand his condition. We—my siblings and I—remain that entire day at his side. That evening, Les suggests that Dad might like to hear stories about my hike.

The next evening, when Dad and I are alone, I hold his left hand and speak of the PCT. He squeezes my hand with every story. There are many. With so much to share between father and son at a time like this, I yearn for him to speak. But it cannot be.

The trail stories wane. My talk drifts to family and familiar memories.

"We're optimistic that you'll recover Dad, but we won't know for awhile. I'm happy to be here with you."

Time passes. I don't notice when, but the hand squeezing stops. Only when my talk returns to the PCT does Dad squeeze again. I get a hint of something.

"Dad, my place is here. We'll soon know how you're doing." He remains motionless. Is this a message?

I'm direct. "Dad, are you surprised that I'm here?" He answers with his hand. "Did you expect me to be hiking?" Quicker now, he squeezes again.

"Dad, I can't do that." He has no reaction.

"Do you really mean that?" His clasp is immediate.

My heart wells up inside my chest and then rises to constrict my throat. My eyes blur with tears. How could he, in his terrifying situation, consider me? Still holding hands, we remain motionless for minutes. Needing proof, I struggle to speak.

"Dad, one for no, two for yes—should I return to the PCT?" His two-squeeze answer is crystal clear. Yet I vacillate. Is it selfish? Fair? Should I? Long minutes pass in silence. Suddenly, my doubts become resolve. I'll hike for us. I want to finish more than ever. "Dad, I'll do it." Squeeze, squeeze.

The power of this moment will never leave me.

Airplane and bus return me to Skykomish. At my motel, I retrieve and stuff my backpack for the trail. Sleep is fitful.

After hitching to Stevens Pass, I set off alone. Six days have passed. My hiking buddies are almost in Manning Park. The beautiful North Cascades invite one to linger, but I'm hauling ass.

Those next days are a blur. Though I encounter others, I hike and sleep alone. The Cascades remain cloudy, damp, and cold. Still trail fit, strong after six days' rest, I blow away the miles and elevation changes. My intention to slow down near Canada is out the window. Not even the purity and magnificence of the Glacier Peak Wilderness can tempt me to linger. My destination is paramount, dwarfing the journey. Canada and Dad draw me ahead, up and over rocky Cascade ridges, across tumbling rivers, north.

Totally out of communication, my mind returns often to Dad. Vivid mental images of him in his hospital bed, unmoving, battling to breathe, invade my days and nights. I dream of that dim room, his silent struggle, and that he may recover.

Time crawls at Bridge Creek Ranger Station while I hang around for the morning Forest Service bus to Stehekin. When the driver briefly stops for salmon and waterfalls viewing, I fight for patience. Only the Stehekin Bakery wins my interest.

We finally arrive in Stehekin, and Meadow Ed greets me. After asking my trail name and taking a hurried photograph on the bakery steps, he directs me to the satellite phone. "You have an urgent message from your daughter Shari."

The news is dire. Dad, learning that recovery chances were bleak, confirmed his decision against artificial life support. Recently vigorous, loving life, enjoying especially his family and friends, he is waiting to die. He is expected to live approximately seven days.

The next morning, reaching Rainy Pass, I hesitate only for the outhouse. Turning back is not an option, regardless of the snowstorm. Drifting up to a foot on the ridges, snow continues for much of the next three days. Between crests, I am soaked to the waist by cedars and huckleberry bushes, only to be refrozen by icy wind at the next ridge. The sun never shows its face. Harts Pass is a snowy blur. The beauty of red and burgundy huckleberries, yellow larch, green cedars, and lacy ice etched into rocks can't slow me. The unlocked yurt at Windy Pass holds me barely long enough for lunch. Only moving warms me.

On my last night out, when that brutal dampness reaches midthigh, my polypro underwear and wool socks barely do their jobs. Camped by mistake on a windy ridge, tent pitched directly on snow, I never get warm. I count every hour. Giving up before daylight, fighting darkness, frigid hands, and bad temper, I stuff my backpack and hurry ahead.

The pristine beauty of these northern woods and mountains escapes me. I want only to finish. In midafternoon, switchbacking through thick trees, I catch sight of the strange, narrow, cleared, and perfectly straight border marching over the hills and through the forest. The Monument 78 minitower, materializing in a clearing, stops me cold. The PCT ends here. I've made it! With overflowing emotions and trembling hands, my attempt at photography fails. Just in time, others arrive from behind, and I pose with the monument for my own camera.

I rush ahead. The truth of eight miles with an unwelcome elevation gain stands between me and civilization. Impatient, along this final trail, I just want it over with. Bipolar emotions reel through me, first joy, then letdown. My life-changing experience is over. Real life crashes in. I'm a horse headed back to the barn. Seeming to get nowhere, I move too fast. Finally at Manning Park Lodge, exhausted, I learn that Dad is battling but sinking. I need to get the hell out of here.

I arrived in Wisconsin thirty hours before Dad passed. I will always trust that he knew of my finish. He died when all six of his kids were in his room at the same time—the first time we'd all been together in thirty years. Each of us lost in our own thoughts, we wished for only his peace and dignity. When his labored breathing suddenly ceased, we felt only relief. Sadness would come later, and still does. A relationship becomes instantly clear when someone passes. Only the relationship itself, forever unchangeable, lives on.

Five years earlier, before either Helen or I had even dreamed of doing a thru hike, Dad and I had stood on a peaceful rocky slope near Upper Lost Lake in the Sierra Nevada. This alpine lake, a few miles south of Carson Pass, is my favorite place for connecting to our planet and contemplating the vast universe. I spread some of Dad's ashes on that rocky slope. Someday mine will rest there as well.

And into eternity, we'll share the most wonderful gift I ever received.

Goodbye, Dad, and thank you.

ON BREAKING CAMP AND BEING LOST

By David Wagoner

A lifelong resident of Washington, and an inveterate explorer and lover of the rainy woods and swollen rivers of the Pacific Northwest, David Wagoner captures many of its splendors in his poetry. In many of his books, such as Sleeping in the Woods *and* Traveling Light, *Wagoner focuses specifically on the hiker's and camper's experience in the backcountry. In the first poem included here, "Breaking Camp," he captures that familiar experience for the PCT hiker, of making a spot of ground into home for the night, and returning it to its wildness in the morning. In the second poem, "Lost," he offers both sound practical advice for the unfortunate PCT hiker who loses the trail as well as sagelike wisdom for anyone exploring the deep and damp forests of the Northwest. Whether we have lost our way or not, as we break camp each morning, many of us could benefit from slowing down, listening, observing, and waking up to the complex interwoven threads of life surrounding us on the trail. We should always "turn to look back once," Wagoner advises us, and remember to "stand still." That's hard advice to follow though, for many mile-eating, trail pounding, thru and section hikers, but it's also advice that always seems to pay off in the end. Many PCT hikers know this, of course, and it is why we come, why we struggle and strive and work so hard to get lost in the wilderness: because we know, deep in our hearts, that it is only by getting lost that we can truly find ourselves.*

SOURCE: From *Traveling Light: Collected and New Poems.* © 1999 by David Wagoner. Reprinted with permission of the poet and the University of Illinois Press.

BREAKING CAMP

Having spent a hard-earned sleep, you must break camp in the mountains
At the break of day, pulling up stakes and packing,
Scattering your ashes,
And burying everything human you can't carry. Lifting
Your world now on your shoulders, you should turn
To look back once
At a place as welcoming to a later dead-tired stranger
As it was to your eyes only the other evening,
As the place you've never seen
But must hope for now at the end of a day's rough journey:
You must head for another campsite, maybe no nearer
Wherever you're going
Than where you've already been, but deeply, starkly appealing
Like a lost home: with water, the wind lying down
On a stretch of level earth,
And the makings of a fire to flicker against the night
Which you, traveling light, can't bring along
But must always search for.

LOST

Stand still. The trees ahead and bushes beside you
Are not lost. Wherever you are is called Here,
And you must treat it as a powerful stranger,
Must ask permission to know it and be known.
The forest breathes. Listen. It answers,
I have made this place around you.
If you leave it, you may come back again, saying Here.
No two trees are the same to Raven.
No two branches are the same to Wren.
If what a tree or bush does is lost on you,
You are surely lost. Stand still. The forest knows
Where you are. You must let it find you.

THE HIGH ADVENTURE OF ERIC RYBACK

By Eric Ryback

No compilation of Pacific Crest Trail stories would be complete without an excerpt from Eric Ryback's account of his 1970 walk from Canada to Mexico. Instead of attending high school graduation, seventeen-year-old Ryback was beginning his walk south in the snowbound North Cascades. Ryback's story, not without its controversies, has served as an inspiration for countless hikers since. Among the challenges Ryback and other early thru hikers had to overcome was the reality that the PCT was no more than a concept, virtually a line on paper, for many miles. It was not until 1993 that the trail was officially declared to be complete. Also, over the years fewer and fewer thru hikers have begun their PCT trek in the north and walked south; Ryback's account of his very eventful first day underscores why. Spring seldom arrives by June in this corner of the world, and 1970 was no exception.

It was six o'clock in the morning, June 10, when I mounted the approach trail to the Pacific Crest and the American border. I was choked with excitement and pride. I had by my own initiative, my own planning, and even mostly my own funds brought myself to this point. I had served my apprenticeship in the Appalachians; now I faced the master's test on the Pacific Crest.

I encountered intermittent patches of snow along the entire length of the trail that led to the first pass and the crest. I moved downward toward the American border. The roar of the water increased in volume as the valley

Source: Excerpted from *The High Adventure of Eric Ryback: Canada to Mexico on Foot*, by Eric Ryback (Chronicle Books, 1971). Reprinted by permission of the author.

floor drew nearer, rising to a deafening pitch as it echoed off the granite walls and resounded along the entire length of the gorge. The valley floor was wet and muddy; and as I trudged toward the river, my heavy pack pushed my boots deep into the mud. Then I was along-side the river, its rushing waters crashing against huge shining boulders and thrusting frothy tongues far above my head.

After surveying the entire area, I plotted a route across the stream, using the scattered boulders as stepping stones. When I reached the other bank, I concluded that in the future it would be better for me to stay on the crest as much as possible in order to avoid the gorges and their raging rivers. Although I knew that rapids such as these could literally pound a person to pieces on the rocks, my worst fear was that if I ever did fall in, my boots would become soaked; and the wetness and rubbing of sock against foot would cause blistering—one problem I did not need. My trek down to this river, however, had a symbolic importance; for theoretically I had just entered the United States of America, and my journey had begun.

Monument 78, marking the border, was supposed to be located here; but scanning the area, I could not see it. In fact, I didn't really know what to look for; the only photograph I had ever seen of it was in some Forest Service literature in which a horse was standing in front of it. That wasn't much to go on.

I followed the trail along the river in hopes of finding it, and after walking about 100 yards, I spotted a small bronze marker standing at the edge of the trail. It was Monument 78, the beginning of the trail. I sat down next to the marker and ate my lunch as a kind of celebration. My plans called for the day to terminate here; but with only 12 miles behind me and the entire trail and afternoon before me, I decided to put in some extra miles.

My shoulders had begun to ache, but I refused to acknowledge it; and after lunch, I once again mounted the trail. After turning away from the river, the trail began a steady rise into the snow. At first, there were only small, isolated patches clinging to the base of trees and tiny protected gullies; but as I continued upward the trail was covered, so that I had to follow the contour of the mountain under the assumption that the trail would take that course. Although the snow was probably about eight feet deep, there were only a few inches of powder snow, and the hard crust beneath it supported me and actually made the walking easier than if I'd been on the bare rock.

Four miles of hiking brought me to Castle Pass, which, like a window, revealed the whole of the Cascades to me. My panoramic view extended hundreds of miles, with range upon endless range of massive mountains and three brilliantly contrasting colors—black rock, white snow, and blue sky.

I made good time walking over the snow along the three-mile stretch from Castle to Hopkins Pass. But by this time, with 18 miles behind me, my boots were wet from the melting snow, and my condition was generally miserable. Gloves, one item that hadn't been on my check list, were my greatest need at this point. The wind and cold had forced my hands into the protection of my pockets, and, as a result, I surrendered much of my balance. I tripped often trying to keep balanced without my arms; and whenever it happened, the 80 pounds on my back was like a pendulum, swaying me back and forth. The outcome was decided by the speed with which I could remove my hands and regain my balance. A couple of times, my reaction was too slow and I toppled over.

Exhausted, frozen, and hungry, I decided that Hopkins Pass had to be my bivouac for the night, even though there were still a few hours of daylight remaining. A few thousand feet beyond was Lakeview Ridge, which would put me at the very summit of the range; but between me and the ridge there was a steep, unmarred ice field extending 2000 feet up to the summit. It would be a treacherous climb in my condition, plus the probability of an even more exposed campsite, warned me against going any further. Below me lay Hopkins Lake, a sheet of ice embedded in the rock and rimmed by boulders. Beyond were the Cascades, snow-covered and waiting.

I sat down with my back to the ledge to rest and to study the ice field that I would have to tackle in the morning. There weren't any visible hand-holds or natural trails on which to cross it. Was there any other route? I scanned the area but could see none.

My thoughts were suddenly interrupted by a new sound that rose over the whistle of the wind. Turning toward the strange sound, I saw a pack of snarling coyotes across the frozen lake. A deer was trapped among them, its brown coat changing color with the blood that seeped from its wounds. The deer stumbled and fell to the ground as the coyotes continued their assault. I watched their butchery in horror until I was struck with the terrible thought that the same thing could happen to me. It wasn't likely; I knew that. Still, the grim scene below upset and frightened me. I decided to move to Lakeview Ridge and get the ice field between them and me.

By the time I had re-shouldered my pack, the coyotes were devouring their prey and the snow was stained with blood. I approached the ice field and found that it was a plane of packed snow—a giant crusted snow drift—reclining at a 75-degree angle from the ridge to the bank of the lake below. The large black boulders at the edge of the lake were a chilling sight, if I fell down this slope, there wouldn't be much left of me after I struck the rocks. The coyotes or the ice field and boulders? I preferred the ice field as my adversary.

I pressed my boot into the smooth, icy snow, gaining a secure foothold; then I stepped forward and pressed the other foot into place. The decision to cross the ice field was made. Cutting footholds into the snow with my boots at every step and zigzagging my way up the snowy incline, I could feel my complete exhaustion. It would be a 20-mile day when I finally made it to the top of Lakeview Ridge.

When I reached the middle of the field, I began to have the feeling I wasn't going to make it; but I kept going, forcing myself to take each new cautious step. I had perhaps 10 feet to go when I gathered all of my waning strength and thrust forward to reach the firm footing of the ridge. Too eager, I stepped flatly on top of the snow and sunk into it an inch or so, losing my leverage. I tried to correct my mistake by edging my foot in [in order] to form a ridge. But this altered my balance; and when I took a second step, I fell and began sliding helplessly down the icy surface on my pack—like a bobsled out of control.

I remember seeing the entire panorama of the Cascades blurred before me and the dark boulders at the bank of Hopkins Lake rushing toward me. And I remember feeling a deliberate, accepting calm as death swept up from the lake to embrace me. Suddenly, the pack jerked, as if refusing to perish with me without a struggle. My weight had shifted to the right, forcing one of the 4-inch extensions of the aluminum frame into the snow and slowing my descent. It took me only a fraction of a second to realize what was happening and struck with this new hope, I acted instantly and instinctively, throwing all my weight to the right and driving the pole further into the packed slope. It sliced viciously into the snow and ice, throwing up a spray and slowing the pace downward a bit more.

With renewed energy, I threw all of my weight to the right and, flexing my knee, dug my right heel into the ice. My foot was repelled by the speed of the descent, thrusting my leg up almost perpendicular to my body. Again I brought it down; and this time, aided by the pack, my fall was abruptly checked.

A few seconds passed before I even realized that I was saved, at least for the moment. Afraid to move a muscle, I lay frozen in both body and mind. Only my heart reacted, pounding painfully and telling me I was still alive.

I flexed my fingers first, bringing the palms to my side and pushing them into the hard snow. When they seemed secured there, I lifted myself slightly and began carefully to flatten a small area with my feet to serve as a platform. Hands pushing upward and feet digging inward, I slowly began to sit up. Then I slid my rump a few inches down the slope and crouched on the platform I had formed, thighs against calves and knees straight up and trembling.

Gaining security and some calm, I finally stood up, and looked above me. A narrow impression extended downward in the snow about 300 feet from where my feet had given out. The impression became a deep gouge where the pole and finally my heel had brought the death slide to a halt.

Stepping sideways, I embedded one foot a few inches up the slope, formed a second platform, and then brought the other foot up. I was now about two feet closer to the summit. Each step was just as cautiously placed, until, a half hour later, I had climbed the 300 feet back to the summit. The coyotes had long since vanished into the forest, leaving only the red-stained snow and scattered bones to tell the story of one creature that had failed nature's test and lost his life and of another that had passed with a low D and a memorable lesson.

When I was well away from the slope, I sat down to a much-needed rest and a hasty, half-cooked dinner of beef stew. After repacking the stove, I removed my boots and crawled into my sleeping bag with all my clothing on. I wasn't sure how cold it would get after dark, and I had no intention of freezing to death after my earlier bout with eternity.

I closed my eyes, expecting to fall asleep immediately, but I felt uneasy and unable to relax. Something was missing on this first night in the mountains. Then I remembered—it was the fire. At the end of every day on the Appalachian hike, whether the weather was hot or cold, I had built a fire, which became my hearth for the night. I always lay close to its comforting presence, basking in the warmth of the flickering flames and falling asleep with the gentle hiss of the burning wood in my ears. Here in my mountain home to the west, there was nothing but snow and rock and the howling wind. I was alone, and I would sleep alone in the cold blackness.

As I lay huddled and exhausted on top of 7000 feet of rock, swept by wind and snow, 2000 miles away from home, I thought of my high school classmates, who were perhaps at that very moment receiving their diplomas at the ceremony I had passed up for this night on an icy peak in Washington. "Well, congratulations, kids," I said to myself, "and don't worry about me. I just had a little graduation ceremony of my own."

THE LAST SKIES

By Cindy Ross

Due to the sheer length of the trail, and the rugged nature of the country it crosses, it is not uncommon for Pacific Crest Trail hikers to take years, to overcome injuries and illnesses, and to battle enormous odds in order to complete their thru hikes. Nevertheless, whether finished in a Herculean single season or over a decade of patient and persistent section hikes, the honor of having "completed the entire trail" carries more weight in western hiking communities than even the heaviest of packs.

When Cindy Ross arrived at Monument 78 it represented an exceptional achievement of perseverance and determination. Two years earlier, while in the process of walking the trail, she had survived a horrendous, near-fatal fall on the icy north face of Sonora Pass. She returned to finish the journey with her new husband, Todd Gladfelter, only to face her final challenge, the snowbound North Cascades. After a night off the trail, trail angels Ron and Mary Ann returned Cindy and Todd to Rainy Pass, where they began their final stretch. It is here that we pick up Cindy's account.

SEPTEMBER 25

The next morning, Ron and Mary Ann cannot bear to leave us on the road alone, so they both call in sick and accompany us the five miles up to Cutthroat Pass. Moral support. We pile into their junker pickup and head up into the mountains.

"Look, that peak isn't even covered," Ron announces. "You guys will be okay." Todd and I say nothing. We saw the trees on the pass, shrouded in wet,

SOURCE: Excerpted from *Journey on the Crest*, by Cindy Ross (The Mountaineers Books, 1987). Reprinted by permission of the author.

white snow. It hangs on them like cloaks, so thick that their green boughs are barely visible. Nobody's positive wishes can convince us that we will be all right. We just don't know. Nobody knows.

The sky is congested with low, dark, snow-packed clouds. What could it do to us? Strand us? Freeze us? Drive us home before we reach our goal? My mind turns the same thoughts and same fears over and over. Once again, I feel unsure, unstable, uncomfortable, so downright scared.

Chatter slows down to a few brief comments as the four of us climb higher toward Cutthroat Pass. The snow grows deeper and deeper: six inches, twelve inches, eighteen inches. We are placing our feet in boot-holes made by the previous four hikers. Petite Mary Ann sinks in to her upper thighs.

At the top of the pass, we all stop and stare in silence. I've never seen a more hostile looking world. Jagged, gray peaks are drowned in snow. Darker gray clouds rumble with thunder in the heavens. They're warning us. Go down! You don't belong up here! Can't you see the season has changed?

I look over at Ron and Mary Ann. They seem so forlorn, as though they're somehow responsible. We all know it's not going to be okay. Mary Ann shivers in her parka, and I shiver with fear. We embrace and look into each other's eyes. I want them to take me back, but we turn and walk away quickly, not knowing how much time remains before we aren't able to move. Ten miles to our first bail-out route. Ten miles! It looks like it's ready to storm any second. I race along the snow-covered traverse, trying to put the miles behind as fast as I possibly can.

Todd notices my abnormal pace and asks, "Are you scared, honey?'

"Yes."

"You can cry if you want to."

"Don't worry," I answer, as tears fill my eyes.

Cutthroat Pass. How I hate the place. The snow drifts across the traverse. Still I push through, quickly. I am afraid of a white-out. Afraid of getting stuck up here in blowing, piling up snow with no place to camp, for who knows how many days. Fear is pushing me through this.

Camp tonight is low, back in the season of autumn. The colorful, changing leaves are a comfort. With only four days to go, we find that getting to the border is an all-engrossing task. It's all I think about. It's our pot of gold at the end of the rainbow. Walking to Monument 78 at the Canadian border means more to me than anything I've ever done in my life. It has certainly been my most eagerly and persistently sought-after goal, the most difficult, the most energy consuming. Four days. Only four days. But four days are an eternity if they're crowded with fear and uncertainty.

SEPTEMBER 26

We awake to falling snow. Today's bail-out point is memorized—as is every day's. The four guys that camped near us last night left about an hour ago. I watch how fast their prints fill with rapidly falling crystals.

On our ascent to Glacier Pass, I walk up switchbacks that are so tight that I feel like the steel ball in a pinball machine. We keep our heads low to guard against the driving snow. To keep my mind occupied, I repeat catechism prayers that I learned in grade school. Oh, I'm tired. We're pushing to get somewhere, farther, and we are wearing ourselves out trying.

Breaks are even shorter now than when it rained, for there is no place that's dry. Snow is everywhere above the tree line. Our feet have never been colder. The snow lies on top of our leathered toes and melts. When we take breaks, our feet just hang in there, freezing, as soon as the motion stops. The only color in this winter landscape is provided by the golden alpine larches. Their ochre color is striking, even in driving snow. If not for them, this entire scene would look like a black and white photograph.

On a knife-edged ridge, a three-foot cornice has blown into shape and already hardened for the winter. Thick fog and blowing snow conceal any stomach-dropping sights we may have seen. It's just as well. These mountains are far too rugged and inhospitable to look at under these conditions.

Harts Pass tonight. Halfway in. We're in as deep as we can get from the North Cascades highway. The end is just as far ahead as the road is behind us. In camp, the snow turns to hail and then finally stops. Soon a few stars poke out, but we're not fooled. Should it clear, unbelievable low temperatures will follow. Even now we sleep with all our clothes and rain gear on. Once again, we memorize our bail-out route for tomorrow. These advance plans add a fragment of strength.

SEPTEMBER 27

Is twelve degrees cold enough to be considered winter camping? I want to go south this winter! The snow cracks under our feet. Boots, bottles, rain fly—all freeze solid. Oatmeal cools off in the time it takes to lift my spoon and carry it the short distance to my lips. The pain in our feet is severe as we shove them into frozen socks and boots. They hurt even more when we put pressure on them, force them to bend and carry us up the mountain.

The sun has come out, but it doesn't make the cold any more bearable. We're wearing all our clothes. I put my gloved hand up to shield my face from the blustery, blowing wind and look back to see the North Cascades that we just walked though. It makes me shudder. Since crossing Harts Pass, we've noticed a definite change in the mountains. They are gentler, not nearly so craggy and forbidding. We have entered the Pasayten Wilderness. Mount Baker and the horrendous Picket range shield us a bit from the storm. Our mountains look like waves high in the sky, swelling and getting ready to curl and break.

Todd lies by my side, sleeping, while I write. His eyes and mouth are part open and through his mouth comes a soft snore, the way he always sleeps when he's extremely tired. His rust-colored wool balaclava is pulled around his forehead, cheeks, and neck. It's as familiar to me as his hair used to be, for I rarely see his bare head anymore. Our clothes are falling apart. Todd's shorts are downright indecent. My underpants have holes in them almost as big as the leg openings. Our sleeping bags' interiors have completely changed from a medium blue to dirt brown. It's time to go home.

Today is the first day we've considered life after Monument 78. We are a little more confident that we may make it. Only six end-to-enders have made it so far. Everyone we hiked with bailed out when they reached their personal limits. The ones who will make it are the ones who have the passion, the dream to reach the end. No one else in his right mind would put himself through it.

September 28

Early this morning, we begin our climb up to Rock Pass. We walk on two-inch-thick hoarfrost. The frozen, upward-reaching crystals have lifted small stones away from the ground. The frozen strings are solid and support our weight. Deer and marten tracks are deep and well preserved in the now-frozen ground, like star handprints on the sidewalks of Hollywood.

We have been following the footprints of those four guys ever since Stehekin and have been most grateful for their guiding steps. They show the way, reassuring us that they got through and continued on. We follow them from Rock Pass toward Woody Pass and become so accustomed to being led that we pay little attention to where the trail is actually going. Two of these guys are almost twenty-six hundred milers, their footprints are to be trusted.

I don't think much of it when I step across the three small fallen trees across the trail. Strange for trees to be lying here, almost obstructing the way. Still, I ignore it and continue after the boot prints. Todd ignores it, too, follows me and makes no mention of it. The trail degenerates as we traverse around the precipitous slopes of Powder Mountain. Before we even reach snow, the danger becomes great. Our feet walk on a wildly angling trail, forcing our worn-down boot cleats to grip beyond their capabilities. Loose scree and rocks clutter the trail. Something seems wrong.

We never saw the trail this eroded. It's not safe anymore.

"I don't like this, Todd. The trail is really in bad shape. Barely any bed."

"I don't think this is the trail."

We look it up in the guidebook and sure enough it's been abandoned. We cautiously turn around and see the PCT switchback down an avalanche bowl. A faint indentation still comes through on the slope, pristine and unmarred. No boots went that way.

Todd is upset with me for refusing to go across this rotten, abandoned trail, which is considerably shorter than the actual PCT. We will add miles to our day by going back and retracing our steps. I know the other guys made it but it doesn't seem worth it to me. Not on the last day of our hike. But mostly Todd is upset with himself, for not listening to his own intuition when he saw the logs across the trail.

I lead the way across the bowl until the snow gets deeper and the slope steeper. We are at the head of an avalanche area and can look down and trace its regular path for miles. Thousands of trees have been wiped out in a funnel-shaped design when avalanches have roared down the mountain in previous winters. My fear begins to grow. I let Todd go first. Footprints aren't enough. He acts as a plow—dragging his outside foot horizontally as his inner leg cuts deep into the bowl's side, making the bed wide enough for me to walk on. His bare thighs are scraped raw from the cold and cutting crust.

Where would I be were it not for him? All the crying he put up with, my slow pace, my endless picture taking, doing so many of the chores so I could be free to record this trip. He is the very reason I am going to reach Canada.

If something had happened to him along the way, say, if he'd fallen again and had to return home, I would not have continued on alone. Nor would he have gone on without me. Reaching the end would not have mattered anymore. We're partners. We're a team. Getting to Canada for one of us is important only if the other is by our side.

After we get across the bowl, we examine the map for more north-facing slopes. Devil's Staircase is a narrow segment of trail that makes tight switch-backs down a knife-edged, north-facing point.

That is it. After this it will all be over. We'll head downhill into less and less snow. We'll be on our way to the border and safety. But Devil's Staircase is the highest point on the route since the Dana Yelverton shelter back in the Goat Rocks Wilderness.

"DAMMIT!" shouts Todd, as he peers over the edge. "It's drifted shut!" He very cautiously swims through the waist-deep snow, slipping a few times and going dangerously close to the edge. Even now, on our last day, we have to work so hard. I grit my teeth and follow.

As soon as we get down the staircase, we race. We can see the border swath in the forest on the mountain across from us, the dividing line between the two countries. We race toward it—no lingering, no holding back, no attempt to stall.

At last we arrive at the pointed metal monument, breathless. We have made it!

> *What they had done, what they had seen, heard, felt, feared—the places, the sounds, the colors, the cold, the darkness, the emptiness, the bleakness, the beauty. Till they died this stream of memory would set them apart, if imperceptibly to anyone but themselves, from everyone else.*
> *—Bernard DeVoto*

CONCLUSION:
ENDINGS AS BEGINNINGS

What the Caterpillar calls the end of the world
The Master calls a butterfly.
—Richard Bach, *Illusions*

When we crest a high pass and find a new world unveiled on the far side, when a thru hiker completes the length of the trail, when we must retire from our hiking days . . . each of these endings also represents a beginning. Many hikers, like the editors of this collection, have enjoyed long love affairs with the Pacific Crest Trail, relationships that have spanned the years and have included the start and finish of a number of different hikes. So, many of us know from experience that every ending holds within it the promise of transformation and the anticipation of a new beginning. Similarly, as you end *The Pacific Crest Trailside Reader*, we hope that it also represents a beginning, whether this means a return to the PCT with new appreciation for the trail and your time on it, or writing and sharing your own story and insights with others, or embarking on a new life adventure. Regardless of where your feet take you from here, we hope you'll carry this collection and its stories with you, in either your pack or your memory.

LESSONS LEARNED
This three-year project has immensely enriched our own appreciation for the PCT; we have new eyes for the history, the ecology, and the hiker experiences that unfold along every mile of the trail. Just as these stories have encouraged our introspection, we expect that you will have drawn your own lessons from the stories included in this anthology.

Here are a few of those insights and reminders that we will take with us:

We can accomplish more than we ever thought possible. Whether Hawk Greenway as he rode his horse north through Oregon and much of Washington, or Larry Hillberg returning to the trail to complete his thru hike urged on by his dying father, or a young Tom Marshburn finishing the trail at the Mexican border, we can and do exceed the limitations we create for ourselves.

We can overcome our fears. Whether it is the example of Suzanne Finney as she scaled Forester Pass, or Barbara Egbert's crossing of Egg Butte, or Eric Ryback's first day on the trail, we can and do conquer our fears.

The PCT is an unparalleled part of our national natural heritage. David Rains Wallace, Wallace Stegner, William O. Douglas, and others capture the magic of the wildlands transited by the PCT. The PCT allows relatively convenient access to majestic wilderness on a well-maintained trail, buffered from the political instability and security concerns present in many wild places around the world.

It requires the vigilance of all to ensure the preservation of the PCT. Robert Birkby contrasts the construction of the PCT with Christo's temporary installations. Charles Bergman documents the impact of civilization on the precarious existence of fauna such as the condor, and Justice Dwyer's injunction halted some of the most aggressive logging practices. These stories remind us that the PCT and its wilderness corridor are fragile. We have a responsibility to participate in the protection and conservancy of the trail.

The PCT experience is even more about our transformation than the wilderness experience. Walker Abel captures this metamorphosis in his students. Charlotte Mauk muses about it in "Homecoming." David Green, Dawn Hanseder, Mark Larabee, and many others touch on the personal growth that occurs along the PCT.

In the daily lives of most of us, we have little exposure to silence and darkness. Paul Bogard's perspectives on night and the richness that comes with true darkness, and Anicca Cox's comments on the quiet of the wilderness, are reminders of two of the special gifts of an experience on the PCT.

We need to tell our stories. We are, by our very nature, storytellers. The oral traditions that have for millennia served as means of entertaining, transmitting knowledge, and preserving history remain an important part of PCT culture. In contemporary times, blogs, journals, and written accounts complement the spoken word. This tradition is captured in stories as diverse as the mythology in "Coyote Places the Stars" and the lessons embedded in Ray Echols's "A Sierra Storm," to the unabashed entertainment of "Air Streaming Off the Crest." It is through stories that we define ourselves as human beings.

THE SEVENTH GENERATION

In the course of these two volumes, we have shared much about our own PCT experiences. Rees has fundamentally grown old with the trail. Since his first exposure to the PCT thirty years ago, Rees has married, became a parent, worked, and retired. Throughout that span of time, he has regularly returned to the PCT. Even his trail names reflect the passage of time and his evolution as a backpacker. From Boris to Mr. Question to Uncle Rico and ultimately to being a part of Team Geezer. In "Walking in 5-7-5," Rees shares a little of his effort to pass the torch to the next generation in his household.

Corey, nearly twenty years Rees's junior, first came to the trail during 1998 as a doctoral student at the University of Nevada, Reno. He was so profoundly affected by the trail that he made it a central figure in his dissertation, and he began leading university classes and work crews on the trail. He has worked to imbue in college students a deep understanding of sustainability and to pass along his love for the trail to his young sons, Hunter and Bodie.

As we shared in the introduction to this volume, our belief in the importance of stewardship is such that we have committed that all of our profits from this project will be returned to the trail. It is for Chisa, Mei Lan, Hunter, and Bodie, and their children, and their children's children—so that they too may be able to walk and enjoy their own experiences on the Pacific Crest Trail.

This perspective is expressed so beautifully in the Great Law of the Iroquois, which asks that decisions today be made to benefit those seven generations into the future. "We are looking ahead, as is one of the first mandates given us as chiefs, to make sure and to make every decision that we make relate to the welfare and well-being of the seventh generation to come ....What about the seventh generation? Where are you taking them? What will they have?" wrote Oren Lyons, chief of the Onondaga Nation (quoted in *American Indian Environments*, Syracuse University Press, 1980).

TRAIL STORIES: A LIVING, BREATHING COLLECTION

We recognize that the ninety-some stories brought together in this anthology are but a small fraction of the Pacific Crest Trail's literary canon, past, present, and future. We hope that hiker-writers will continue to develop their tales for a broader audience, spreading the love for and appreciation of this national treasure. And, we hope that you will share them with us, because this ending is just a beginning.

CONTRIBUTING WRITERS

WALTER BAILEY lived in the West at the close of the nineteenth and opening of the twentieth century and, among other things, wrote about the old Barlow Road, which wound its way across the Cascades just south of Mount Hood, in northern Oregon.

ROBERT BIRKBY is author of *Lightly on the Land: The SCA Trail Building and Maintenance Manual* (The Mountaineers Books, 1996), the current edition of *The Boy Scout Handbook* (Boy Scouts of America, 2009), and many other environmental publications. As a crew leader and wilderness work skills instructor, he has had a hand in maintaining trails across America, including the PCT. His current efforts include helping design a network of trails around Siberia's Lake Baikal. He has thru hiked the Appalachian Trail and much of the PCT.

PAUL BOGARD teaches writing and environmental literature at Wake Forest University in Winston-Salem, North Carolina. He still owns the small house in Reno that he bought when he began graduate school, and he brings his writing, dog, and hiking boots back west as often as he can.

AMANDA CARTER graduated from Humboldt State University in Arcata, California, where she spent her summers as a child. The Pacific Northwest has inspired and shaped her perspective on nature writing and has schooled her in the lessons that can be learned from outdoor experiences. Carter currently teaches writing at the College of the Redwoods in Eureka, California.

ELLA E. CLARK (1896–1984) taught at Washington State University from 1927 to 1961 and traveled the Pacific Northwest extensively, recording the stories and myths of First Nation peoples. She also served as a fire lookout for the US Forest Service for several years during World War II, studying the flora and fauna of the Cascades in great detail. She is best known as an author and editor who collected and recorded a wide variety of Native American literature, published in three separate volumes, *Indian Legends of the Pacific Northwest* (University of California Press, 1953), *Indian Legends of Canada* (McClelland & Stewart; Bailey & Swinfen, 1960), and *Indian Legends from the Northern Rockies* (University of Oklahoma Press, 1966).

ANICCA COX is from the high deserts of New Mexico but fell in love with the West Coast as a young woman. She enjoys returning there often to enjoy the ocean and the spectacular wilderness it provides. Cox teaches writing at the University of New Mexico in Taos.

ROBERT H. COX, on a weeklong hike in the Olympic wilderness, was warned by a park ranger, "It is not six miles. It is eighteen miles with two mountain passes to cross and sometimes no trail. You will never make it." This was the beginning of Cox's many high-country hikes.

ELIZABETH DODD teaches creative writing and literature at Kansas State University. Her most recent book, *In the Minds Eye: Essays across the Animate World* (University of Nebraska Press, 2008), won the Best Creative Book Award from the Association for the Study of Literature and Environment in 2009.

WILLIAM O. DOUGLAS (1898–1980) was the longest-serving justice in the history of the Supreme Court, with a term lasting over thirty-six years. He grew up in Yakima, Washington, often working alongside migrant farm workers to support the family, witnessing widespread injustice, which spurred him on to a legal career. An avid outdoorsman, who thru hiked the Appalachian Trail, Douglas famously argued in the 1972 case *Sierra Club v. Morton* that trees should have legal standing, advocating for "the conferral of standing on environmental objects to sue for their own preservation."

WILLIAM L. DWYER (1929–2002), known in Seattle as a renaissance man, was a judge, an author, an actor, an outdoorsman who scrambled up many Cascade peaks, a part owner of an oyster house, a collector of art, and a lover of history and Shakespeare who cited both in numerous rulings. Dwyer was a trial lawyer for thirty-four years before serving for fifteen years on the federal bench.

CAROLYN "SWEET GOAT MAMA" EDDY is a member of the board for the North American Packgoat Association. She is also a PCT trail angel in the northern Oregon area. She and her goats volunteer for the Wilderness Steward Program on Mount Hood.

BARBARA EGBERT is a freelance writer and editor and author of *Zero Days: The Real-Life Adventures of Captain Bligh, Nellie Bly, and 10-year-old Scrambler on the Pacific Crest Trail* (Wilderness Press, 2007). She lives in northern California with her husband and daughter.

KACI ELDER is a writer, hiker, and stage artist with a variety of publications and performances to her credit. More importantly, she is remembering how to see the world freshly, like a child, although she still thinks too much. Her home is the Hobbit House in the Klamath-Siskiyou watershed.

DAVID FOSCUE rode the PCT on his horse, Stub, from 1991 to 1998. He is a former president of the Pacific Crest Trail Association and a retired Washington superior court judge.

DAVID GREEN is principal of UnCommon Knowledge, a speechwriting and strategic communications consultancy in the New York City area. He has written speeches for senior executives at Hewlett-Packard, Mercedes-Benz USA, and Johnson & Johnson, among others—all while being an involved father of thirteen-year-old twin boys. He is not sure which activity is the more demanding.

HAWK GREENWAY, at age twenty-one, found himself managing the 250,000-acre Mountain-Island Ranch along the Colorado River. He has been a bush pilot, a hunter's guide, and a graduate student in forest management. Greenway currently lives in Colorado, where he manages the nonprofit Alfred Braun Hut System, a collection of backcountry ski huts above 11,000 feet just west of the Continental Divide. He serves on the local Open Space and Trails Board, where he works to protect open space, agriculture, and public access to public lands. But he misses his horseback days on the PCT.

TOM "BULLFROG" GRIFFIN has finished about one-third of the PCT as a section hiker, including most of the trail in his home state of Washington. Prior to his current position as an editor for Rick Steves's guidebooks, Griffin worked as a magazine editor, a newspaper reporter, a public relations specialist, and a Berlitz teacher in Europe. He is the author of *The University of Washington Experience* (University of Washington, 2003) and lives in Seattle with his wife, Julie.

HERMANN GUCINSKI retired from the research arm of the US Forest Service and, along with his wife, Barbara, completed section hiking the PCT in 2007. They also section hiked the Appalachian Trail, finishing in 2009, and have walked 800 miles of the Continental Divide Trail (mostly in Colorado). Hermann enjoys writing, photography, and flying (he earned his pilot's license on his sixty-ninth birthday in 2009).

CHRIS HALL grew up in the foothills of the Sierra Nevada in the South Yuba River watershed and now makes his home in Humboldt County. He has published a number of reviews, a couple of poems, and he has hiked a few western trails. "There and Back Again" is his second published piece of place-based creative nonfiction.

DAWN "GARBANZO" HANSEDER grew up in the wilds of Wisconsin. She set her sights on a PCT thru hike while volunteering with the Nevada Conservation Corps. Since then, she has done conservation work at places like Glen Canyon National Recreation Area and Gila Cliff Dwellings National Monument. She currently teaches middle school science with Teach for America. Hanseder intends to hike the miles she missed on the PCT and to start some spreadsheets for her upcoming Appalachian Trail thru hike with her dog Stink and newly adopted canine friend Wheeler.

LARRY HILLBERG retired from IBM and currently works as a computer consultant living in Colfax, California. A regular hiker in the Sierra Nevada, Hillberg also enjoys his time as a volunteer broadcaster and music show host on the community radio station KVMR in Nevada City.

BOB HOLTEL got the idea for running the entire PCT while at a summer running camp at Mammoth Lakes. The high school cross-country team that Holtel coached also trained on the PCT most days. Holtel recruited crew and pacers for his PCT run, including his longtime friend Court Mumford, and some twenty-five years ago was the first to run the length of the PCT. He is currently attempting to be the oldest person to run the entire trail, with his goal to reach the Mexican border exactly on his eightieth birthday.

REES HUGHES retired in 2008 after working in higher education for more than three decades. It has allowed him to increase the rate at which he is completing the PCT, one of his life goals. He and his wife, Amy, have two daughters and live happily in Arcata, California, with easy access to wildlands.

GREG "STRIDER" HUMMEL is currently a geologist and father of five children, living in southern California. In 1977 he hiked the incomplete PCT. He is the president of the Annual Day Zero Pacific Crest Trail Kickoff (ADZPCTKO) and of the American Long Distance Hiking Association–West.

DAVID KOLB was born in 1924 in Baltimore, Maryland. He served in the US Army from 1943 to 1946 in Europe, graduated from West Virginia University with a bachelor's in forestry and a master's in botany (ecology). He currently lives in Tigard, Oregon.

MARK LARABEE is a Pulitzer Prize–winning reporter and the managing editor of *The Communicator*, the magazine of the Pacific Crest Trail Association. He lives in Portland, Oregon, with his wife, Carol.

DENNIS LARSEN is a retired history teacher residing in Olympia, Washington. For the past decade, he has researched and written about Ezra Meeker and early Pacific Northwest pioneers.

URSULA K. LE GUIN is a prolific writer of science fiction and fantasy as well as adult realism, poetry, and young adult and children's literature. Le Guin has been decorated with awards and followed by fans in a multitude of genres. The daughter of California anthropologist Alfred Kroeber, Le Guin carries on a strong intellectual heritage. She is perhaps best known for her *Earthsea* series for young adults, and she is often hailed as one of the most imaginative authors of our time.

COREY LEE LEWIS makes his home with his two sons, Hunter and Bodie, in the heart of Redwood Country on the North Coast of California. Author of *Reading the Trail: Exploring the Literature and Natural History of the California Crest* (University of Nevada Press, 2005), Corey is a longtime trail builder, hiker, and lover of the PCT.

KEITH A. "ST. ALFONZO" LIKER finally finished his lifetime project of hiking the PCT in sections on September 18, 2009.

BARRY LOPEZ is an award-winning and widely ranging travel and nature writer. He completed graduate work at the University of Oregon and now makes his home in his beloved western state. Early works such as *Of Wolves and Men* (Touchstone, 1978) and *Arctic Dreams* (Charles Scribner's Sons, 1986) established him as an authoritative author of natural history, while such works as *Crow and Weasel* (North Point Press, 1990) and *Lessons from the Wolverine* (University of Georgia Press, 1997) cemented his status as a powerful writer of fiction.

BARNEY "SCOUT" MANN thru hiked the PCT in 2007 with his wife, Sandy "Frodo" Mann. They observed their thirtieth wedding anniversary on top of Forester Pass, the trail's high point. Scout is a San Diego–based writer and retired attorney.

GEORGE PERKINS MARSH (1801–1882) was a diplomat, literary historian, and writer who has often been called America's first environmentalist. He is most well-known for his book *Man and Nature* (Charles Scribner, 1864), an early work in ecology and the effects of deforestation.

ANN MARSHALL has an exceptional hiking pedigree. Her mother, Louise, was a founder of the Washington Trails Association (WTA) and cofounder of the American Hiking Society, serving as its president in the late 1980s. Marshall herself served as editor of *The Signpost*, the magazine of the WTA, for twelve years and subsequently started the magazine *Pack and Paddle* in 1991. Ann continues to live in western Washington.

PATRICK F. MCMANUS was born in Idaho, educated in the backwoods of the West, and schooled at Washington State University in Pullman, where he worked as an editor until taking a teaching post at Eastern Washington University in Cheney.

McManus has been a frequent contributor to *Field and Stream* and *Outdoor Life*, recounting his many misadventures with dry and sardonic wit. His humorous tales have been collected in over a dozen books, ranging from *A Fine and Pleasant Misery* (Holt, Rinehart and Winston, 1978) to *They Shoot Canoes Don't They?* (Holt, Rinehart and Winston, 1981), *The Deer on the Bicycle* (Eastern Washington University Press, 2000), and *The Bear in the Attic (Henry Holt and Company, 2002).*

MOURNING DOVE (HUM-ISHU-MA) (1888–1936) is best known for her novel *Cogewa the Half-Blood* (Four Seas Company, 1927) and her collected myths and legends, *Coyote Stories* (The Caxton Printers, 1933). She was born to a Colville mother and a half Okanagan, half Irish father. "Mourning Dove" is a translation of her Native name, Hum-ishu-ma, while her less used English name was Christal Quintasket.

JOEL PALMER (1810–1881) was an Oregon Territory pioneer who traveled westward in 1845. He wrote a popular immigrant guidebook in 1847 (*Journal of Travels Over the Rocky Mountains to the Mouth of the Columbia River*), cofounded Dayton, Oregon, and served as a controversial Indian Affairs administrator. After Oregon became a state, Palmer served in both branches of the Oregon Legislative Assembly. He was selected as Speaker of the Oregon House of Representatives for one session in 1862 and in 1870 lost a bid to become governor of Oregon.

JIM REA retired from a varied career that included being a philosophy professor and an electronics wholesaler. After thirty years of not hiking, Rea joined an outdoors club for a Grand Canyon hike. Hooked, he repeated the trip and wanted more. The following year he hiked the first four hundred miles of the PCT.

CINDY ROSS AND TODD GLADFELTER, after hiking the PCT, went on to handcraft a log home from scratch, grow much of their own organic food, and raise two children, whom they led across the Continental Divide Trail as babes, along with a string of llamas. Ross's sixth book, *Scraping Heaven: A Family's Journey along the Continental Divide* (Ragged Mountain Press, 2003), is the story of their five-summer, 3100-mile trek over the rooftop of North America. Ross is currently working on a new book about how to use the whole (natural) world to educate our children and instill a lifelong love of learning in them.

ERIC RYBACK chronicled his 1970 hike from Canada to Mexico in *The High Adventure of Eric Ryback* (Chronicle Books, 1971), capturing the imagination of a generation of hikers. No other text has had a more profound impact on the visibility of and interest in the PCT. After a thru hike of the Appalachian Trail the year before, Ryback began his PCT adventure at the conclusion of high school. In 2008, after a long hiatus, Ryback was reunited with the PCT community at the Annual Day Zero Pacific Crest Trail Kickoff (ADZPCTKO) and has since joined the board of the Pacific Crest Trail Association.

JEFFREY P. SCHAFFER made his first backpack trip in 1962 at age nineteen, traversing the Grand Canyon. In 1964 he began climbing in Yosemite National Park, where he has completed some seventy different roped ascents, including several first ascents. In 1972, he began work on his first book for Wilderness Press. Since then, he has written and contributed to more than a dozen guidebooks and has mapped about four thousand miles of trail. Today, he teaches natural sciences courses at San Francisco Bay Area community colleges, does Sierran geomorphic research, lead-climbs both outdoors and in climbing gyms, and lives the good life with his wife in the Napa Valley.

GEORGE AND PATRICIA SEMB hiked the PCT from 1996 through 1999 and have written two books describing day hikes that cover 85 percent of the trail—*Day Hikes on the Pacific Crest Trail: California* (2000) and *Day Hikes on the Pacific Crest Trail: Oregon and Washington* (2000), both published by Wilderness Press. Pat and George both retired from teaching at the University of Kansas in 2010. Pat now works in the insurance industry and George in the investment industry.

HOWARD SHAPIRO has been section hiking the PCT since 1981. Having completed the Washington and Oregon sections, he is slowly making his way through California. When not hiking with his friends Rees Hughes and Jim Peacock, Shapiro teaches school in Burlington, Washington.

WALKIN' JIM STOLTZ (1953–2010) set off on his last wild hike on September 3, 2010, at the conclusion of a heroic battle with cancer. He was widely known for his unique combination of long-distance hiking, original songwriting, photography, and painting. At the forefront of many environmental causes throughout the United States, Walkin' Jim founded the nonprofit MUSE (Musicians United to Sustain the Environment) with Craig Wagner and Joyce Rouse.

WILLIAM L. SULLIVAN is the author of ten books, including a five-book 100 Hikes guidebook series that covers every significant trail in Oregon. He has also written numerous articles about Oregon, including the "Oregon Trails" feature column for Eugene's *Register-Guard*. A fifth-generation Oregonian, Sullivan began hiking at the age of five and has been exploring new trails ever since.

KIM TODD is the author of *Chrysalis, Maria Sibylla Merian and the Secrets of Metamorphosis* (Harcourt, 2007), and *Tinkering with Eden: A Natural History of Exotic Species in America* (W. W. Norton, 2001). Her essays and articles have appeared in *Orion, Sierra, Backpacker,* and *Grist,* among other places. She teaches literary nonfiction at Penn State, the Behrend College, in Erie, Pennsylvania.

DAVID WAGONER is a prolific poet and novelist, winner of several writing awards, and is perhaps best known for his environmental poetry. His published works include *Staying Alive* (Indiana University Press, 1966), *Sleeping in the Woods* (Indiana University Press, 1974), and *Traveling Light* (University of Illinois Press, 1999), just to name a few. He taught creative writing at the University of Washington and is enamored of the Pacific Northwest country, which he calls home.

LYNN WUNISCHE and her husband, Dave, live close to Section G of the Oregon PCT. They have hiked it, along with most of the Columbia Gorge trails, in combinations of overnight and day hikes. In 2006, they spent a month hiking from Timberline Lodge to Crater Lake. When they are not hiking, they ride their recumbent bikes and guide for Upward Trails.

INDEX

ABOUT THE EDITORS

COREY LEE LEWIS was raised on frequent and extended camping, backpacking, and horsepacking trips in the Rocky Mountains of Colorado and Wyoming. Family tradition and practice defined summer as a time for being at high elevations, jumping in cold streams fed by snow-melt, and reveling in the smell of sage, pine, and campfire smoke. Born in Fort Collins, Colorado, Corey moved with his family to a small farm in eastern Kansas when he was ten years old; he has been returning to the western mountains ever since.

Corey first encountered the PCT in 1998 while earning his PhD from the University of Nevada, Reno and working for the Nevada Conservation Corps. The long trail immediately took hold of his heart and became a major feature in both his professional work and personal life. For eight years, Corey led trail crews working on and around the PCT, and taught field-based college classes in environmental studies along its length. His first book, *Reading the Trail: Exploring the Literature and Natural History of the California Crest* (2005), discusses the methods he developed during these years for uniting experiential education and conservation along the trail.

Corey teaches environmental writing and literature at Humboldt State University and continues to lead students in the field. He returns each season to the high country of the PCT with his two sons, Hunter and Bodie.

REES HUGHES has been section hiking the PCT since 1981. Growing up in Kansas he found the lure of the mountains irresistible so he traded the flatlands for Seattle, the Olympics, and the Cascades. He has walked his way through some of the most stunning regions on Earth—from the top of Kilimanjaro to the arid interior of Australia, from the pilgrimage route up Sri Pada

in Sri Lanka to the picturesque Cornish coast, from the Himalayas to the Andes—but he insists there is nothing he has found to equal the Pacific Crest Trail's unique blend of access, wildness, and diversity. And, despite dalliances with ultralight, he still finds a tent and a book to be worth their weight.

The evolution of Rees' trail names reflects the manner in which he has aged with the PCT these past thirty years . . . from Boris to Uncle Rico to Mr. Question to Team Geezer. He hopes, however, that he is more akin to fine wine or cheese than a threadbare shirt or the old horse relegated to the pasture.

Rees has lived for the last twenty-five years in Northern California, with his wife, Amy, and their two daughters, Chisa and Mei Lan. He retired from Humboldt State University in 2008.

OTHER TITLES YOU MIGHT ENJOY
FROM THE MOUNTAINEERS BOOKS

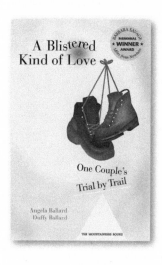

A BLISTERED KIND OF LOVE
Angela and Duffy Ballard

A young couple's account of their four-and-a-half months of PCT bliss: 6,300,000 steps, 528 doses of ibuprofen, 180 Snickers bars, 36 popped blisters, and more.

100 CLASSIC HIKES IN OREGON,
2ND EDITION
Douglas Lorain

A full-color guide to the most spectacular hikes and overnight outings Oregon has to offer.

100 CLASSIC HIKES: WASHINGTON, 3RD EDITION
Craig Romano

Gorgeous color photos bring 100 of the finest hikes in Washington to life.

THE ZEN OF WILDERNESS AND WALKING
Edited by Katharine Wroth

Inspirational and/or humorous quotes—plus, it's a flip book!

BACKCOUNTRY COOKING DECK
Dorcas Miller

Fifty recipes for camp and trail on 4" x 5½" cards.

The Mountaineers has more than 600 outdoor recreation books in print. For details, visit www.mountaineersbooks.org.

THE MOUNTAINEERS, founded in 1906, is a nonprofit outdoor activity and conservation organization whose mission is "to explore, study, preserve, and enjoy the natural beauty of the outdoors . . . ." Based in Seattle, Washington, it is now one of the largest such organizations in the United States, with seven branches throughout Washington State.

The Mountaineers sponsors both classes and year-round outdoor activities in the Pacific Northwest, which include hiking, mountain climbing, ski-touring, snowshoeing, bicycling, camping, canoeing and kayaking, nature study, sailing, and adventure travel. The Mountaineers' conservation division supports environmental causes through educational activities, sponsoring legislation, and presenting informational programs.

All activities are led by skilled, experienced volunteers, who are dedicated to promoting safe and responsible enjoyment and preservation of the outdoors.

If you would like to participate in these organized outdoor activities or programs, consider a membership in The Mountaineers. For information and an application, write or call The Mountaineers Program Center, 7700 Sand Point Way NE, Seattle, WA 98115-3996; phone 206-521-6001; visit www.mountaineers.org; or email clubmail@mountaineers.org.

The Mountaineers Books, an active, nonprofit publishing program of The Mountaineers, produces guidebooks, instructional texts, historical works, natural history guides, and works on environmental conservation. All books produced by The Mountaineers Books fulfill the mission of The Mountaineers. Visit www.mountaineersbooks.org to find details about all our titles and the latest author events, as well as videos, web clips, links, and more!

The Mountaineers Books
1001 SW Klickitat Way, Suite 201
Seattle, WA 98134
800-553-4453
mbooks@mountaineersbooks.org

NATIONAL GEOGRAPHIC

KIDS™

ALMANAC 2013

NATIONAL
GEOGRAPHIC

WASHINGTON, D.C.

National Geographic Children's Books
gratefully acknowledges the following people for their help with the
National Geographic Kids Almanac 2013.

Curtis Malarkey, Julie Segal, and Cheryl Zook
of the National Geographic Explorers program;
Truly Herbert, National Geographic Communications;
and Chuck Errig of Random House

Amazing Animals

Suzanne Braden, Director, Pandas International

Dr. Rodolfo Coria, Paleontologist, Plaza Huincul, Argentina

Dr. Sylvia Earle,
National Geographic Explorer-in-Residence

Dr. Thomas R. Holtz, Jr., Senior Lecturer, Vertebrate Paleontology,
Dept. of Geology, University of Maryland

Dr. Luke Hunter, Executive Director, Panthera

"Dino" Don Lessem, President, Exhibits Rex

Kathy B. Maher, Research Editor,
NATIONAL GEOGRAPHIC magazine

Kathleen Martin, Canadian Sea Turtle Network

Barbara Nielsen, Polar Bears International

Andy Prince, Austin Zoo

Christopher Sloan

Julia Thorson, translator, Zurich, Switzerland

Dennis vanEngelsdorp, Senior Extension Associate, Pennsylvania
Department of Agriculture

Awesome Adventure

Jen Bloomer, Media Relations Manager,
The National Aquarium in Baltimore

Dereck and Beverly Joubert,
National Geographic Explorers-in-Residence

Culture Connection

Dr. Wade Davis,
National Geographic Explorer-in-Residence

Deirdre Mullervy, Managing Editor,
Gallaudet University Press

Super Science

Tim Appenzeller, Chief Magazine Editor, NATURE

Dr. José de Ondarza, Associate Professor,
Department of Biological Sciences, State University
of New York, College at Plattsburgh

Lesley B. Rogers, Managing Editor,
NATIONAL GEOGRAPHIC magazine

Dr. Enric Sala, National Geographic Visiting Fellow

Abigail A. Tipton, Director of Research (former),
NATIONAL GEOGRAPHIC magazine

Erin Vintinner, Biodiversity Specialist,
Center for Biodiversity and Conservation at the
American Museum of Natural History

Barbara L. Wyckoff, Research Editor,
NATIONAL GEOGRAPHIC magazine

Wonders of Nature

Anatta, NOAA Public Affairs Officer

Dr. Robert Ballard,
National Geographic Explorer-in-Residence

Douglas H. Chadwick, wildlife biologist and contributor to
NATIONAL GEOGRAPHIC magazine

Drew Hardesty, Forecaster, Utah Avalanche Center

Going Green

Eric J. Bohn, Math Teacher, Santa Rosa High School

Stephen David Harris, Professional Engineer,
Industry Consulting

Catherine C. Milbourn, Senior Press Officer, EPA

Brad Scriber, Senior Researcher,
NATIONAL GEOGRAPHIC magazine

Cid Simões and Paola Segura,
National Geographic Emerging Explorers

Dr. Wes Tunnell, Harte Research Institute for
Gulf of Mexico Studies, Texas A&M
University–Corpus Christi

History Happens

Sylvie Beaudreau, Associate Professor, Department of History,
State University of New York

Elspeth Deir, Assistant Professor, Faculty of Education, Queens
University, Kingston, Ontario, Canada

Dr. Gregory Geddes, Lecturer, Department of Global Studies, State
University of New York–Orange, Middletown-Newburgh, New York

Dr. Fredrik Hiebert, National Geographic Visiting Fellow

Micheline Joanisse, Media Relations Officer,
Natural Resources Canada

Dr. Robert D. Johnston,
Associate Professor and Director of the
Teaching of History Program,
University of Illinois at Chicago

Dickson Mansfield, Geography Instructor (retired),
Faculty of Education, Queens University, Kingston,
Ontario, Canada

Tina Norris, U.S. Census Bureau

Parliamentary Information and Research Service,
Library of Parliament, Ottawa, Canada

Karyn Pugliese, Acting Director, Communications, Assembly of
First Nations

Geography Rocks

Dr. Mary Kent, Demographer,
Population Reference Bureau

Dr. Walt Meier, National Snow and Ice Data Center

Dr. Richard W. Reynolds,
NOAA's National Climatic Data Center

United States Census Bureau, Public Help Desk

Dr. Spencer Wells,
National Geographic Explorer-in-Residence

Carl Haub, Senior Demographer, Conrad Taeuber Chair of Public
Information, Population Reference Bureau

Glynnis Breen, National Geographic Special Projects